GRAMMAR AND BEYOND 3B

Second Edition

with Academic Writing

Randi Reppen

Laurie Blass

Susan Iannuzzi

Alice Savage

CAMBRIDGE
UNIVERSITY PRESS

CAMBRIDGE
UNIVERSITY PRESS

University Printing House, Cambridge CB2 8BS, United Kingdom

One Liberty Plaza, 20th Floor, New York, NY 10006, USA

477 Williamstown Road, Port Melbourne, VIC 3207, Australia

314–321, 3rd Floor, Plot 3, Splendor Forum, Jasola District Centre, New Delhi – 110025, India

79 Anson Road, #06–04/06, Singapore 079906

Cambridge University Press is part of the University of Cambridge.

It furthers the University's mission by disseminating knowledge in the pursuit of education, learning and research at the highest international levels of excellence.

cambridge.org
Information on this title: cambridge.org/9781108779821

© Cambridge University Press 2021

First published 2013
Second edition 2021

20 19 18 17 16 15 14 13 12 11 10 9 8 7 6 5 4 3 2 1

Printed in Dubai by Oriental Press

A catalogue record for this publication is available from the British Library

ISBN Student's Book 3B with Online Practice 978-1-108-77982-1

Additional resources for this publication at www.cambridge.org/grammarandbeyond

About the Author

Randi Reppen is Professor of Applied Linguistics and TESL at Northern Arizona University (NAU) in Flagstaff, Arizona. She has over 20 years' experience teaching ESL students and training ESL teachers, including 11 years as the Director of NAU's Program in Intensive English. Randi's research interests focus on the use of corpora for language teaching and materials development. In addition to numerous academic articles and books, she is the author of *Using Corpora in the Language Classroom* and a co-author of *Basic Vocabulary* in Use, 2nd edition, both published by Cambridge University Press.

Laurie Blass has more than 25 years' experience teaching and creating materials for ESL students in the United States and abroad. She is currently a full-time materials developer with a special interest in ESL for academic success and educational technology. Laurie is co-author of *Writers at Work: From Sentence to Paragraph*, published by Cambridge University Press, among many other titles.

Susan Iannuzzi has been teaching ESL for more than 20 years. She has trained English teachers on five continents and consulted on the national English curricula for countries in Africa, Asia, and the Middle East. She has authored or co-authored more than 10 English courses in use today. *Grammar and Beyond* is her first publication with Cambridge University Press.

Alice Savage is an English Language Teacher and Materials Writer. She attended the School for International Training in Vermont and is an author on the Read This! series, published by Cambridge University Press. She lives in Houston, Texas with her two children.

Advisory Panel

The ESL advisory panel has helped to guide the development of this series and provided invaluable information about the needs of ESL students and teachers in high schools, colleges, universities, and private language schools throughout North America.

Neta Simpkins Cahill, Skagit Valley College, Mount Vernon, WA
Shelly Hedstrom, Palm Beach State College, Lake Worth, FL
Richard Morasci, Foothill College, Los Altos Hills, CA
Stacey Russo, East Hampton High School, East Hampton, NY
Alice Savage, Lone Star College-North Harris, Houston, TX

Scope and Sequence

Unit	Theme	Grammar	Topics
PART 1 The Present and the Past			
UNIT 1 page 2	First Impressions	Simple Present and Present Progressive	Simple Present vs. Present Progressive (p. 4) Stative Verbs (p. 8) Special Meanings and Uses of Simple Present (p. 12)
UNIT 2 page 18	Global Marketing	Simple Past and Past Progressive *Used To, Would*	Simple Past vs. Past Progressive (p. 20) Time Clauses with Simple Past and Past Progressive (p. 22) *Used To* and *Would* (p. 26)
PART 2 The Perfect			
UNIT 3 page 34	Success	Present Perfect and Present Perfect Progressive	Present Perfect (p. 36) Present Perfect vs. Simple Past (p. 40) Present Perfect vs. Present Perfect Progressive (p. 43)
UNIT 4 page 52	Nature vs. Nurture	Past Perfect and Past Perfect Progressive	Past Perfect (p. 54) Past Perfect with Time Clauses (p. 59) Past Perfect Progressive (p. 62)
PART 3 The Future			
UNIT 5 page 68	Looking Ahead at Technology	*Be Going To*, Present Progressive, and Future Progressive	*Be Going To*, Present Progressive, and Simple Present for Future (p. 70) *Will* and *Be Going To* (p. 73) Future Progressive (p. 76)
UNIT 6 page 84	Business Practices of the Future	Future Time Clauses, Future Perfect, and Future Perfect Progressive	Future Time Clauses (p. 86) Future Perfect vs. Future Perfect Progressive (p. 91)

Avoid Common Mistakes	Academic Writing
Remembering the simple present with stative verbs; avoiding the base form of the verb when using the present progressive	**Plagiarism and Academic Honesty** • Avoid plagiarism
Remembering the base form of the verb after *would* and *used to*; remembering the simple past for specific events in the past; remembering the past progressive for background information	**Expository Writing** Writing prompt: *How has globalization changed your country?* • Topic sentences • Support statement with details • Use tables to organize information
Remembering correct subject–verb agreement with present perfect; remembering been for the present perfect progressive	• Essay structure • Write effective thesis statements • Write the introductory paragraph
Remembering when to use the past perfect or past perfect progressive	• Write the first draft • Revise and edit
Remembering *be* with *be going to*; remembering when to use the future progressive, the simple present, or the present progressive	**Comparison and Contrast** Writing prompt: *Compare learning a language with studying math. How do you think the study of these subjects will change over time with new technology?* • Use Venn diagrams • Brainstorm topics and ideas
Avoiding the future form in the time clause; remembering *will* with the future perfect	• Use transitions to show comparison and contrast • Structure a comparison-and-contrast essay

Unit	Theme	Grammar	Topics
PART 4 Modals and Modal-like Expressions			
UNIT 7 page 98	Learning How to Remember	Social Modals	Modals and Modal-like Expressions of Advice and Regret (p. 100) Modals and Modal-like Expressions of Permission, Necessity, and Obligation (p. 103) Modals and Modal-like Expressions of Ability (p. 108)
UNIT 8 page 114	Computers and Crime	Modals of Probability: Present, Future, and Past	Modals of Present Probability (p. 116) Modals of Future Probability (p. 118) Modals of Past Probability (p. 122)
PART 5 Nouns and Pronouns			
UNIT 9 page 128	Attitudes Toward Nutrition	Nouns and Modifying Nouns	Nouns (p. 130) Noncount Nouns as Count Nouns (p. 134) Modifying Nouns (p. 138)
UNIT 10 page 146	Color	Articles and Quantifiers	Indefinite Article, Definite Article, and No Article (p. 148) Quantifiers (p. 151)
UNIT 11 page 162	Unusual Work Environments	Pronouns	Reflexive Pronouns (p. 164) Pronouns with *Other / Another* (p. 167) Indefinite Pronouns (p. 170)
PART 6 Gerunds and Infinitives			
UNIT 12 page 176	Getting an Education	Gerunds	Gerunds as Subjects and Objects (p. 178) Gerunds After Prepositions and Fixed Expressions (p. 181) Gerunds After Nouns + *of* (p. 185)
UNIT 13 page 192	Innovative Marketing Techniques	Infinitives	Infinitives with Verbs (p. 194) Infinitives vs. Gerunds (p. 197) Infinitives After Adjectives and Nouns (p. 200)

Avoid Common Mistakes	Academic Writing
Remembering *have* + the past participle after a modal; remembering *be* in *be allowed to* and *be supposed to*	• Use modals in academic writing • Write the first draft
Avoiding *must* with future probabilities; remembering *be* + verb + *-ing* with the progressive with modals	• Revise and edit
Avoiding plural noncount nouns; remembering plural forms for count nouns	**Opinion Writing** Writing prompt: *Is disease prevention the responsibility of individuals and their families or of the government?* • Use T-charts to brainstorm and organize ideas • Use precise nouns and adjectives
Avoiding *much* with plural nouns; remembering articles before singular occupations	• Use transitions to show opposing ideas • Add sentence variety • Structure an opinion essay • Use quantifiers and pronouns to hedge
Remembering to form reflexive pronouns with object pronouns; remembering to use singular verb forms with indefinite pronouns	• Plan the essay • Write the first draft • Revise and edit
Remembering to use a gerund after a preposition; remembering to use a singular verb with a gerund subject	**Summary-Response** Writing prompt: *Summarize the article "Creating a Successful Logo." Then choose a logo and analyze it in terms of the criteria in the article.* • Use an outline • Summarize • Write the summary paragraph
Avoiding verb + *that* clauses after *want*; remembering correct word order with a negative form of an infinitive	• Determine and apply criteria • Respond to an article • Write the response • Revise and edit

Unit	Theme	Grammar	Topics
PART 7 Questions and Noun Clauses			
UNIT 14 page 208	Geographic Mobility	Negative Questions and Tag Questions	Negative Questions (p. 210) Tag Questions (p. 212)
UNIT 15 page 222	Cultural Values	*That* Clauses	*That* Clauses (p. 224) Agreement Between *That* Clauses and Main Clauses (p. 227) *That* Clauses After Adjectives and Nouns (p. 229)
UNIT 16 page 236	Inventions They Said Would Never Work	Noun Clauses with *Wh-* Words and *If / Whether*	Noun Clauses with *Wh-* Words (p. 238) Noun Clauses with *If / Whether* (p. 240) Noun Clauses in Direct and Indirect Questions (p. 243)
PART 8 Indirect Speech			
UNIT 17 page 248	Human Motivation	Direct Speech and Indirect Speech	Direct Speech (p. 250) Indirect Speech (p. 253) Indirect Speech Without Tense Shift (p. 256) Other Reporting Verbs (p. 258)
UNIT 18 page 266	Creative Problem Solving	Indirect Questions; Indirect Imperatives, Requests, and Advice	Indirect Questions (p. 268) Indirect Imperatives, Requests, and Advice (p. 270)
PART 9 The Passive			
UNIT 19 page 276	English as a Global Language	The Passive (1)	Active vs. Passive Sentences (p. 278) Verbs and Objects with the Passive (p. 282) Reasons for Using the Passive (p. 282)
UNIT 20 page 290	Food Safety	The Passive (2)	The Passive with *Be Going To* and Modals (p. 292) *Get* Passives (p. 295) Passive Gerunds and Infinitives (p. 298)

Avoid Common Mistakes	Academic Writing
Remembering the auxiliary verb + *not* in negative questions; remembering an auxiliary verb + a pronoun in tag questions	**Argumentative Writing** Writing prompt: *Which is more important when choosing a home: location or size?* • Negative and tag questions in academic writing • Identify arguments and reasons • Brainstorm and organize in a T-chart
Avoiding a comma before a *that* clause; remembering a complete verb in *that* clauses; remembering a subject in *that* clauses	• Connect information • Support arguments
Remembering to use statement word order for a noun clause with a *wh-* word; avoiding using *either* instead of *whether*	• Register in academic writing • Argumentative essay structure • Write the first draft • Revise and edit
Remembering to change the form of the verb in indirect speech; remembering quotation marks with direct speech	**Argumentative Writing Using Graphs and Tables for Support** Writing prompt: *Using what you know about the job market, what is a good choice for a career path with a secure future? Include information from graphs or tables to support your choice.* • Understand and use graphs and tables • Brainstorm topics and ideas • Use reporting verbs to introduce evidence
Remembering to use infinitives in indirect imperatives; remembering to use an object pronoun or noun after *tell*	• Analyze information in graphs and other visuals • Make and evaluate claims • Add indirect advice from experts • Write body paragraphs
Remembering a form of *be* in passive sentences; remembering to put *be* before the subject in questions	• Make a logical appeal in the introductory paragraph • Use active and passive voice to discuss visuals • Write the first draft
Avoiding the base form of the verb after *be* in passive sentences	• Use passive voice in academic writing • Revise and edit

Unit	Theme	Grammar	Topics
PART 10 Relative Clauses (Adjective Clauses)			
UNIT 21 page 304	Alternative Energy Sources	Subject Relative Clauses (Adjective Clauses with Subject Relative Pronouns)	Identifying Subject Relative Clauses (p. 306) Nonidentifying Subject Relative Clauses (p. 309) Subject Relative Clauses with *Whose* (p. 312)
UNIT 22 page 320	Biometrics	Object Relative Clauses (Adjective Clauses with Object Relative Pronouns)	Identifying Object Relative Clauses (p. 322) Nonidentifying Object Relative Clauses (p. 325) Object Relative Clauses as Objects of Prepositions (p. 326)
UNIT 23 page 332	Millennials	Relative Clauses with *Where* and *When*; Reduced Relative Clauses	Relative Clauses with *Where* and *When* (p. 334) Reduced Relative Clauses (p. 338)
PART 11 Conditionals			
UNIT 24 page 346	Media in the United States	Real Conditionals: Present and Future	Present Real Conditionals (p. 348) Future Real Conditionals (p. 351) Real Conditionals with Modals, Modal-like Expressions, and Imperatives (p. 354)
UNIT 25 page 362	Natural Disasters	Unreal Conditionals: Present, Future, and Past	Present and Future Unreal Conditionals (p. 364) Past Unreal Conditionals (p. 368) Wishes About the Present, Future, and Past (p. 371)

Avoid Common Mistakes	Academic Writing
Using *which*, *that*, and *who* correctly; avoiding a second subject in the relative clause	**Expository Writing** Writing prompt: *Explain the advantages and disadvantages of three types of renewable energy and decide which would work best in your country or region.* • Organize ideas in a table • Use relative clauses to add information and avoid repetition
Avoiding commas for an identifying object relative clause; avoiding *what* in relative clauses	• Introduce advantages and disadvantages • Build coherence • Order ideas in an essay • Write the first draft
Avoiding a preposition before *when*; remembering a subject in *where* clauses	• Write the concluding paragraph • Revise and edit
Remembering the simple present in *if* clauses in future real conditionals; avoiding *when* to describe possible future conditions	**Argumentative Writing** Writing prompt: *Research an aging but culturally or historically important building in your city or country. What do you think should be done with it and why?* • Build support for an argument • Maintain paragraph unity • Brainstorm and organize ideas
Remembering a subject in *if* clauses	• Integrate information from multiple sources • Use impersonal statements • Use conditionals to support ideas • Write the first draft • Revise and edit

Unit	Theme	Grammar	Topics
PART 12 Connecting Ideas			
UNIT 26 page 378	Globalization of Food	Conjunctions	Connecting Words and Phrases with Conjunctions (p. 380) Connecting Sentences with Coordinating Conjunctions (p. 384) Reducing Sentences with Similar Clauses (p. 388)
UNIT 27 page 396	Consumerism	Adverb Clauses and Phrases	Subordinators and Adverb Clauses (p. 398) Reducing Adverb Clauses (p. 401) Subordinators to Express Purpose (p. 403)
UNIT 28 page 408	Technology in Entertainment	Connecting Information with Prepositions and Transitions	Connecting Information with Prepositions and Prepositional Phrases (p. 410) Connecting Information with Transition Words (p. 413)

Avoid Common Mistakes	Academic Writing
Avoiding *either* when joining ideas with *and*; avoiding *too* after a negative verb	**Comparison and Contrast** Writing prompt: *Not all products and services fit the same business model. Some might have a more successful introduction in a mobile setting. For others, a mobile setting would not be appropriate. Compare and contrast two products or services regarding their potential as mobile businesses.* • Use signal words and phrases to compare and contrast • Use Venn diagrams
Remembering to spell *even though* as two words; avoiding *even* in adverb clauses	• Organize comparisons and contrasts • Write concisely • Write body paragraphs
Avoiding *in the other hand*	• Connect the conclusion to the introduction • Write the first draft • Revise and edit

Appendices   A1
Glossary of Grammar Terms   G1
Index & Credits   I1

Introduction to *Grammar and Beyond*, 2nd edition

Grammar and Beyond is a research-based and content-rich grammar and academic writing series for beginning to advanced-level students. The series focuses on the most commonly used English grammar structures and practices all four skills in a variety of authentic and communicative contexts.

Grammar and Beyond is Research-Based

The grammar presented in this series is informed by years of research on the grammar of written and spoken English as it is used in college lectures, textbooks, academic essays, high school classrooms, and conversations between instructors and students. This research, and the analysis of over one billion words of authentic written and spoken language data known as the *Cambridge International Corpus*, has enabled the authors to:

- Present grammar rules that accurately represent how English is actually spoken and written

- Identify and teach differences between the grammar of written and spoken English

- Focus more attention on the structures that are commonly used, and less on those that are rarely used, in writing and speaking

- Help students avoid the most common mistakes that English language learners make

- Choose reading topics that will naturally elicit examples of the target grammar structure

- Introduce important vocabulary from the Academic Word List

Special Features of *Grammar and Beyond*

Realistic Grammar Presentations

Grammar is presented in clear and simple charts. The grammar points presented in these charts have been tested against real-world data from the *Cambridge International Corpus* to ensure that they are authentic representations of actual use of English.

Data from the Real World

Many of the grammar presentations and application sections include a feature called Data from the Real World. Concrete and useful points discovered through analysis of corpus data are presented and practiced in exercises that follow.

Avoid Common Mistakes

Every unit features an Avoid Common Mistakes section that develops students' awareness of the most common mistakes made by English language learners and gives them an opportunity to practice detecting and correcting these errors. This section helps students avoid these mistakes in their own work. The mistakes highlighted in this section are drawn from a body of authentic data on learner English known as the *Cambridge Learner Corpus*, a database of over 35 million words from student essays written by non-native speakers of English and information from experienced classroom teachers.

Academic Vocabulary

Every unit in *Grammar and Beyond* includes words from the Academic Word List (AWL), a research-based list of words and word families that appear with high frequency in English-language academic texts. These words are introduced in the opening text of the unit, recycled in the charts and exercises, and used to support the theme throughout the unit. By the time students finish each level, they will have been exposed several times to a carefully selected set of level-appropriate AWL words, as well as content words from a variety of academic disciplines.

Academic Writing

Every unit ends with an Academic Writing section. In Levels 1 through 3, this edition of *Grammar and Beyond* teaches students to write academically using writing cycles that span several units. Each writing cycle is organized around a writing prompt and focuses on a specific type of academic writing, such as argumentative, expository, and summary-response. Students move through the steps of the writing process - Brainstorm, Organize, Write, Edit - while learning and practicing new writing skills and ways to incorporate the unit grammar into their writing. In Level 4, the entire scope and sequence is organized around the types of essays students write in college, and focuses on the grammar rules, conventions, and structures needed to master them.

Series Levels

The following table provides a general idea of the difficulty of the material at each level of *Grammar and Beyond*. These are not meant to be interpreted as precise correlations.

	Description	TOEFL IBT	CEFR Levels
Level 1	Beginning	20 – 34	A1 – A2
Level 2	Low Intermediate to Intermediate	35 – 54	A2 – B1
Level 3	High Intermediate	55 – 74	B1 – B2
Level 4	Advanced	75 – 95	B2 – C1

Student Components

Student's Book with Online Practice

Each unit, based on a high-interest topic, teaches grammar points appropriate for each level in short, manageable cycles of presentation and practice. Academic Writing focuses on the structure of the academic essay in addition to the grammar rules, conventions, and structures that students need to master in order to be successful college writers. Students can access both the Digital Workbook and Writing Skills Interactive using their smartphones, tablets, or computers with a single log-in. See pages xx–xxv for a Tour of a Unit.

Digital Workbook

The Digital Workbook provides additional online exercises to help master each grammar point. Automatically-graded exercises give immediate feedback for activities such as correcting errors highlighted in the Avoid Common Mistakes section in the Student's Book. Self-Assessment sections at the end of each unit allow students to test their mastery of what they learned. Look for [ ] in the Student's Book to see when to use the Digital Workbook.

Writing Skills Interactive

Writing Skills Interactive is a self-grading course to practice discrete writing skills, reinforce vocabulary, and give students an opportunity with additional writing practice. Each unit has:

- Vocabulary review
- Short text to check understanding of the context
- Animated presentation of target unit writing skill
- Practice activities
- Unit Quiz to assess progress

Teacher Resources

A variety of downloadable resources are available on Cambridge One (cambridgeone.org) to assist instructors, including the following:

Teacher's Manual

- Suggestions for applying the target grammar to all four major skill areas, helping instructors facilitate dynamic and comprehensive grammar classes
- An answer key and audio script for the Student's Book
- Teaching tips, to help instructors plan their lessons
- Communicative activity worksheets to add more in-class speaking practice

Assessment

- Placement Test
- Ready-made, easy-to-score Unit Tests, Midterm, and Final in .pdf and .doc formats
- Answer Key

Presentation Plus

Presentation Plus allows teachers to digitally project the contents of the Student's Books in front of the class for a livelier, interactive classroom. It is a complete solution for teachers because it includes easy-to-access answer keys and audio at point of use.

Acknowledgments

The publisher and authors would like to thank these reviewers and consultants for their insights and participation:

Marty Attiyeh, The College of DuPage, Glen Ellyn, IL

Shannon Bailey, Austin Community College, Austin, TX

Jamila Barton, North Seattle Community College, Seattle, WA

Kim Bayer, Hunter College IELI, New York, NY

Linda Berendsen, Oakton Community College, Skokie, IL

Anita Biber, Tarrant County College Northwest, Fort Worth, TX

Jane Breaux, Community College of Aurora, Aurora, CO

Anna Budzinski, San Antonio College, San Antonio, TX

Britta Burton, Mission College, Santa Clara, CA

Jean Carroll, Fresno City College, Fresno, CA

Chris Cashman, Oak Park High School and Elmwood Park High School, Chicago, IL

Annette M. Charron, Bakersfield College, Bakersfield, CA

Patrick Colabucci, ALI at San Diego State University, San Diego, CA

Lin Cui, Harper College, Palatine, IL

Jennifer Duclos, Boston University CELOP, Boston, MA

Joy Durighello, San Francisco City College, San Francisco, CA

Kathleen Flynn, Glendale Community College, Glendale, CA

Raquel Fundora, Miami Dade College, Miami, FL

Patricia Gillie, New Trier Township High School District, Winnetka, IL

Laurie Gluck, LaGuardia Community College, Long Island City, NY

Kathleen Golata, Galileo Academy of Science & Technology, San Francisco, CA

Ellen Goldman, Mission College, Santa Clara, CA

Ekaterina Goussakova, Seminole Community College, Sanford, FL

Marianne Grayston, Prince George's Community College, Largo, MD

Mary Greiss Shipley, Georgia Gwinnett College, Lawrenceville, GA

Sudeepa Gulati, Long Beach City College, Long Beach, CA

Nicole Hammond Carrasquel, University of Central Florida, Orlando, FL

Vicki Hendricks, Broward College, Fort Lauderdale, FL

Kelly Hernandez, Miami Dade College, Miami, FL

Ann Johnston, Tidewater Community College, Virginia Beach, VA

Julia Karet, Chaffey College, Claremont, CA

Jeanne Lachowski, English Language Institute, University of Utah, Salt Lake City, UT

Noga Laor, Rennert, New York, NY

Min Lu, Central Florida Community College, Ocala, FL

Michael Luchuk, Kaplan International Centers, New York, NY

Craig Machado, Norwalk Community College, Norwalk, CT

Denise Maduli-Williams, City College of San Francisco, San Francisco, CA

Diane Mahin, University of Miami, Coral Gables, FL

Melanie Majeski, Naugatuck Valley Community College, Waterbury, CT

Jeanne Malcolm, University of North Carolina at Charlotte, Charlotte, NC

Lourdes Marx, Palm Beach State College, Boca Raton, FL

Susan G. McFalls, Maryville College, Maryville, TN

Nancy McKay, Cuyahoga Community College, Cleveland, OH

Dominika McPartland, Long Island Business Institute, Flushing, NY

Amy Metcalf, UNR/Intensive English Language Center, University of Nevada, Reno, NV

Robert Miller, EF International Language School San Francisco – Mills, San Francisco, CA

Marcie Pachino, Jordan High School, Durham, NC

Myshie Pagel, El Paso Community College, El Paso, TX

Bernadette Pedagno, University of San Francisco, San Francisco, CA

Tam Q Pham, Dallas Theological Seminary, Fort Smith, AR

Mary Beth Pickett, Global-LT, Rochester, MI
Maria Reamore, Baltimore City Public Schools, Baltimore, MD
Alison M. Rice, Hunter College IELI, New York, NY
Sydney Rice, Imperial Valley College, Imperial, CA
Kathleen Romstedt, Ohio State University, Columbus, OH
Alexandra Rowe, University of South Carolina, Columbia, SC
Irma Sanders, Baldwin Park Adult and Community Education, Baldwin Park, CA
Caren Shoup, Lone Star College – CyFair, Cypress, TX
Karen Sid, Mission College, Foothill College, De Anza College, Santa Clara, CA
Michelle Thomas, Miami Dade College, Miami, FL
Sharon Van Houte, Lorain County Community College, Elyria, OH

Margi Wald, UC Berkeley, Berkeley, CA
Walli Weitz, Riverside County Office of Ed., Indio, CA
Bart Weyand, University of Southern Maine, Portland, ME
Donna Weyrich, Columbus State Community College, Columbus, OH
Marilyn Whitehorse, Santa Barbara City College, Ojai, CA
Jessica Wilson, Rutgers University – Newark, Newark, NJ
Sue Wilson, San Jose City College, San Jose, CA
Margaret Wilster, Mid-Florida Tech, Orlando, FL
Anne York-Herjeczki, Santa Monica College, Santa Monica, CA
Hoda Zaki, Camden County College, Camden, NJ

We would also like to thank these teachers and programs for allowing us to visit:

Richard Appelbaum, Broward College, Fort Lauderdale, FL
Carmela Arnoldt, Glendale Community College, Glendale, AZ
JaNae Barrow, Desert Vista High School, Phoenix, AZ
Ted Christensen, Mesa Community College, Mesa, AZ
Richard Ciriello, Lower East Side Preparatory High School, New York, NY
Virginia Edwards, Chandler-Gilbert Community College, Chandler, AZ
Nusia Frankel, Miami Dade College, Miami, FL
Raquel Fundora, Miami Dade College, Miami, FL
Vicki Hendricks, Broward College, Fort Lauderdale, FL
Kelly Hernandez, Miami Dade College, Miami, FL
Stephen Johnson, Miami Dade College, Miami, FL
Barbara Jordan, Mesa Community College, Mesa, AZ
Nancy Kersten, GateWay Community College, Phoenix, AZ
Lewis Levine, Hostos Community College, Bronx, NY
John Liffiton, Scottsdale Community College, Scottsdale, AZ
Cheryl Lira-Layne, Gilbert Public School District, Gilbert, AZ
Mary Livingston, Arizona State University, Tempe, AZ

Elizabeth Macdonald, Thunderbird School of Global Management, Glendale, AZ
Terri Martinez, Mesa Community College, Mesa, AZ
Lourdes Marx, Palm Beach State College, Boca Raton, FL
Paul Kei Matsuda, Arizona State University, Tempe, AZ
David Miller, Glendale Community College, Glendale, AZ
Martha Polin, Lower East Side Preparatory High School, New York, NY
Patricia Pullenza, Mesa Community College, Mesa, AZ
Victoria Rasinskaya, Lower East Side Preparatory High School, New York, NY
Vanda Salls, Tempe Union High School District, Tempe, AZ
Kim Sanabria, Hostos Community College, Bronx, NY
Cynthia Schuemann, Miami Dade College, Miami, FL
Michelle Thomas, Miami Dade College, Miami, FL
Dongmei Zeng, Borough of Manhattan Community College, New York, NY

Tour of a Unit

ACADEMIC WRITING FOCUS

appears at the beginning of the unit.

GRAMMAR IN THE REAL WORLD

presents the unit's grammar in a realistic context using relatable texts.

UNIT 17 Direct Speech and Indirect Speech
Human Motivation

1 Grammar in the Real World

ACADEMIC WRITING

Argumentative writing using graphs and tables for support

A What makes people work hard at their jobs? Read the article about employee motivation. What type of reward is particularly effective in motivating workers?

B Comprehension Check Complete the chart. Check (✓) whether each reward is external or internal.

	External Reward	Internal Reward
1 Pay raise		
2 Feeling successful		
3 Freedom to work independently		
4 Good salary		
5 Good grades		

C Notice Find similar sentences in the article and complete the sentences below.

1 Lionel Messi _____, "Money is not a motivating factor… My motivation comes from playing the game I love."

2 Daniel Pink, the author of a book on motivation, _____ an audience once that Google was a great example of a company that supported autonomy.

3 Pink _____ the audience that Google News and Gmail had been created during this free time.

Each sentence tells what someone says. Which sentence gives the actual words of the speaker? How do you know?

WORKPLACE MOTIVATION

Motivation is the desire to do something. Soccer star Lionel Messi **said**, "Money is not a motivating factor… My motivation comes from playing the game I love." Messi meant that he enjoys playing soccer more than making millions of dollars. Can that be true? What other factors are important in motivating people?

Many psychologists believe that there are two types of rewards that affect motivation: external rewards and internal rewards. External rewards are rewards that someone gives you. A pay raise is a common external reward. A good grade at school is also an example of an external reward. Internal rewards are connected to the feelings people have about the work they do. The satisfaction you get when you do something well is an internal reward. Researcher Frederick Herzberg (1923–2000) studied motivation in the workplace for many years. Herzberg **said that** employers must think about factors that affect employees' feelings of satisfaction. Herzberg **explained that** working conditions and relationships among co-workers affect workers' motivation. Therefore, employers need to create an environment that makes employees feel safe, valued, and accepted.

Some studies on workplace motivation have focused on autonomy, which is the freedom to work independently. This is an important internal reward. Daniel Pink, the author of a book on motivation, **told** an audience once **that** Google was a good example of a company that supported autonomy. One day each week, Google engineers focus on their own ideas. Pink **informed** the audience **that** Google News and Gmail had been created during this free time.

Research also shows that appreciation is a powerful reward. In his book *The 1001 Rewards and Recognition*[1] *Fieldbook*, Bob Nelson described a study on the effects of appreciation on motivation. The study **asked**, "What motivates you?" Workers ranked the importance of 65 motivating factors. Nelson **indicated that** appreciation for their work ranked first for the workers.

The subject of worker motivation is complex. People expect fair pay for their work. However, research **shows that** people find internal rewards more meaningful than a high salary.

[1]**recognition:** special positive attention

NOTICE ACTIVITIES

draw students' attention to the structure, guiding their own analysis of form, meaning, and use.

GRAMMAR PRESENTATION

begins with an overview that describes the grammar in an easy-to-understand summary.

CHARTS

provide clear guidance on the form, meaning, and use of the target grammar, for ease of instruction and reference.

---

5 Other Reporting Verbs

Grammar Presentation

| Although *say* is the most common reporting verb, many other verbs can introduce indirect speech. | The president *explained* that our company's workers deserved higher pay.
The president *told us* that our company's workers deserved higher pay. |

5.1 Other Reporting Verbs

A *Tell* is a common reporting verb. Always use a noun or object pronoun after *tell*.	The president *said* that he was doing a great job. The president *told him* that he was doing a great job.
B You can use these verbs in place of *say*: *admit, announce, complain, confess, exclaim, explain, mention, remark, reply, report, state,* and *swear*. When used with an object, the object comes after *to*.	"The workers need recognition," said the manager. The manager *admitted* that the workers needed recognition. He *swore to us* that he'd be on time in the future.
C You can use these verbs in place of *tell*: *assure, convince, inform, notify,* and *remind*. Always use a noun or object pronoun with these verbs.	The president *told the managers,* "All workers need to be creative." The president *reminded them* that all workers need to be creative.

▸ Reporting Verbs: See page A11.

🌐 **DATA FROM THE REAL WORLD**

| Commonly used reporting verbs in formal writing include *claim, explain, find, show, state,* and *suggest*. | The author *claimed that* internal motivation was more effective than external motivation.
The results of the study *showed that* money was not always an effective way to motivate employees. |

🔊 Grammar Application

Exercise 5.1 Other Reporting Verbs

Complete the excerpt from an email about a presentation on cultural differences in motivation. Circle the correct verbs.

> Wei **said / told** me that he had attended a presentation on the cultural differences that affect motivation. He **said / told** that an expert on motivation gave the presentation. He **said / told** me that the expert was Dr. Ghosh.
>
> He **reminded / mentioned** me that we had read one of her articles in class.
>
> Anyway, Dr. Ghosh **said / informed** the group that the typical workplace included people with various cultural backgrounds. She **explained / reminded** that these workers had different expectations. She **informed / explained** the group that these workers often had different motivations.
>
> At the same time, Dr. Ghosh **reminded / remarked** that there was no one way to motivate all workers. She **admitted / reminded** that in multicultural settings, it was even more complicated.
>
> She **stated / reminded** the group that managers shouldn't make generalizations about cultures. She **assured / remarked** that the "human touch," getting to know employees as individuals, was the best way to motivate them.

DATA FROM THE REAL WORLD

takes students beyond traditional information and teaches them how the unit's grammar is used in authentic situations, including differences between spoken and written use.

GRAMMAR APPLICATION

Keeps students engaged with a wide variety of exercises that introduce new and stimulating content.

QR CODES

give easy access to audio at point of use in class or for review.

CONTEXTUALIZED PRACTICE

moves from controlled to open-ended, teaching meaningful language for real communicative purposes.

THEME-RELATED EXERCISES

boost fluency by providing grammar practice in a variety of different contexts.

Exercise 5.2 More Reporting Verbs

A Listen to the conversation about a presentation on cultural differences in classrooms. Complete the sentences with the words you hear.

David What happened in class today?

Mira We had a guest speaker. He _told us_ about the importance of motivation in
(1)
the language classroom. He _____ there are two kinds of
(2)
motivation: intrinsic and extrinsic.

David Right. Last week, the professor _____ there were two different
(3)
types, and she gave examples.

Mira Yes. So anyway, the speaker _____ he had done a study of
(4)
students in Japan and students in the United States. He _____
(5)
both groups had native-speaking English teachers. He _____
(6)
the purpose of the study was to see whether the teachers' remarks had a negative
effect on the motivation of the Japanese students.

David What did he find out?

Mira He _____ the study found four ways in which the teachers'
(7)
behavior had a negative effect on Japanese students' motivation.

David Did he give any examples?

Mira He _____ classroom discussion is one area where there are
(8)
key differences. He _____ in the Japanese classroom, students
(9)
generally listen more and talk less.

David And as we know from our reading, Porter and Samovar _____
(10)
in the U.S. classroom, some students speak up spontaneously, and that a lot of
teachers encourage discussion.

Mira Right. So, he _____ when a teacher criticizes a Japanese group
(11)
for not participating, it has a bad effect on motivation.

B Listen again and check your answers.

260 Unit 17 Direct Speech and Indirect Speech

HOW TO USE A QR CODE

1 Open the camera on your smartphone.

2 Point it at the QR code.

3 The camera will automatically scan the code. If not, press the button to take a picture.

* Not all cameras automatically scan QR codes. You may need to download a QR code reader. Search "QR free" and download an app.

AVOID COMMON MISTAKES

is based on a database of over 135,000 essays, students learn the most common mistakes English language learners make.

EDITING TASK

gives learners an opportunity to identify and correct the commonly made errors, helping develop self-editing skills needed in their university studies.

ACADEMIC WRITING

concentrates on specific stages of the writing process: Brainstorm, Organize, Write, Edit

---

C Over to You Compare the behavior of American and Japanese students to students from another culture that you are familiar with. Use sentences with indirect speech.

The speaker said that in the Japanese classroom, students listen more and talk less. That is true in my culture, too. Students show respect that way.

6 Avoid Common Mistakes ⚠

1 For verbs such as *admit, announce, complain, explain,* and *mention,* the object pronoun comes after the preposition *to.*

to us
He explained ~~us~~ the objective.

2 Change the form of the verb in indirect speech in most cases.

had
He claimed that they ~~followed~~ the directions.

3 Use beginning and ending quotation marks with direct speech.

The director said, "All designers may work from home on Fridays."

Editing Task

Find and correct the mistakes in the paragraphs about a memorable event.

One of the highlights of my life happened through an experience at work. It started when my manager announced us some interesting news. He said, I am starting a company band. Then he asked, "Who wants to join?" I mentioned him that I had played guitar for many years. He said, You should definitely try out.

5 On the day of tryouts, I was a little nervous because everyone played extremely well. After I auditioned, the manager thanked me and explained me that he will let me know soon.

I forgot about it, so I was very surprised when I got a phone call from my manager a few days later. He said, You can play lead guitar. I said, Wow! That's great! After that, the band practiced a few times a week. A few months later, we played

10 at the company party. We were nervous, but we played well. The president of the company spoke to me later and said I have a lot of talent. I was embarrassed by his compliment, but I said I am proud to play for the company. I will never forget that experience.

---

7 Academic Writing

Argumentative Writing Using Graphs and Tables for Support

Brainstorm Organize Write Edit

In this writing cycle (Units 17–20), you will write an argumentative essay that uses graphs or tables to answer the prompt below. In this unit (17), you will analyze an essay with graphs and then brainstorm ideas about the topic.

Using what you know about the job market, what is a good choice for a career path with a secure future? Include information from graphs or tables to support your choice.

Exercise 7.1 Preparing to Write

Work with a partner. Discuss the questions.

1 Is it important to have a college degree? Why or why not?

2 College tuition in the United States is very expensive. Do you think the benefits of a degree outweigh the costs? Why or why not?

3 A founder of Netscape, an early Internet search company, has said that people who earn a degree in a non-technical field like literature will probably be working in a shoe store upon graduation. Do you agree or disagree? Why or why not?

Exercise 7.2 Focusing on Vocabulary

Read the sentences. Then match the words in bold to the definitions.

1 Steve Jobs, one of the **founders** of Apple Inc., said that quality was more important than quantity.

2 Business leaders **disputed** the government's claim that the number of jobs had grown.

3 The successful campaign against buying the corporation's products **illustrates** the power of the consumer.

4 There is some **ambiguity** in the law, so it is difficult to know if the company did anything wrong.

5 This new technology has the **potential** to change how students learn about science.

6 According to economists, the more you consume something, the more your enjoyment of it will **diminish**. In other words, you will never enjoy it as much as you do when you first buy it.

7 The consequences of the economic crash **extend** beyond the city to the whole country.

a _____ (v) to disagree with

b _____ (n) the state of being unclear or having more than one possible meaning

c _____ (n) people who establish an organization

d _____ (v) to decrease in size or importance

e _____ (v) to go further

f _____ (n) the possibility to develop and succeed

g _____ (n) an example that explains something

What Is the Value of a College Education?

Benjamin Franklin, one of the founding fathers of the United States, once said, "An investment in knowledge pays the best interest." These days, a college education is a significant investment, so it makes sense to consider carefully whether it is worth the time and money. In good economic times and bad, and in spite of

5 its rising cost, the answer appears to be "yes." Figure 1, from the Organization for Economic Cooperation and Development (OECD), shows that around the world the number of people getting a college education is rising steadily.

A college education has a broad and positive impact. People with a college degree are by far the most likely to enter and remain in the labor force. In OECD

10 countries, average participation in the labor force for those who never completed high school is about 59%. The OECD reports that for those with a high school degree, the figure is about 78%, and for college graduates, it is about 84%. They also state that college graduates earn more than those with only a high school degree. In the United States, a new high school graduate earned on average

15 less than $30,000 per year in 2017, whereas those with a college degree made over $52,000. Over a lifetime, that difference adds up to about a million dollars. Figure 2 **illustrates** that the impact of a college degree on income in selected OECD countries can be dramatic.

The consequences of getting—or not getting—a college education **extend**

20 beyond income. There is a strong association between education and health. Chronic¹ diseases, such as heart disease and diabetes, pose the greatest risks to public health in developed countries today. These diseases are caused, at least partly, by lifestyle choices, such as poor diet or smoking. In general, people with higher levels of education make healthier lifestyle choices and have greater access

25 to high-quality healthcare.

It is evident that a college degree provides an economic advantage, but not all degrees have the same earning power. Most analysts suggest that degrees in STEM fields (science, technology, engineering, and math) have the greatest **potential** impact on future income. In the United States, a college graduate with, for example,

30 a chemical engineering degree can expect to earn about $70,000 annually, whereas a graduate with a literature or art degree may be lucky to get $36,000 for an entry-level position. Marc Andreessen, the **founder** of the internet company Netscape, once declared that someone who studies a non-technical field like literature will probably end up "working in a shoe store."

35 Yet, technology married with liberal arts . . . that yields the results that make our hearts sing." Other major employers in the technology field agree. Industry leaders say that employees from the liberal arts are often good at managing **ambiguity**, unlike engineers, who tend to see situations in black and white. Liberal arts graduates can see a problem from multiple perspectives.

It is interesting to note that the income gap between liberal arts and STEM graduates gradually **diminishes** as they continue in their careers.

40 In fact, liberal arts degrees are quite common among the world's most highly paid workers. About one-third of the directors of Fortune 500 companies have a liberal arts background. Students, parents, politicians, and industry leaders may argue over which are the most valuable degrees, but the value of a college degree in general cannot be **disputed**.

¹**chronic** (adj) lasting for a long time, especially something bad

Figure 1 Percentage of Population (25–64) with a College Education

Source: Organization for Economic Cooperation and Development (OECD), Online Education Database, retrieved September 13, 2019, from https://stats.oecd.org/index.aspx. See Digest of Education Statistics 2018, table 603.20.

■ 2000
■ 2017

Figure 2 Level of Earnings Relative to Education

Source: OECD (2019), Education and earnings: Level of earnings relative to median earnings, by educational attainment, OECD.Stat, https://stats.oecd.org/index.aspx?DataSetCode=EAG_EARNINGS, accessed on August 1, 2019.

■ At or below the median income
■ More than 2x the median income

LEARNER OUTCOMES

are mapped out at the beginning of each writing cycle and section.

REAL WORLD MODEL

incorporates the unit grammar into common types of writing for students to understand and analyze.

SKILL BOXES

provide clear explanations of carefully selected writing skills.

WRITING TASK

helps students develop their academic writing at various stages of the writing process.

Direct Speech and Indirect Speech

Exercise 7.3 Comprehension Check

Read the text on page 263. Work with a partner. Discuss the questions.

1 Summarize the main argument of the text.
2 What benefits of a college degree are mentioned in the text?
3 According to Figure 1, what three countries had the highest percentage of citizens with a college education?

Exercise 7.4 Noticing the Grammar and Writing

Work with a partner. Complete the tasks.

1 Underline the first sentence. Why does the writer use a quote to introduce the topic?
2 Find another quote in the text. How does the writer introduce the quote?
3 Look at Figure 1. What is the writer's purpose in using this graph?
4 Look at Figure 2. What is the writer's purpose in using this graph?
5 What is the source of the information in the graphs?

Understanding and Using Graphs and Tables

Information in academic texts is often presented through graphs and tables. Writers include these to support their ideas or argument. It is important to understand and interpret the information in your graphs and tables, and to draw inferences and conclusions for your reader.

Exercise 7.5 Applying the Skill

Work with a partner. Ask and answer the questions about the information in Table 1.

Table 1. The 100 Best Jobs in the U.S., with Median Salary

Rank	Job Title	Median Salary
1	Software Developer	$101,790
4	Dentist	$165,120
14	Surgeon	$208,000
28	IT Manager	$139,220
42	Lawyer	$119,250
62	Hairdresser	$24,850
66	Medical Assistant	$32,480
76	High School Teacher	$59,170
88	Massage Therapist	$39,990

Source: U.S. News and World Report 2018

1 What information does the table present?
2 What can you infer from the table?
3 In addition to salary, what other factors do you think make a job a "best job"?

My Writing

Argumentative Essays with Graphs or Tables as Support

In argumentative essays, writers present their position, reasons, and supporting evidence. Evidence used in graphs and tables should come from credible sources, such as educational or research institutions, government websites, and respected news organizations.

Exercise 7.6 Brainstorming Topics and Ideas

1 Work with a partner. Make a copy of the chart and complete it.

  • Column 1: Write the names of three careers.
  • Column 2: Write relevant information from the reading, Table 1, and other credible sources you find. Include the name of the source in parentheses.
  • Column 3: Make notes about the career and the information you found.

Career	Information (Name of Source)	Notes

2 In your opinion, which of the careers is the best choice for a financially secure future? Why?

Using Reporting Verbs to Introduce Evidence

Writers use reporting verbs to introduce evidence. Reporting verbs also show readers how the writer feels about the evidence. **Neutral reporting verbs** show a more neutral feeling towards the evidence.

The report **said** that the number one skill employers are looking for is flexibility.

Strong reporting verbs show a strong feeling towards the evidence.

The report **asserted** that the number one skill employers are looking for is flexibility.

Neutral reporting verbs: advise, accept, acknowledge, recognize, encourage, interpret, analyze, examine, investigate, consider, evaluate
Strong reporting verbs: argue, assert, convince, emphasize, indicate, persuade, refute, show, state, stress, support, warn

Exercise 7.7 Applying the Skill

Use the information from Exercise 7.6 to write a paragraph that asserts which career would best lead to a secure future. Include a topic sentence, at least two reasons for your argument with supporting details and evidence, and a concluding sentence. Use at least one reporting verb to introduce evidence.

Kahoot!

for Grammar and Beyond
cambridge.org/kahoot/grammarandbeyond

What is Kahoot!?
Kahoot! is a game-based learning platform that makes it easy to create, share and play fun learning games and trivia quizzes in minutes. Students can play Kahoot! on any mobile device or laptop with an internet connection.

What can you use kahoots for?
Kahoots can be used for review, formative assessment or homework.

When should you play Kahoot?
You can use a kahoot before starting the unit as a diagnostic, during the unit as formative assessment, or at the end of a unit to test student knowledge.

To launch a live game in the classroom, simply click on "play" when launching kahoot.

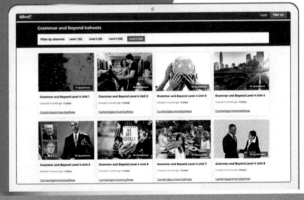

Quiz Your English app

Quiz Your English is a fun new way to practice, improve, and test your English by competing against learners from all around the world. Learn English grammar with friends, discover new English words, and test yourself in a truly global environment.

- Learn to avoid common mistakes with a special section just for *Grammar and Beyond* users
- Challenge your friends and players wherever they are
- Watch where you are on the leaderboards

Negative Questions and Tag Questions

Geographic Mobility

1 Grammar in the Real World

A Have you moved very often in your life? If so, why did you move? Read the interview about geographic mobility. What are some of the reasons why people move?

B Comprehension Check **Answer the questions.**

1 What are some reasons why people move long distances?

2 What are some reasons why people stay nearby when they move?

3 Why is the mobility rate in Russia lower than in the United States?

C Notice **Find the sentences in the article and complete them.**

1 Professor, you **have been** interested in geographic mobility for

a long time, _____ you?

2 Mobility **isn't** easy to explain, _____ it?

Look at the verbs you wrote and the verbs in bold. What do you notice about the use of *not*?

Geographic Mobility
ACROSS CULTURES

Interviewer Today we're speaking with two specialists in geographic mobility. They will discuss some reasons why people move from one place to another. Professor O'Neill is from
5 Carlow University in the United States, and Professor Tabenkin is from Zala University in Russia. Let's start with Professor O'Neill. Professor, you have been interested in geographic mobility for a long time,
10 **haven't you**?

O'Neil Well, yes. When I was a boy, my best friend moved away, and that affected me deeply. As I grew older, I saw more people move away. I noticed that the population
15 decrease affected local businesses. As a result, I got interested in the choices people make about moving.

Interviewer People are very mobile and are moving a lot. But most people aren't moving long
20 distances, **are they**? **Isn't** that curious?

O'Neil Yes. That's interesting. In fact, I've been studying the connection between moving and distance recently. Every year, about 11.6 percent of people in the United States
25 move, and of these, about 14.8 percent move to a different state.

Interviewer **Doesn't** that surprise you?

O'Neil No, not really. Often, people who change jobs have to move long distances. On
30 the other hand, people looking for better housing usually stay near their original home. And people who relocate[1] for family reasons may move far away or stay nearby.

Interviewer So, I guess it depends on the situation,
35 **doesn't it**?

O'Neil That's right. It's more complicated than you may think. For example, my wife was living in California when we met. When we got married, she moved a long distance to live
40 with me in Chicago. Now her sister, who lives near Chicago, is expecting a baby. She and her husband plan to move a short distance to be closer to us.

Interviewer Professor Tabenkin, people in Russia have
45 the same issues, **don't they**?

Tabenkin To a certain extent, yes. It's harder to find housing in Russia, so people tend to move less frequently. In fact, the mobility rate in Russia is less than 2 percent. In my
50 research, I found that young people often decide not to move because available, affordable housing would take them further from family.

Interviewer OK. But **don't** people sometimes have to
55 move long distances for economic reasons?

Tabenkin Yes, that's true. Personally, I had to move a very long distance ten years ago because there were no jobs nearby. However, my experience doesn't seem to be the norm.[2]

Interviewer 60 Mobility isn't easy to explain, **is it**? Thank you both for your thoughts on this issue.

---

[1]**relocate:** move to a new place   [2]**norm:** an expected situation or a situation considered to be typical

2 Negative Questions

Grammar Presentation

Negative questions are similar to *Yes/No* questions in that they begin with an auxiliary verb, a modal, or a form of *be*.	*Haven't you moved recently?* *Aren't there many reasons why people move?*

2.1 Forming Negative Questions

A Negative questions usually begin with a contraction.	*Don't you live around here?* *Can't you help me move?* *Wasn't he living in Chicago?*
B The full form of *not* in negative questions is very formal. The word *not* comes between the subject and the main verb.	*Were they **not** living in Chicago?* *Have you **not** moved recently?*
C With a contraction, use *are* instead of *am* with *I*. Use *am* when you use the full form.	*Aren't I correct?* *Am I not correct?*

2.2 Using Negative Questions

A Use negative questions when you think the information is true and you expect people to agree.	*Don't people often move when they change jobs?* (My experience tells me people often move when they change jobs.) *Isn't it unusual for people to move in Russia?* (I've read that it's unusual to move in Russia.)
B Use negative questions to show surprise or disbelief.	*"Tom has changed his major to English."* *"Really? **Isn't he still planning to work at a bank?**"*
C Use negative questions to show annoyance or anger.	*Didn't you say you would call me?* (I'm angry that you didn't call me.) *Shouldn't Bob have finished that report by now?* (I'm annoyed because Bob hasn't finished the report.)

2.3 Answering Negative Questions

Respond to a negative question just as you would a regular *Yes/No* question. Typically, we answer negative questions with *yes* or *no* and an explanation.	*"Don't you want to move?"* (Do you want to move?) *"**Yes**, I do. I'd like to live somewhere else."* *"**No**, I don't. I really want to stay here."*

Grammar Application

Exercise 2.1 Negative Questions

A family is packing for a big move. Complete the negative questions with the correct form of the words in parentheses.

1 _____Didn't I tell_____ (I told) you to be careful with that lamp?

2 _____ (you have been listening) to what I've been saying?

3 _____ (you can stop) texting and help me?

4 _____ (you should have bought) bigger boxes?

5 _____ (I am) correct that you promised to help?

6 _____ (you were going to take) the baby to the neighbor's?

Exercise 2.2 More Negative Questions

Read the sentences about moving and migration. Then write negative questions with the information in parentheses. Use contractions when possible.

1 A lot of people left Ireland in the 1800s.
   Didn't a lot of people leave because of a famine?
   (You heard that a lot of people left because of a famine.)

2 Hope of employment brings a lot of immigrants to rich countries.
   _____
   (You heard that good schools have made rich countries more attractive, too.)

3 Some people move great distances.
   _____
   (You heard that some people move great distances to reunite with family members.)

4 Some corporations require their employees to move to another country.
   _____
   (You think that this is happening more because of globalization.)

5 People are able to move around more freely because of globalization.
   _____
   (You heard that the laws are changing to allow even more movement.)

Geographic Mobility **211**

Pair Work Read the chart on migration in the United States. Study it for 30 seconds. Then cover it. What details can you remember? Ask your partner negative questions. Then switch roles and answer your partner's negative questions.

A   *Haven't 60 percent of men moved?*

B   *Yes, that's right.*

A   *And haven't 50 percent of college graduates moved?*

B   *Actually, no, 77 percent of college graduates have moved.*

People Who Move: Percentages of people who have moved at least once in their lifetimes	% of People Who Have Moved	% of People Who Have Never Moved
Total	63	37
By Gender		
Men	60	40
Women	65	35
By Education		
College graduates	77	23
High school graduates	56	44

▶ www.pewsocialtrends.org/2008/12/17/who-moves-who-stays-put-wheres-home

3 Tag Questions

Grammar Presentation

Use tag questions to confirm information or ask for agreement.	*You're a professor, aren't you?* *He hasn't been studying, has he?*

3.1 Forming Tag Questions

A The verb in a tag question is an auxiliary verb, a modal, or a form of *be*.	*Your parents have never moved, have they?* *She got the job, didn't she?* *You can't stay, can you?*

3.1 Forming Tag Questions *(continued)*

B The pronoun in a tag question agrees with the subject.	*The students* will be on time, won't **they**? *Your sister* lives close by, doesn't **she**?
Use *it* when the subject is *that* or *something*.	*That's* amazing information, isn't **it**?
Use *they* when the subject is *someone* or *everyone*.	*Someone* recorded the interview, didn't **they**? *Everyone* respects the professor, don't **they**?
C Use an affirmative tag with a negative statement.	NEGATIVE STATEMENT AFFIRMATIVE TAG They *don't live* in Chicago, **do they**? You*'re not* from Russia, **are you**?
Use a negative tag with an affirmative statement.	AFFIRMATIVE STATEMENT NEGATIVE TAG Geography *is* interesting, **isn't it**? Her sister *moved* to Chicago, **didn't she**?

3.2 Answering Tag Questions

A In negative tags, we expect the listener to answer *yes*, but it is possible to answer *no*.	*"They moved from Miami to Chicago, <u>didn't they</u>?"*
	    *"**Yes**, they got jobs in Illinois."* (That's right, they moved.)
	    *"Actually, **no**."* (That's not right. They didn't move.)

B In affirmative tags, we expect the listener to answer *no*, but it is possible to answer *yes*.	*"They didn't move from Miami to Chicago, <u>did they</u>?"*
	    *"**No**, they decided to stay."* (You're right, they didn't move.)
	    *"**Yes**, they had to move for work."* (Actually, they did move.)

C You cannot answer *Yes . . . not*.	*"They didn't move from Miami to Chicago, <u>did they</u>?"* *"**Yes, they did**."* OR *"**No, they didn't**."* NOT *"~~Yes, they didn't.~~"*

Grammar Application

Exercise 3.1 Tag Questions

Match the statements and tags about a friend who is moving.

1 Erica and her family are moving overseas, _d_   a do they?

2 You knew about their move, _____   b didn't you?

3 Erica's company is relocating to London, _____   c aren't you?

4 Erica's husband won't get a new job, _____   d aren't they?

5 They don't have a place to live yet, _____   e don't I?

6 Erica will get an international driving permit, _____   f isn't it?

7 I have a lot of information about their move, _____   g will he?

8 You're giving them a going-away party, _____   h won't she?

Exercise 3.2 Tags

Complete the questions about the stresses of moving. First underline the subject and circle the auxiliary verb in each sentence. Then write the correct tag.

1 <u>Moving</u> (can) be stressful as well as expensive, _can't it_ ?

2 People can sometimes deduct moving costs from their income taxes, _____ ?

3 Things have sometimes disappeared from a moving truck, _____ ?

4 Your friends will give you boxes, _____ ?

5 Everyone should read reviews of a moving company before hiring one, _____ ?

6 Marta has been disorganized since the move, _____ ?

7 Vinh and Ahn weren't moving today, _____ ?

8 It's been a stressful time for you, _____ ?

Exercise 3.3 Statements in Tag Questions

Complete the questions about people who are moving. Use the words in parentheses with the correct verb forms.

1 _____ _Mary is retiring to Florida_ _____ , isn't she?
        (Mary / retire / Florida)

2 _____ , hasn't he?
        (Raul / relocate / London)

3 _____ , didn't she?
        (Annette / attend school / France)

4 _____ , won't they?
        (Miriam and Amir / turn down the promotion / New York)

5 _____ , did you?

(You / like / the air quality / Hong Kong)

6 _____ , will he?

(Bernard / take the children / with him / Texas)

Exercise 3.4 Answering Tag Questions

Complete the conversations with the expected answers.

Conversation 1

| Paolo | I'm interviewing for a job in New York. |
| | You grew up there, didn't you? |

Luis	_____Yes, I did_____ . What do you want
	(1)
	to know?

| Paolo | Well, I'm worried about housing. Apartments |
| | aren't cheap there, are they? |

| Luis | _____ . They're also hard to find. |
| | (2) |

Conversation 2

| Phoebe | You've read the article on migration patterns for class today, haven't you? |

| Alex | _____ . It was interesting. |
| | (3) |

| Phoebe | Oh, good. You don't have time to tell me about it before class, do you? |

| Alex | _____ . But I can send you a link to the article. |
| | (4) |

Conversation 3

| Claudia | I heard the company is moving to Dallas, Texas. Some of us will have to move, |
| | won't we? |

| Jun | _____ . I'll know exactly who next week. |
| | (5) |

| Claudia | You have family there, so you won't mind moving, will you? |

| Jun | _____ . My family's excited. |
| | (6) |

Conversation 4

| Fen | There are a lot of new families moving into the neighborhood, aren't there? |

| Bin | _____ . I'm glad to see new faces. |
| | (7) |

| Fen | It's nice to see a lot of young children around again, isn't it? |

| Bin | _____ . It's wonderful! |
| | (8) |

Geographic Mobility **215**

Use rising intonation in the tag when you are not certain your statement is true.	"Moving wasn't difficult, *was it*?" "Yes, it was!" "There won't be a quiz tomorrow, *will there*?" "No, there won't."
Use falling intonation when you expect the listener to agree with you.	"His research is really boring, *isn't it*?" "Yes, it is." "You didn't go to class, *did you*?" "No, I didn't."

A Listen and repeat the questions in the chart above.

B Listen to the conversations about a student moving far away to attend college. Draw the intonation pattern above the tag. Then write *U* if the speaker is uncertain of the information or *E* if the speaker is expecting agreement.

Conversation 1

1 You're not still thinking about going to college in Pennsylvania, are you? *U*

2 But that college doesn't offer the major you want, does it? _____

Conversation 2

3 Your son is thinking of going to college far from home, isn't he? _____

4 Duquesne University is in Pittsburgh, isn't it? _____

Conversation 3

5 You're excited about moving to Pennsylvania for college, aren't you? _____

6 You're not worried about moving so far from home, are you? _____

Conversation 4

7 Your son is worried about moving so far from home, isn't he? _____

8 But you and your wife feel OK about him moving so far away, don't you? _____

C Pair Work Find out information about your partner by asking tag questions. Use both intonation patterns. Use rising intonation when you are uncertain and falling intonation when you expect agreement.

A *You're from Egypt, aren't you?*

B *Yes, I am. You're studying culinary arts, aren't you?*

A *Actually, no. My major is geography.*

4 Avoid Common Mistakes ⚠

1 **In negative questions, use the auxiliary verb + *not*.**

Didn't she
~~She no~~ call you?

2 **Answer negative questions the same way as regular *Yes/No* questions.**

"Aren't you coming with us?"

No, I'm not.
"~~Yes.~~" (I'm not coming.)

Yes, I am.
"~~No.~~" (I'm coming.)

3 **In tag questions, remember to use an auxiliary verb + a pronoun in the tag.**

wasn't it
The research was old, ~~no~~?

4 **In the tag, use an auxiliary verb that agrees with the main verb + the correct pronoun for the subject.**

aren't they
They are still living in their hometown, ~~isn't it~~?

Editing Task

Find and correct six more mistakes in the conversation about economic mobility.

    A   That article on economic mobility in America was really interesting, ~~no~~? *wasn't it*

    B   It sure was. Some of the facts were surprising, isn't it? I was especially surprised that

          there is more economic mobility in countries like France and Germany.

    A   I was, too. I thought there was more mobility here. By the way, don't you have a class

5   right now?

    B   Yes. I'm finished for today. I'm free for the evening.

    A   But you're working tonight, no?

    B   No, I quit my job.

    A   Really? Why? You no like it?

10   **B**   The job was fine. The truth is I'm moving to Florida with my family at the end of the

          semester, so I'm really busy.

    A   You're kidding! Why? Your family no like it here?

    B   They like it here, but there aren't many good jobs. We're moving where the jobs are.

    A   But you only have one semester left, isn't it?

15   **B**   That's right, but I have to go with them.

5 Academic Writing

Argumentative Writing

Brainstorm > Organize > Write > Edit

In this writing cycle (units 14-16), you will write an argumentative essay that answers the prompt below. In this unit (14), you will analyze an argumentative text and start brainstorming ideas about your topic.

Which is more important when choosing a home: location or size?

Exercise 5.1 Preparing to Write

Work with a partner. Discuss the questions.

1 Why might people move from one location to another?
2 What are the most beautiful buildings in your country? Describe them.
3 How do you feel about modern architecture? Give an example.
4 In your opinion, which is more important in architecture, beauty or function?

Exercise 5.2 Focusing on Vocabulary

Read the sentences and choose the best definition for the words in bold.

1 The **function** of an architectural drawing is to show what a building will look like after construction.
   a complexity or detail
   b purpose
2 Box-like buildings without windows or unique features can seem very **depressing**, can't they?
   a making you feel unhappy and without hope
   b making you feel physically weak and less active
3 When you see a magnificent work of art, such as a painting or a beautiful building, the creativity behind it can be **inspiring**.
   a causing eagerness to learn or do something
   b informative or educational
4 Not taking care of public parks and buildings **reflects** badly **on** a city and its government.
   a reacts to
   b damages
5 That architect has a wonderful **reputation** in her field; she is widely admired by many other architects.
   a the general opinion that people have about someone
   b a collection of works
6 He **demonstrated** the new construction technique for the public.
   a criticized or disapproved of something
   b showed how to do something; explained

Form or Function?

At the start of the twentieth century, Louis Sullivan, one of the creators of modern architecture, said that "form follows **function**." The term *functionalism* is used to suggest that the
5 idea behind architecture focuses primarily on the purpose or use of a building. That seems to mean that the look of a building is unimportant, doesn't it? On the contrary, many people feel that beauty is the most important factor in architectural design.
10 In the modern world, it seems that most architects try to combine the two ideas, aiming to create buildings that are both functional and **inspiring** in their beauty. This goal is often difficult to achieve, however. Don't we create buildings to serve the
15 needs in our lives? If so, the role that function plays should always be prioritized over form.

Many people believe that architects have a wider responsibility to society than just designing functional buildings. Beautiful, well-constructed
20 buildings are a symbol of a civilized[1] society, and they **reflect** well on the **reputation** of a business or owner. Ugly public buildings, on the other hand, can project a negative image of the organization. Don't you agree? People say
25 that living or working in an ugly place creates a **depressing** and uninspiring environment. In contrast, an attractive building can make people feel happier and increase their motivation to work.

The beauty of a building is important; however,
30 the reason for creating a building in the first place—its use—is even more important, isn't it? When building an airport terminal, for example, you need to think of the needs of passengers as well as planes. Passengers want to get to
35 their plane as quickly as they can, and planes need to be parked in a way that maximizes their ease of use. A solution to this challenge is that many airport terminals have a circular shape with satellite areas. Residential homes need to have
40 enough space for a family, art galleries need wall space to show pictures, and factories need to produce goods as efficiently as possible. Each type of building has a different function, and, therefore, it has a different form.

45 There is no reason that architecture cannot be both functional and beautiful, is there? Yet in practice, this can cause problems. The International Style of the 1920s and 1930s, an example of which is the Guggenheim Museum in
50 New York, was supposed to combine beauty with function. Many consider the museum's white spiral ramp beautiful, but there have been complaints that it is impractical, as it is difficult to stand back to view the art. Also, the ramp is so narrow that it
55 can become overcrowded. The Farnsworth House by Ludwig Mies van der Rohe is another icon of beautiful design that **demonstrate**s the idea that "less is more." However, critics have attacked it for a lack of privacy because of the huge glass
60 windows. It also has a leaky flat roof and has been repeatedly flooded. It seems that even these two celebrated designs have problems with functionality.

If architects focus only on function, buildings
65 may be cold, ugly, and uninteresting. There is no doubt that a building with a beautiful form is something we can all appreciate. However, an attractive design that does not consider the practical needs of the people who live or work in
70 the building is also problematic. For this reason, shouldn't functional needs be addressed before visual ones? This issue of practicality is the most important feature of the buildings we live in, work in, and visit. Therefore, function must outweigh
75 form when an architect plans a building.

[1]**civilized:** having a well-developed way of life and social systems

Read the text on page 219. Work with a partner. Discuss the questions.

1 What is the main idea of the reading?

2 What are two examples of buildings that are beautiful but not completely practical?

3 What are two problems that may occur when a building only focuses on function?

Exercise 5.4 Noticing the Grammar and Writing

Work with a partner. Complete the tasks.

1 Highlight six questions in the text.

2 Underline the last sentence in the first paragraph. What is the purpose of this sentence?

3 What is the writer's view about architecture?

4 What reasons and examples does the writer give to support this view?

5 Where might this text appear? Explain your answer.

Negative and Tag Questions in Academic Writing

Negative questions and tag questions are not common in academic writing. They are generally found in less formal writing, like editorials, blogs, or popular magazines.

Exercise 5.5 Applying the Skill

Revise two negative questions and two tag questions in the text to make them appropriate for academic writing. You may need to combine more than one sentence when you revise the negative questions.

1 _____

2 _____

3 _____

4 _____

Argumentative Essays

In an argumentative essay, a writer looks at several viewpoints on a topic and attempts to give reasons to persuade the reader that one of those viewpoints is better than the others.

Exercise 5.6 Identifying Arguments and Reasons

1 Work with a partner. Review the text on page 219, and complete the T-chart.

2 In each column, which reason is the most persuasive? Which is the least persuasive? Why?

Writer's Argument:	Opposing Argument:
Reasons:	Reasons:

My Writing

Exercise 5.7 Brainstorming and Organizing

Work with a partner. Complete the tasks.

1 Many people choose a home based on its location or size. Why are these important considerations when selecting a home?

2 Write the reasons for considering location in the first column of the T-chart.

3 Write the reasons for considering size in the second column of the T-chart.

4 Look at your T-chart. Which do you feel is more important? Explain your answer.

Location	Size

Exercise 5.8 Writing an Argumentative Paragraph

Use your answers in Exercise 5.7 to write a paragraph about the importance of either location or size. Include a topic sentence, at least two reasons for your argument with supporting details, and a concluding sentence.

That Clauses

Cultural Values

1 Grammar in the Real World

ACADEMIC
WRITING

Argumentative
writing

A Is it possible to identify "typical" American values? Theories exist about the values Americans hold today – and why. Read the article about one view of American values. Do you agree with the writer's point of view?

B Comprehension Check Match the two parts of the sentences.

1 According to some historians, the difficulty of living on the frontier led to _____

2 Survival under difficult circumstances may have led to _____

3 The lack of towns and traditions may have led to _____

a optimism.

b the value of hard work.

c individualism.

C Notice Find the sentences in the article and complete them.

1 Many Americans _____ they must work hard in order to be happy.

2 Traditionally, American children _____ they are responsible for their own lives.

3 Not all historians _____ frontier life influenced modern American values.

How many subjects are in each of these sentences? What word connects the two clauses?

U.S. Cultural Values

Values are beliefs held in common by members of a group. They often come from shared experiences. For example, some historians assert[1] **that the settlement of the American**
5 **West in the nineteenth century shaped many American values. These include the importance** of hard work, optimism, and individualism.

Countless U.S. children have learned in school **that hard work is essential**. In fact,
10 many Americans believe **that they must work hard in order to be happy**. How did this belief develop? According to some researchers, as Americans moved deeper into the continent, they discovered **that the West was mostly**
15 **wilderness**.[2] Their lives were difficult, and they had to work hard to survive. Some historians are convinced **that their success helped form a general belief in the value of hard work**.

Furthermore, many Americans believe **that**
20 **they should have a positive view of the future**. A few historians suggest **that this perspective helped put men on the moon**. What is the origin of this optimism? Some research suggests **that struggles on the frontier[3] encouraged this**
25 **attitude**. People found **that they could survive, even in difficult situations**.

Another common belief about Americans is **that they are individualistic**. Traditionally, American children have learned **that they are**
30 **responsible for their own lives**. This way of thinking supports the idea **that every person can succeed through hard work**. In addition, Americans tend to believe **that they can start over when they make mistakes**. Why
35 do they feel this way? It is the belief of some historians **that this idea developed as a result of frontier life**. Because there were few towns and traditions, settlers created their own rules. Each new settlement developed its own ways
40 of getting things done. When settlements faced problems, they had no choice but to try new and different approaches.

Not all historians agree **that frontier life influenced modern American values**.
45 Furthermore, the United States is becoming more and more culturally diverse all the time. Undoubtedly, this is already affecting the values held by its citizens. In what way might American values change?

---

[1]**assert:** to state an opinion

[2]**wilderness:** an area of land that has not been farmed or had towns and roads built on it

[3]**frontier:** the western area of the United States that did not have many white settlers from the eastern part of the United States

2 That Clauses

Grammar Presentation

Noun clauses function like nouns in sentences. They often begin with the word *that*.

Many people believe that they must work hard in order to be happy.

2.1 Forming *That* Clauses

A *That* clauses have their own subject and verb.

MAIN CLAUSE		THAT CLAUSE	
SUBJECT	VERB	SUBJECT	VERB

Many Americans think that anyone can succeed.

B In conversation and informal writing, *that* is often omitted. In academic writing, *that* is usually not omitted.

Most people recognize cooperation is important. (informal)

Most people recognize that cooperation is important. (formal)

2.2 Using *That* Clauses

Use *that* clauses after the following verbs that express mental activity:

assume, believe, decide, discover, expect, feel, find (out), guess, hear, hope, imagine, know, learn, notice, read, realize, recognize, say, see, show, suppose, think, understand

Can we <u>assume</u> that the core values have remained basically the same?

Some people <u>believe</u> that hard work brings happiness.

I've <u>discovered</u> that some cultures don't have a positive view of the future.

I <u>read</u> that American values developed during the colonial period.

Grammar Application

Exercise 2.1 Forming *That* Clauses

Combine the sentences about employees in the United States. Use *that* clauses.

1 Many Americans notice something. They are working harder but have less money.

   Many Americans notice that they are working harder but have less money.

2 In fact, recent research has found something. Hard work doesn't always lead to wealth.

   In fact, recent research has found that hard work doesn't always lead to wealth.

3 Many older Americans are realizing something. They are unable to retire after working hard all their lives.

Many older Americans are realizing that they are unable to retire after working hard all their lives.

4 Many employees assumed something. Their companies would reward them for their hard work.

Many employees assumed that their companies would reward then for their hard work,

5 Researchers recently reported something. Job satisfaction has declined in recent years.

Researchers recently reported that job satisfaction has declined in recent years.

6 Employers are beginning to understand something. It is important to give people some freedom at work.

Employers are beginning to understand that it is important to give people some freedom at work.

Exercise 2.2 Using *That* Clauses Without *That*

Over to You Do you believe that money makes people happy? Why or why not? Write five sentences. Use *that* clauses but do not use *that* in your sentences. Then share your sentences with a partner.

A *I don't think money makes people happy because having money causes many problems.*

B *I disagree. I believe you need a certain amount of money to feel secure, and this makes people happy.*

Exercise 2.3 Using *That* Clauses

A Write statements with *that* clauses using the words in parentheses.

1 Europeans work fewer hours than Americans. (I / understand)

   I understand that Europeans work fewer hours than Americans.

2 The average European gets about two months' vacation every year. (Michael / read)

   _____

3 The average American works 46 weeks per year. (international labor statistics / show)

   _____

4 Culture may be one reason for the difference in attitudes toward work. (some experts / believe)

   _____

5 Europeans tend to value leisure more highly than Americans.
(a group of scholars / found)

_____

6 Americans tend to value earning money more highly than Europeans.
(some scholars / believe)

_____

7 Many Americans seem to use possessions as a measure of success.
(a professor at Gradina University / wrote)

_____

B Group Work **As a group, talk about differences between Americans and Europeans. You may also include another culture that you know about. Discuss the following questions, or use your own ideas.**

- How much vacation time do Americans usually get?
- How much vacation time do Europeans usually get?
- How much vacation time do people from other cultures usually get?
- Who tends to relax on vacation?
- Who tends to bring work to do on vacation?

Use the following verbs in your discussion:

believe	hear	imagine	read	see	suppose	think

A _I've heard that Americans get less vacation time than Canadians._
B _I think that's true. My brother lives in Canada, and he told me the same thing._

3 Agreement Between *That* Clauses and Main Clauses

Grammar Presentation

<table>
<tr>
<td>Use a past form in a *that* clause when the verb refers to a past event. When it refers to a present event or state, use a present form.</td>
<td>Some historians believe that American values developed a long time ago. (present belief about a past action)

Some historians believe that early American history explains certain American values. (present belief about a present state)</td>
</tr>
</table>

3.1 That Clauses in Sentences with Present Verbs in the Main Clause

<table>
<tr>
<td>A When the main clause is in the present, use a present form in the *that* clause to express a fact or general truth.</td>
<td>Many Americans <u>feel</u> that nothing <u>is</u> impossible.

Some cultures <u>think</u> that cooperation <u>is very important</u>.</td>
</tr>
<tr>
<td>B When the main clause is in the present, use a past form in the *that* clause to describe a past event.</td>
<td>Some historians <u>don't think</u> that early American history <u>influenced</u> American culture.</td>
</tr>
<tr>
<td>C When the main clause is in the present, use a future form in the *that* clause to describe a future event.</td>
<td>I <u>assume</u> that you <u>are going to do</u> more research.</td>
</tr>
</table>

3.2 That Clauses in Sentences with Past Verbs in the Main Clause

<table>
<tr>
<td>A When the main clause is in the past, use a past form in the *that* clause to describe an event or idea that happened at the same time as the event in the main clause.</td>
<td>Nineteenth-century Americans <u>knew</u> that hard work <u>was</u> necessary.

My professor <u>noticed</u> that many students <u>were writing</u> about the nineteenth century.</td>
</tr>
<tr>
<td>B When the main clause is in the past, use a present form in the *that* clause to express a universal truth or a fact that applies to the present.</td>
<td>Who <u>discovered</u> that the Earth <u>is</u> round and not flat?

Scientists <u>discovered</u> that DNA <u>holds</u> the code for life.

When I started living on my own, I <u>found out</u> that life <u>is</u> sometimes very hard.</td>
</tr>
<tr>
<td>C Use the past perfect or past perfect progressive when the event in the *that* clause happened before the event in the main clause.</td>
<td>I <u>discovered</u> that she <u>had been copying</u> my history research for years!

I <u>heard</u> that she <u>had failed</u> the test.</td>
</tr>
</table>

D Use *would* or *was/were* going to when the event of the *that* clause happened after the event of the main clause.

I <u>heard</u> that a famous historian <u>would be speaking</u> at the conference.

We <u>discovered</u> that we <u>were going to study</u> twentieth-century history.

Grammar Application

Exercise 3.1 *That* Clauses in Sentences with Present Verbs in the Main Clause

Complete the sentences about the influence of Latin American cultures on mainstream U.S. culture. Use a *that* clause with the correct verb form. Sometimes more than one answer is possible.

1 Anthropologists agree / there be / links between Latin American cultures and U.S. culture (present for general truth)

Anthropologists agree that there are links between Latin American cultures and U.S. culture.

2 Research / shows / contemporary Latin American cultures / have / roots in African, European, and indigenous cultures (present for general truth)

Research shows that contemporary Latin American cultures have roots ~

3 Sociologists / believe / Latin American cultures / influence / world culture as well as U.S. culture (past event)

Sociologists believe that Latin American cultures influenced world ~

4 Many musicologists / agree / modern U.S. music / be / derived in part from Latin American cultures (present for general truth)

Many musicologists agrees that modern U.S. music is derived ~

5 Many language experts / assert / Spanish speakers / contribute / a great many words to the English language (past event)

Many language experts asserts that Spanish speakers contributed a great ~

6 Most sociologists / agree / Latin American cultures / continue / to influence U.S. culture (future for future action)

Most sociologists agree Latin American cultures are going to continue to ~

Exercise 3.2 *That* Clauses in Sentences with Past Verbs in the Main Clause

Listen to part of a lecture on westward movement in nineteenth-century North America. Complete the sentences with the words you hear.

In the nineteenth century, many people _**believed that**_ Americans _**had**_ the right
            (1)   (2)
to expand across the continent. John Quincy Adams, the sixth president of the United States,

thought that one large country _would be_ good for all Americans.
      (3)   (4)

However, some people ___knew that___ the westward
(5)
expansion ___would have___ some negative consequences.
(6)
For example, some people ___were aware that___ westward
(7)
expansion ___was having___ a negative impact on Native
(8)
American culture. In fact, some Americans at the time
___felt that___ the U.S. government ___was taking___
(9)   (10)
Native American land unfairly. They also ___pointed out that___
(11)
westward expansion ___was leading to___ many wars, such as the Mexican-American War of
(12)
1836. Most people ___did not realize that___ Americans ___were destroying___ native plants and
(13)   (14)
wildlife as well.

Exercise 3.3 Agreement Between *That* Clauses and Main Clauses

Group Work Do Internet research on how a culture, such as Irish-American or Latin American culture, has influenced culture in the United States or Canada. Write statements with *that* clauses. Use simple present for general truths, simple past for past events, and future for future action. Share your sentences with your group members. Use the following phrases in your sentences:

- I learned / discovered / found that . . .
- Another area that . . .

- For example, . . .
- A recent study showed / found that . . .

I learned that Indian culture has influenced American culture. One area that Indian culture has influenced is entertainment. Many film specialists agree that Bollywood movies are influencing American movies.

4 *That* Clauses After Adjectives and Nouns

Grammar Presentation

That clauses can follow some adjectives and nouns.	*I'm sure that a cultural group shares at least some values.* *I have the feeling that our values are quite different.*

4.1 That Clauses After Adjectives

A You can use a *that* clause after adjectives that express certainty or emotion.	*I'm <u>certain</u> that I haven't read enough about American culture.* *The conference organizers were <u>pleased</u> that he accepted the invitation.*

4.1 That Clauses After Adjectives (continued)

B You can use *that* clauses after *It + be +* certain adjectives. These adjectives often express emotions or degrees of certainty. They include:

certain, clear, evident, (un)fortunate, interesting, (un)likely, surprising, understandable

<u>It is evident</u> *that many other cultures have influenced U.S. culture.*

<u>It is unfortunate</u> *that many students don't know more about their country's history.*

<u>It is unlikely</u> *that we'll finish the unit by the next class.*

<u>It is understandable</u> *that historians disagree about the development of cultural values.*

4.2 That Clauses After Adjectives

A You can use *that* clauses after nouns that express thoughts and ideas, such as *belief, feeling, impression,* and *possibility*.

It was our <u>impression</u> that the historian was wrong.

There was no <u>possibility</u> that he was going to convince us.

B You can use noun *+ be + that* clauses with these commonly used nouns: *concern, difference, hope, idea, impression, point, problem, saying,* and *views*.

The <u>concern was</u> that we would never find out the truth.

The <u>point is</u> that the United States is a very large country.

The <u>problem is</u> that very individualistic people can find it hard to work in a group.

🌐 **DATA FROM THE REAL WORLD**

Research shows that the following nouns frequently occur with *that* clauses:

assumption, belief, claim, conclusion, doubt, fact, hope, idea, impression, possibility, report, suggestion, view

*Is it your **assumption** that we cannot find jobs in other companies?*

*We came to the **conclusion** that he would never understand our point of view.*

🖥 Grammar Application

Exercise 4.1 That Clauses After Adjectives

Complete the magazine interview with a cultural studies expert. For each item, use the words in parentheses with the correct form of *be* and a *that* clause.

U.S. CULTURE AND THE WORLD

Interviewer Some experts are studying culture, and they have expressed some concerns. What are they concerned about?

Dr. Green *They are concerned that U.S. culture may have a negative impact on global culture.*
(1. they / concerned / U.S. culture may have a negative impact on global culture)

Interviewer Why are they worried?

Dr. Green Some people are worried that Americanization is making everything the same.
(2. some people / worried / Americanization is making everything the same)

Interviewer Why do they think this?

Dr. Green They are aware that Hollywood and fast-food chains are influencing culture.
(3. they / aware / Hollywood and fast-food chains are influencing culture)

Interviewer What's your opinion?

Dr. Green I am convinced that culture is a two-way street.
(4. I / convinced / culture is a two-way street)

Interviewer Why do you think that?

Dr. Green I am positive that other cultures influence U.S. culture as much as U.S. culture influence them.
(5. I / positive / other cultures influence U.S. culture as much as U.S. culture influences them)

Interviewer Can you give some examples?

Dr. Green A lot of people are surprised that the French invented movies
(6. a lot of people / surprised / the French invented movies)

Interviewer What else?

Dr. Green They are surprised that the British invented one of the original fast foods, fish and chips.
(7. they / surprised / the British invented one of the original fast foods, fish and chips)

Interviewer So what can we conclude?

Dr. Green I am sure that we all benefit from global cultural exchange.
(8. I / sure / we all benefit from global cultural exchange)

A Group Work **Complete the answers to these questions about the spread of U.S. culture worldwide. Explain your answers.**

1 Is the exportation of U.S. culture to the rest of the world a good thing?

It is my belief that *the exportation of U.S. culture is in some ways a good thing and in some ways a bad thing*   .

2 Survey your group members: Do you think that most people outside of the United States have a favorable opinion of U.S. popular culture?

It is our feeling that _____

_____.

3 Does your group think that most people outside of the United States have good feelings about American fast-food restaurants opening up in cities around the world?

It is our group's impression that _____

_____.

B Over to You **Read the results of a survey about the exportation of U.S. culture. Write three sentences about the survey results. Use the following adjectives: *amazed, disappointed, glad, pleased, relieved, surprised*. Discuss your reactions with a partner.**

What is your opinion of U.S. popular culture, such as music, TV shows, and movies?

Very favorable	21%
Somewhat favorable	39%
Somewhat unfavorable	25
Very unfavorable%	14%
No Answer	1%

I'm not surprised that most people have mixed feelings about U.S. culture.

I'm surprised that about 40 % people have unfavorable feelings about U.S. culture. more than I thought

I'm glad that more than 20 % people really like U.S. culture

I'm disappointed that 14% people don't like U.S. culture.

5 Avoid Common Mistakes ⚠️

1 **Do not use a comma before a *that* clause.**

Their parents are pleased~~,~~ that they are getting married.

2 **Remember that *that* clauses need a complete verb.**

I noticed that she ∧was leaving.

3 ***That* clauses must have a subject.**

Records show that ∧many settlers hoped to return east later.

4 **In academic writing, do not omit *that*.**

Some cultures believe ∧that individuals should put other people first.

Editing Task

Find and correct six more mistakes in the paragraphs about a famous American of the mid-nineteenth century.

Settlers from the east who traveled across the American West in the mid-nineteenth century understood ∧that they faced a difficult journey across deserts and mountains. They knew~~,~~ that the trip would take years and that some people lose their lives. However, they were optimistic.

5 Michael T. Simmons was one of those determined travelers. Someone told him to go to the Pacific Northwest for new opportunities. He sold his business to pay for the supplies that he and his family needed. He knew that the area was largely unknown. He also knew that ∧it was dangerous. This did not stop him.

When Simmons and his group reached Oregon, he announced that ∧he was~~was~~ going to continue north. The Hudson's Bay Trading Company heard the news, and they discouraged him. However, Simmons was certain~~,~~ that the trip ∧was going to be successful, and he did not listen. Instead, he continued north as planned. After he arrived, he helped to establish the first settlement in the territory that is now known as Washington State. Documents show that Simmons built the first mill using water
15 from the Tumwater waterfall for power. For this, he is sometimes called the father of Washington industry.

6 Academic Writing

Argumentative Writing

Brainstorm > Organize > Write > Edit

In Unit 14, you analyzed a text and brainstormed ideas for the prompt below. In this unit (15), you will continue brainstorming and start organizing your ideas by connecting information and supporting arguments.

> Which is more important when choosing a home: location or size?

Connecting Information

When you present an argument, you need to connect the information clearly and logically. To do this, there are several ways to refer back to a previous sentence with the same topic.

Countless U.S. children have learned that **hard work** is essential. In fact, many Americans believe that they must **work hard** in order to be happy.

Work hard in the second sentence is a rewording of *hard work* in the first sentence. **Rewording** connects the sentences and helps avoid unnecessary repetition.

Writers also use reference words such as *this, that, these, those*, or reference phrases like *that is why, for this reason*, or *in spite of this* to connect information and avoid repetition.

Traditionally, American children have learned that they are responsible for their own lives. **This** way of thinking supports the idea that every person can succeed through hard work.

Exercise 6.1 Applying the Skill

Complete the paragraph with the correct words and phrases from the box.

for this reason	in spite of	this	those

    U.S. culture has spread all over the world. (1)_____ concerns many people for a number of reasons. North American movies, music, and TV programs often give a false impression of life in the U.S. (2)_____, some experts warn that this "Hollywood culture" does not accurately reflect American society and can lead to misunderstandings of U.S. citizens. (3)_____ who say it is inaccurate believe that Hollywood portrays a glamorous life in which everyone is beautiful, rich, and happy. Others argue this is not a real concern. (4)_____ the portrayal of America in popular movies, people around the globe are well aware of the struggles many Americans encounter.

Supporting Arguments

Writers need to think about how to support an argument by following it with specific facts or observations that can persuade the reader.

Point of view: Working hard is the most important value that Americans have.

Not a specific fact or observation → not very persuasive: This is because it is good to work hard.

A specific observation → much more persuasive: People who work hard are more financially secure and contribute more to their community.

Exercise 6.2 Understanding the Skill

Read the numbered sentences. Choose the follow-up sentence that sounds more persuasive.

1 Having an optimistic view of the future is an important value.
   a This is because you will be happier.
   b If you are positive, you are likely to accomplish more things.

2 People need to know the history of their country.
   a It is sad that people do not know their country's history.
   b When you understand your country's history, you better understand its values.

3 The exportation of American culture is positive.
   a It is good because people want to know more about American culture.
   b When a culture is exported, people learn and understand more about others.

Exercise 6.3 Applying the Skill

Work with a partner. Read the opinions. Think of a supporting statement for each one.

1 The best way to learn about American culture is to watch movies.

2 People who are very individualistic do not work well with others.

3 Americans place too much importance on work, and not enough on family.

My Writing

Exercise 6.4 Organizing Ideas

1 Work in a small group. Review your paragraphs from My Writing in Unit 14. Who believes choosing a home for size is more important? Who believes choosing a home for location is more important?

2 Create a new T-chart about the advantages of the size and location of a home. Write all the reasons that you can think of in each column.

3 As a group, organize the reasons from strongest to weakest.

4 Write down any ideas that you can use in your essay.

16 Noun Clauses with *Wh-* Words and *If/Whether*

Inventions They Said Would Never Work

1 Grammar in the Real World

A Have you ever thought of inventing something? If so, what was it? Read the article about inventors. What obstacles did Edison and the Wright brothers face?

B Comprehension Check **Answer the questions.**

1 Why did people doubt Thomas Edison?
2 How did Edison convince the world of his accomplishment?
3 What were the obstacles the Wright brothers faced?

C Notice **Find the sentences in the article and complete them.**

1 No one knew exactly _____ .

2 Second, the success of inventors often depended on

_____ .

3 He could not predict _____ .

Look at the sentences again. Answer the questions.

1 In sentence 1, what type of question is the missing clause similar to?

   a an information question   **b** a *Yes/No* question

2 In sentences 2 and 3, what type of question is the missing clause similar to?

   a an information question   **b** a *Yes/No* question

INVENTIONS PEOPLE SAID WOULD NEVER WORK

Throughout history, new ideas have often faced skepticism[1] from society. Skepticism, however, has never stopped the creation of new inventions. Three important American inventors, Thomas Edison and
5 Orville and Wilbur Wright, faced strong public doubt, but they persevered,[2] and the results were the invention of the electric light bulb and the airplane.

While Edison may now be considered a brilliant inventor, in his lifetime he faced much criticism. Most
10 inventors in his day would not announce an invention until they had a model. Edison, however, stated that he had invented the light bulb, but he had no actual evidence for it. Thus, scientists doubted **what he said**. Also, most inventors had a schedule
15 for their projects, but Edison did not. No one knew exactly **when he would complete it**. Moreover, his experiments failed repeatedly, and this added to the skepticism. However, in 1882, Edison succeeded in lighting up an entire New York neighborhood,
20 and the world finally understood **what he had accomplished**.

Many inventors in the early 1900s wondered **whether it was possible to fly**. The Wright brothers proved **what others doubted** by inventing the first

25 airplane. However, they faced many obstacles along the way. First, most inventors were highly educated, but the Wright brothers had little formal education. Second, the success of inventors often depended on **whether they had financial support**. The
30 Wright brothers had none. Finally, most inventors publicized their research, but the Wright brothers did not. No one knew exactly what they were doing. Consequently, the public did not believe that the Wright brothers would succeed. Wilbur himself was
35 not sure **what would happen**. He could not predict **if their airplane would fly or not**. Then, in 1903, the Wright brothers flew their airplane for 12 seconds in Kitty Hawk, North Carolina. No one could believe **what they were seeing**. Five years later in France,
40 they flew another plane higher and longer.

Inventors almost always face public disbelief. Some people have trouble believing that new ideas are possible, but they certainly are. No one can be sure about **what the future holds**.

---

[1]**skepticism:** doubting the truth or value of an idea or belief

[2]**persevere:** continue doing something in a determined way despite difficulties

2 Noun Clauses with *Wh-* Words

Grammar Presentation

Noun clauses with *wh-* words can act as subjects, direct objects, or objects of prepositions.	*What they wanted* was financial support. The inventor understood *how we should build the machine.* I learned about *how many inventions are made every year.*

2.1 Forming Noun Clauses with *Wh-* Words

A Noun clauses with *wh-* words use statement word order (subject + verb).	*I've just realized what he did!* *I don't know when Edison invented the light bulb.*
B When noun clauses with *wh-* words *who*, *what*, and *which* act as subjects, they take a singular verb.	*What happened next is going to surprise you.*

2.2 Using Noun Clauses with *Wh-* Words

A Noun clauses with *wh-* words often appear after the following verbs: Thoughts and opinions: *consider, know, remember* Learning and perception: *figure out, find out, see, understand, wonder* Emotions: *care, doubt, hate, like, love*	*I don't remember who invented the airplane.* *We need to figure out why our invention failed.* *Our professor cares how we do our work.*
B Noun clauses with *wh-* words often follow verbs + prepositions, including *care about, decide on, find out about, forget about, know about, learn about, read about,* and *see about.*	*We shouldn't forget about which inventions succeeded and which didn't.* *I read about where Edison grew up.*

2.3 Reduced Noun Clauses with Infinitives

Noun clauses with *wh-* words can often be reduced to *wh-* word + infinitive. Common infinitives used this way include *to ask, to consider, to decide, to figure (out), to find (out), to forget, to know, to learn, to remember, to say, to see, to show, to understand,* and *to wonder.*

We're not sure who/whom[1] <u>to ask</u> for information.
= We're not sure who/whom[1] we should ask for information.

I don't know what <u>to say</u> about your invention.
= I don't know what I can say about your invention.

[1] The use of *whom* is infrequent, except in very formal writing.

Grammar Application

Exercise 2.1 Noun Clauses with *Wh-* Words

A Listen to the conversation among a group of students doing Internet research on recent inventions and inventors. Complete the sentences with the noun clauses you hear.

Peter OK, let's start with Randi Altschul.

Larry I don't know _who Randi Altschul is_ .
(1)

Paula Neither do I. I don't know _____ .
(2)

Peter I know _____ . She invented the disposable
(3)
cell phone.

Paula I'm impressed! I wonder _____ .
(4)

Larry I don't know.

Peter Got it! It says here her cell phone wasn't working well, and she felt like throwing it away.

Larry Let's find out _____ .
(5)

Peter It says here she got a patent for it in 1999.

Larry I just found out _____ at the
(6)
time. It was Florida.

Paula I wonder _____ .
(7)

Peter It says here that it was only 2 inches by 3 inches – kind of like a credit card.

Larry I wonder _____ .
(8)

Peter It was made of recycled paper.

PHONE-CARD-PHONE™
Working Model

B Pair Work With a partner, talk about what you know or don't know about other inventions. Use the verbs in A with *wh-* noun clauses.

I know when the smartphone was invented. It was in 2007. I remember what company first made it, but I don't know who invented it.

Exercise 2.2 Reduced Noun Clauses with *Wh-* Words + Infinitives

Some college students are talking to a business adviser about their new product. Rewrite the sentences with *wh-* words + infinitives.

1 We don't know where we should start.

    We don't know where to start.

2 Amy wonders where she could find a good patent lawyer.

3 I don't know how I can find a manufacturer for our product.

4 Binh is wondering who he can ask for money for our invention.

5 I'll figure out who we can contact for financial advice.

6 I wonder what we should charge for our product.

3 Noun Clauses with *If/Whether*

Grammar Presentation

Noun clauses can begin with *if* or *whether*. These noun clauses are similar in some ways to *Yes/No* questions, but they follow statement (subject + verb) word order.	I'm not sure *if the Wright brothers invented the airplane*. He doesn't know *whether we will get money for our experiment*.

3.1 Forming Noun Clauses with *If / Whether*

A Use statement word order (subject + verb) for noun clauses with *if/whether*.	*I don't know if the public will accept our idea.* *I don't know whether Edison really invented the light bulb.*
B You can use the words *or not* at the end of both *if* and *whether* clauses.	*The scientist didn't know if/whether you would understand her invention or not.*
Or not can immediately follow *whether*, but not *if*.	*The scientist didn't know whether or not you would understand her invention.* NOT *The scientist didn't know if or not you would understand her invention.*
C You can use *if/whether* to introduce two options.	*We don't know whether the new phone or the new tablet will come out first.*

3.2 Using Noun Clauses with *If / Whether*

A You can use noun clauses with *if/whether* after the following verbs: Thoughts and opinions: *decide, know, remember* Learning and perception: *figure out, find out* Emotions: *care, doubt, matter, mind*	*I haven't decided if I'm going to write a report about the Wright brothers.* *He can't find out if Edison first tried the light bulb in New York.* *They doubted whether anyone would steal their idea.*
B You can also use noun clauses with *whether* after verbs + prepositions, including *care about, decide on, find out about, forget about, know about,* and *read about.* You cannot use *if* after prepositions.	*You should forget about whether you'll make a lot of money with that invention.* NOT *You should forget about if you'll make a lot of money with that invention.*
C You can use an infinitive with *whether*. You cannot use an infinitive with *if*.	*He didn't know whether to share his discovery.* (= He didn't know whether he should share his discovery.) NOT *He didn't know if to share his discovery.*

🌐 DATA FROM THE REAL WORLD

Noun clauses with *if* are much more frequent than noun clauses with *whether*. *Whether* is more frequent in writing than in speaking.

Grammar Application

Combine the sentences. Use a noun clause with *if* or *whether*. Sometimes more than one answer is possible.

1 Scientists have not decided something. Is time travel possible?

   Scientists have not decided whether time travel is possible.

2 Many people don't know something. Do some robots think like humans?

   Many people don't know whether some robots think like humans.

3 Many people don't know this. Can we invent a non-polluting fuel?

   Many people don't know if we can invent a non-polluting fuel.

4 We can't remember this. Has anyone invented a self-cleaning house?

   We can't remember whether anyone has invented a self-cleaning house.

5 Many people don't know about this. Are hybrid cars good for the environment?

   Many people don't know if hybrid cars are good for the environment.

6 Scientists haven't figured this out. Are there other planets humans can live on?

   Scientists haven't figured whether there are other planets humans can live on.
   out

A Read the inventor's list of questions about her invention. Rewrite the questions as sentences. Use noun clauses with *if* or *whether*.

1 Can I really invent a solar-powered car?

   I don't know if I can really invent a solar-powered car.

2 Will it take a long time to invent it?

   I don't know if it will take a long time to invent it.

3 Am I smart enough to do it by myself?

   I don't know whether I am smart enough to do it by myself.

4 Do people really want solar-powered cars?

   I don't know if people realy want solar-powered cars.

5 Will a solar-powered car work on cloudy days?

   I don't know if a solar-powered car will work on cloudy days.

6 Is my car going to be too expensive?

   I don't know whether my car is going to be too expensive.

B Read more questions from the inventor in A. Rewrite the questions as sentences. Use *whether or not* with an infinitive.

1 Should I get some help?

   I can't decide whether or not to get some help.

2 Should I take out a loan from the bank?

   _____

3 Should I patent my idea first?

   _____

4 Should I see a lawyer?

   _____

 # 4 Noun Clauses in Direct and Indirect Questions

Grammar Presentation

Wh- noun clauses and noun clauses with *if* and *whether* can be used in direct and indirect questions.	*Do you know when New York got electricity?* (direct question) *I was wondering when New York got electricity.* (indirect question)

4.1 Forming Direct and Indirect Questions

A Direct questions with noun clauses have question word order and end with a question mark. Common phrases include: *Do you know . . . ? Can you tell me . . . ? Would you know . . . ?*	*Do you know **who invented the first calculator**?* *Are you trying to find out **if Edison was born in this country**?* *Can anyone tell me **if Edison was born in Scotland**?*
B Indirect questions with noun clauses have statement word order and end with a period. Common phrases include: *I want to find out . . . I'd like to know . . . I don't know why . . .*	*I have been wondering **what a patent is**.* *My group really needs to find out **if the Wright brothers had financial support for their invention**.* *I'd like to know **if people need to get patents for their inventions**.*

▸▸ Verbs and Fixed Expressions that Introduce Indirect Questions: See page A10.

Grammar Application

Complete the interview with artist and inventor Crispiano Columna. Rewrite the questions in parentheses as noun clauses in direct and indirect questions. Sometimes more than one answer is possible.

ArtOnline	I'm wondering *if you are both an artist and an inventor* .
	(1 Are you both an artist and an inventor?)
Crispiano Columna	Yes, I'm both.
ArtOnline	I'd like to know _____ .
	(2 What is your most famous invention?)
Crispiano Columna	I make sculptures that you can wear as gloves.
ArtOnline	I was wondering _____ .
	(3 Can you show us an example?)
Crispiano Columna	Yes, I'm wearing a pair right now.
ArtOnline	I was wondering _____ .
	(4 Did you study art in college?)
Crispiano Columna	No. In fact, I studied literature.
ArtOnline	I'd like to know _____ .
	(5 How did you become an artist?)
Crispiano Columna	I taught myself. I learned about color and drawing from books.
ArtOnline	I'd like to know _____ .
	(6 What was your first invention?)
Crispiano Columna	I invented a toy airplane for my nephew when I was a teenager.

A Look at the pictures of inventions. Write one indirect question about each picture. Use the following phrases:

I wonder / I'm wondering . . .   I'd like to know . . .   I'm interested in knowing . . .

The hair protector	The food cooler	The baby mop	The butter stick

I wonder who invented the hair protector.

1 _____

2 _____

3 _____

4 _____

B Pair Work Take turns reading your questions.

5 Avoid Common Mistakes ⚠

1 **Remember that a noun clause with a *wh-* word follows statement word order.**

                                      will

No one knows what ~~will~~ the next great invention ∧ be.

2 **Be careful to spell *whether* correctly.**

                                            whether

The success of the invention depended on ~~wether~~ people would buy it.

3 **Do not confuse *whether* and *either*.**

                                                 whether

The newest electronic devices will always tempt us, ~~either~~ we like them or not.

Editing Task

Find and correct the mistakes in the paragraphs about the importance of the Internet.

     Many inventions make life more convenient, but the Internet is the most essential one today. The Internet is a part of daily life. Although some people worry about ~~wheather~~ *whether* this fact is harmful or not, many agree that they do not know what would they do if they could not go online.

5   First of all, the Internet helps people communicate instantly with family and friends who are far away. In the past, people had to write a letter or pay for a long-distance call to find out how were they doing. While they waited, they worried about whether their loved ones were all right. Now there are many ways to contact people and find out if they are well.

10   In addition, the Internet helps people find information. If we want to know what is the temperature in Seoul today, we only have to type the question. Also, it is very easy to look for employment, research solutions to a problem, and even find out wether a movie is playing nearby.

     It is too early to tell either the Internet causes serious long-term problems for
15 society or not. To me, it seems extremely valuable because it connects me to people I care about and to information I need.

6 Academic Writing

Argumentative Writing

Brainstorm > Organize > **Write** > **Edit**

In Unit 15, you learned ways to connect information and support your arguments for the prompt below. In this unit (16), you will write, revise, and edit your essay.

Which is more important when choosing a home: location or size?

Register in Academic Writing

The types of language used in informal writing and in formal, academic writing are very different. Academic writers use more precise, technical words and more formal phrases and linking words.

They usually avoid slang, colloquial expressions, first-person pronouns, contractions, exclamation points, abbreviations like *etc.*, and negative and tag questions.

Exercise 6.1 Applying the Skill

Replace the informal words and phrases in bold in the paragraph with academic words and phrases from the box.

a great deal of	benefits	critical	fundamentally	reduce	undoubtedly

   I'm sure that the greatest invention of all time is the microwave. The microwave **basically** makes our lives easier. It has a number of **good things**. First, with a microwave, we can prepare **lots of** food in a very short time. Microwaves **cut down** our meal preparation time, which is useful in our busy lives. Next, microwaves are small, and this is **really important** if you have a small kitchen.

Argumentative Essay Structure

Argumentative essays often follow the structure below.
- **Introductory Paragraph**
- **Body Paragraph 1**: Argument #1 in favor of your choice being more important
- **Body Paragraph 2**: Argument #2 in favor of your choice being more important
- **Body Paragraph 3** (if necessary): Argument #3 in favor of your choice being more important
- **Concluding Paragraph**

My Writing

Exercise 6.2 Applying the Skill

1 Write your point of view.

2 Review your notes and T-charts from My Writing in Units 14 and 15. Choose the 2–3 strongest arguments for your body paragraphs. Think of reasons and support for them.

3 Write your thesis statement.

4 Write the first draft of your argumentative essay.

Exercise 6.3 Revising Your Ideas

1 Work with a partner. Use the questions to give feedback on your partner's essay.

- Which of your partner's ideas seem the strongest to you?
- Which of your partner's ideas needs to be explained more clearly?
- What could your partner add or remove to make the essay stronger and clearer?

2 Use the feedback from your partner to revise the ideas and content of your essay.

Exercise 6.4 Editing Your Writing

Use the checklist to review and edit your essay.

Does your essay answer the prompt completely?	
Does your essay follow the argumentative essay structure?	
Does your essay support your point of view with persuasive language and ideas?	
Did you connect information clearly and logically?	
Did you support your argument with specific examples and information?	
Did you use the correct register for an academic essay?	

Exercise 6.5 Editing Your Grammar

Use the checklist to review and edit the grammar in your essay.

Did you use *that* clauses correctly?	
Did you use noun clauses correctly?	
Did you avoid the common mistakes in the charts on pages 217, 233, and 245?	

Exercise 6.6 Writing Your Final Draft

Apply the feedback and edits from Exercises 6.3 to 6.5 to write the final draft of your essay.

17 Direct Speech and Indirect Speech

Human Motivation

1 Grammar in the Real World

A What makes people work hard at their jobs? Read the article about employee motivation. What type of reward is particularly effective in motivating workers?

B Comprehension Check **Complete the chart. Check (✓) whether each reward is external or internal.**

	External Reward	Internal Reward
1 Pay raise		
2 Feeling successful		
3 Freedom to work independently		
4 Good salary		
5 Good grades		

C Notice **Find similar sentences in the article and complete the sentences below.**

1 Lionel Messi _____, "Money is not a motivating factor… My motivation comes from playing the game I love."

2 Daniel Pink, the author of a book on motivation, _____ an audience once that Google was a great example of a company that supported autonomy.

3 Pink _____ the audience that Google News and Gmail had been created during this free time.

Each sentence tells what someone says. Which sentence gives the actual words of the speaker? How do you know?

WORKPLACE MOTIVATION

Motivation is the desire to do something. Soccer star Lionel Messi **said**, "Money is not a motivating factor… My motivation comes from playing the game I love." Messi meant that he enjoys playing soccer more than making millions of dollars. Can that be true? What other factors are important in motivating people?

Many psychologists believe that there are two types of rewards that affect motivation: external rewards and internal rewards. External rewards are rewards that someone gives you. A pay raise is a common external reward. A good grade at school is also an example of an external reward. Internal rewards are connected to the feelings people have about the work they do. The satisfaction you get when you do something well is an internal reward. Researcher Frederick Herzberg (1923–2000) studied motivation in the workplace for many years. Herzberg **said that** employers must think about factors that affect employees' feelings of satisfaction. Herzberg **explained that** working conditions and relationships among co-workers affect workers' motivation. Therefore, employers need to create an environment that makes employees feel safe, valued, and accepted.

25 Some studies on workplace motivation have focused on autonomy, which is the freedom to work independently. This is an important internal reward. Daniel Pink, the author of a book on motivation, **told** an audience once **that** Google was a good example of a company that supported autonomy. One day each 30 week, Google engineers focus on their own ideas. Pink **informed** the audience **that** Google News and Gmail had been created during this free time.

Research also shows that appreciation is a powerful reward. In his book *The 1001 Rewards and* 35 *Recognition[1] Fieldbook*, Bob Nelson described a study on the effects of appreciation on motivation. The study **asked**, "What motivates you?" Workers ranked the importance of 65 motivating factors. Nelson **indicated that** appreciation for their work ranked first for 40 the workers.

The subject of worker motivation is complex. People expect fair pay for their work. However, research **shows that** people find internal rewards more meaningful than a high salary.

---

[1]**recognition:** special positive attention

2 Direct Speech

Grammar Presentation

Direct speech repeats people's exact words.	*Lionel Messi said, "Money is not a motivating factor. … My motivation comes from playing the game I love."*

2.1 Forming Sentences with Direct Speech

A Direct speech consists of a reporting clause and a person's exact words.	REPORTING CLAUSE *Lionel Messi said, "Money is not a motivating factor."*
The most common reporting verb is *said*. Use a comma after the verb.	*Our manager **said**, "Treat the customers like family, and they will come back."*
To quote speech, use quotation marks and a capital letter to begin the direct speech. End the direct speech with punctuation inside the quotation marks.	*My colleague said, "**W**e are going to lead the company in sales next year**!**"*
B The reporting clause can also come at the end or in the middle of direct speech. Notice that the verb can also come before the subject in the reporting clause when the reporting clause comes at the end or in the middle.	*"The company pays its workers fairly," **the president said**.* *"We didn't do well this year," **said Liz**, "so we won't get a sales bonus."*
C Use the verb *asked* to quote a question.	*Mr. Smith **asked**, "What do you hope to accomplish in this job?"*

Grammar Application

Exercise 2.1 Statements in Direct Speech

A Rewrite the quotations about motivation as direct speech. Sometimes more than one answer is possible.

1 in my experience, there is only one motivation, and that is desire –Jane Smiley

   Jane Smiley said, "In my experience, there is only one motivation, and that is desire."

2 the ones who want to achieve and win championships motivate themselves
–Mike Ditka

_____

_____

3 the ultimate inspiration is the deadline –Nolan Bushnell

_____

_____

4 motivation is the art of getting people to do what you want them to do because
they want to do it –Dwight D. Eisenhower

_____

_____

5 I'm a great believer in luck, and I find the harder I work, the more I have of it
–Thomas Jefferson

_____

_____

6 great work is done by people who are not afraid to be great –Fernando Flores

_____

_____

7 nothing great was ever achieved without enthusiasm –Ralph Waldo Emerson

_____

_____

8 you miss 100 percent of the shots you don't take –Wayne Gretzky

_____

_____

9 the journey of a thousand miles begins with a single step –Lao Tzu

_____

_____

B Over to You **Choose two of the quotations, and write a sentence that explains what
each one means.**

*When Jane Smiley said, "In my experience there is only one motivation, and that
is desire," she meant that the only real motivation is wanting to do something.*

C Pair Work **Share your sentences with a partner. Discuss whether you agree or disagree
with your partner's interpretation.**

A Read the transcript of an online discussion about motivating employees. Then rewrite each question as a direct speech question. The information in parentheses tells you where to put the reporting clauses – at the beginning or end of the sentences.

Working Today

Today, motivational expert Camila Valdez is here to answer your questions.

Claire **Is money the best way to get employees to work harder?**
(1)

Camila No. Studies show that appreciation and recognition are the best ways.

Pedro **Do you have guidelines for rewarding employees?**
(2)

Camila Try to match the size of the reward to the size of the accomplishment.

Roxana **When should you give the rewards?**
(3)

Camila It's really best to give them as soon as possible after employees have

accomplished something.

Hong **What are some ways to motivate employees?**
(4)

Camila Give rewards that fit your employees' working style.

Chelsea **Can you give an example of what you mean?**
(5)

Camila Certainly. For example, give a more flexible schedule to working parents.
They will feel more focused at work because they will be able to take care
of their home-related responsibilities.

---

1 (beginning) *Claire asked, "Is money the best way to get employees to*

work harder?"

2 (end) _____

3 (beginning) _____

4 (end) _____

5 (beginning) _____

B Over to You Ask two classmates these questions: Would money motivate you to
work harder? Why or why not? Then write a short report on your interviews with direct
speech statements and questions.

*I talked to Anne and Mike. I asked, "Would money motivate you to work harder?"
Anne said, "No, it wouldn't." I asked, "Why not?" Anne said, "I work to please myself.
That's my reward." Then I asked Mike, "Would money motivate you to work harder?"
Mike said, "Yes, it would."*

3 Indirect Speech

Grammar Presentation

Indirect speech tells what someone says in another person's words. Indirect speech is also called reported speech.	Lionel Messi said, "Money is not a motivating factor." (direct speech) Lionel Messi said that money was not a motivating factor. (indirect speech)

3.1 Forming Indirect Speech

An indirect speech statement consists of a reporting verb such as *say* in the main clause, followed by a *that* clause. The word *that* is optional and is often omitted when speaking.	She said, "The boss is angry." (direct speech) She **said (that)** the boss was angry. (indirect speech)

3.2 Tense Shifting in Indirect Speech

A After a past verb in the reporting clause, the verb form in indirect speech usually changes. The verb shifts to express a past time.

DIRECT SPEECH	INDIRECT SPEECH
She said, "The boss **is** angry."	She said that the boss **was** angry.
He said, "She **is enjoying** the work."	He said that she **was enjoying** the work.
They said, "The store **closed** last year."	They said that the store **had closed** last year.
The manager said, "The group **has done** good work."	The manager said that the group **had done** good work.

B The following forms usually change in indirect speech.

DIRECT SPEECH	INDIRECT SPEECH
He said, "The department **will add** three new managers."	He said that the department **would add** three new managers.
She said, "They **are going to hire** more people soon."	She said that they **were going to hire** more people soon.
The teacher said, "The students **can work** harder."	The teacher said that the students **could work** harder.
Their manager said, "Money **may not be** very important to them."	Their manager said that money **might not be** very important to them.

C The forms of *should, might, ought to*, and *could* are the same in direct and indirect speech.	

DIRECT SPEECH	INDIRECT SPEECH
The boss said, "He should go home."	*The boss said that he should go home.*

D Do not change the form of verbs in general truths or facts.	She said, "Martin Luther King, Jr. **was** a great man." She said (that) Martin Luther King, Jr. **was** a great man. NOT *She said that Martin Luther King Jr.* ~~had been~~ *a great man.*

▶▶ Tense Shifting in Indirect Speech: See page A11.

Grammar Application

Exercise 3.1 Tense Shifts in Indirect Speech

Read the quotes about a psychology course. Then rewrite each quote as indirect speech. Sometimes more than one answer is possible.

1 The professor said, "Psychology 101 includes a unit on motivation."

   The professor said that Psychology 101 included a unit on motivation.

2 A student said, "The class is discussing motivation and personality this week."

_____

_____

3 The professor said, "The class is reading about Abraham H. Maslow's theories on motivation."

_____

_____

4 One student said, "I'm learning a lot in the class."

_____

_____

5 Another student said, "I don't understand the lectures."

_____

_____

6 The teaching assistant said, "The readings have great practical value."

_____

_____

Exercise 3.2 Modals and Future Forms in Indirect Speech

Read the excerpt from a lecture on how to motivate adult learners. Then complete the email. Rewrite each sentence from the lecture as indirect speech. Sometimes more than one answer is possible.

Welcome to Motivating Adult Learners. This class is for people who teach adults. Participants in the course are going to learn all about motivating adult learners. The course will rely heavily on participants' own experiences. Students should come to class prepared to discuss their own experiences. We may occasionally have guest speakers. The course will include presentations, homework, and weekly quizzes. There will be three papers and two oral presentations. Participants can substitute an oral presentation for one of the papers.

To: jake15@cambridge.org
From: marta34@cambridge.org
Subject: First Class Meeting

Hi Jake,

Here's what happened in class today. The instructor welcomed us, and then she said Motivating Adult Learners was for people who teach adult learners.

1 *She said that participants in the course were going to learn all about motivating adult learners.*

2 _____

3 _____

4 _____

5 _____

6 _____

4 Indirect Speech Without Tense Shift

Grammar Presentation

Indirect speech usually includes a shift in verb tense. However, in some cases the form of the verb does not change.	*The president announced that she was going to start an employee program next year.* *The president announced that she is going to start an employee program next year.*

4.1 Keeping the Original Tense in Indirect Speech

You may use the tense in the original direct speech clause when you report statements that are still true now, such as: Facts or general truths	*He said, "A pay raise is a common reward."* *He said that a pay raise is a common reward.*
Habits and routines	*Leo said, "Our meetings always begin on time."* *Leo said that their meetings always begin on time.*
Actions in progress	*Eve said, "I'm studying hard for the exam.* *Eve said that she is studying hard for the exam.*

▶▶ Tense Shifting in Indirect Speech: See page A11.

4.2 Using Present Tense Reporting Verbs

Use a present tense verb in the reporting clause when what was said relates to the present and is still important at the moment of speaking. Keep the same tense as in the quote.	*Everybody always says, "Employees need to be motivated."* *Everybody always says that employees need to be motivated.*

Grammar Application

Exercise 4.1 Keeping the Original Tense in Indirect Speech

Read the quotes from a business meeting. Then rewrite the quotes as indirect speech. Use the same tense as the direct speech. Sometimes more than one answer is possible.

1 "We are trying to improve our new marketing plan."
   –the marketing manager

   The marketing manager said that we are trying
   to improve our new marketing plan.

2 "The client loves it." –the manager

_____

3 "We have always solved these problems in the past." –Janet

_____

4 "Staff satisfaction has been very important." –Janet

_____

5 "Tomorrow, we are going to have a half-day training session on giving constructive feedback." –Rodrigo

_____

_____

6 "We will all work together, as a team." –Rodrigo

_____

Exercise 4.2 Using Present Tense Reporting Verbs

A Complete the sentences. Use the correct form of the verbs in parentheses.

1 My father always says that money __*makes*__ (make) the world go round.

2 My friend Amanda insists that a good night's sleep _____ (be) more important than studying.

3 My aunt says that she _____ (enjoy) doing the work more than making money.

4 My friend says that he _____ (enjoy) having autonomy at work.

5 My colleague says that it _____ (not/be) always easy to stay motivated.

6 My manager says that you _____ always _____ (should/ask) questions if something is not clear.

B Pair Work Discuss the sentences in A. Do you agree with the statements?

5 Other Reporting Verbs

Grammar Presentation

Although *say* is the most common reporting verb, many other verbs can introduce indirect speech.	The president **explained** that our company's workers deserved higher pay. The president **told us** that our company's workers deserved higher pay.

5.1 Other Reporting Verbs

A *Tell* is a common reporting verb. Always use a noun or object pronoun after *tell*.	The president **said** that he was doing a great job. The president **told him** that he was doing a great job.
B You can use these verbs in place of *say*: *admit, announce, complain, confess, exclaim, explain, mention, remark, reply, report, state,* and *swear*.	"The workers need recognition," **said** the manager. The manager **admitted** that the workers needed recognition.
When used with an object, the object comes after *to*.	He **swore** <u>to us</u> that he'd be on time in the future.
C You can use these verbs in place of *tell*: *assure, convince, inform, notify,* and *remind*. Always use a noun or object pronoun with these verbs.	The president **told the managers**, "All workers need to be creative." The president **reminded them** that all workers need to be creative.

▶▶ Reporting Verbs: See page A11.

⊕ **DATA FROM THE REAL WORLD**

Commonly used reporting verbs in formal writing include *claim, explain, find, show, state,* and *suggest*.	The author **claimed that** internal motivation was more effective than external motivation. The results of the study **showed that** money was not always an effective way to motivate employees.

Grammar Application

Complete the excerpt from an email about a presentation on cultural differences in motivation. Circle the correct verbs.

Wei **said** / **told** me that he had attended a presentation on the cultural
(1)
differences that affect motivation. He **said** / **told** that an expert on motivation
(2)
gave the presentation. He **said** / **told** me that the expert was Dr. Ghosh.
(3)
He **reminded** / **mentioned** me that we had read one of her articles in class.
(4)

Anyway, Dr. Ghosh **said** / **informed** the group that the typical workplace
(5)
included people with various cultural backgrounds. She **explained** / **reminded**
(6)
that these workers had different expectations. She **informed** / **explained** the
(7)
group that these workers often had different motivations.

At the same time, Dr. Ghosh **reminded** / **remarked** that there was no one
(8)
way to motivate all workers. She **admitted** / **reminded** that in multicultural
(9)
settings, it was even more complicated.

She **stated** / **reminded** the group that managers shouldn't make
(10)
generalizations about cultures. She **assured** / **remarked** that the "human touch,"
(11)
getting to know employees as individuals, was the best way to motivate them.

A Listen to the conversation about a presentation on cultural differences in classrooms. Complete the sentences with the words you hear.

David   What happened in class today?

Mira   We had a guest speaker. He _told us_ about the importance of motivation in
(1)
the language classroom. He _____ there are two kinds of
(2)
motivation: intrinsic and extrinsic.

David   Right. Last week, the professor _____ there were two different
(3)
types, and she gave examples.

Mira   Yes. So anyway, the speaker _____ he had done a study of
(4)
students in Japan and students in the United States. He _____
(5)
both groups had native-speaking English teachers. He _____
(6)
the purpose of the study was to see whether the teachers' remarks had a negative
effect on the motivation of the Japanese students.

David   What did he find out?

Mira   He _____ the study found four ways in which the teachers'
(7)
behavior had a negative effect on Japanese students' motivation.

David   Did he give any examples?

Mira   He _____ classroom discussion is one area where there are
(8)
key differences. He _____ in the Japanese classroom, students
(9)
generally listen more and talk less.

David   And as we know from our reading, Porter and Samovar _____
(10)
in the U.S. classroom, some students speak up spontaneously, and that a lot of
teachers encourage discussion.

Mira   Right. So, he _____ when a teacher criticizes a Japanese group
(11)
for not participating, it has a bad effect on motivation.

B Listen again and check your answers.

C Over to You Compare the behavior of American and Japanese students to students from another culture that you are familiar with. Use sentences with indirect speech.

The speaker said that in the Japanese classroom, students listen more and talk less. That is true in my culture, too. Students show respect that way.

6 Avoid Common Mistakes ⚠

1 For verbs such as *admit*, *announce*, *complain*, *explain*, and *mention*, the object pronoun comes after the preposition *to*.

to us
He explained ~~us~~ the objective.

2 Change the form of the verb in indirect speech in most cases.

had
He claimed that they ~~follow~~ followed the directions.

3 Use beginning and ending quotation marks with direct speech.

The director said, "All designers may work from home on Fridays."

Editing Task

Find and correct the mistakes in the paragraphs about a memorable event.

One of the highlights of my life happened through an experience at work.
It started when my manager announced ~~us~~ to us some interesting news. He said, I am
starting a company band. Then he asked, "Who wants to join?" I mentioned him that
I had played guitar for many years. He said, You should definitely try out.

5   On the day of tryouts, I was a little nervous because everyone played extremely
well. After I auditioned, the manager thanked me and explained me that he will let
me know soon.

I forgot about it, so I was very surprised when I got a phone call from my
manager a few days later. He said, You can play lead guitar. I said, Wow! That's great!

10 After that, the band practiced a few times a week. A few months later, we played
at the company party. We were nervous, but we played well. The president of the
company spoke to me later and said I have a lot of talent. I was embarrassed by his
compliment, but I said I am proud to play for the company. I will never forget
that experience.

7 Academic Writing

Argumentative Writing Using Graphs and Tables for Support

Brainstorm > Organize > Write > Edit

In this writing cycle (Units 17-20), you will write an argumentative essay that uses graphs or tables to answer the prompt below. In this unit (17), you will analyze an essay with graphs and then brainstorm ideas about the topic.

> *Using what you know about the job market, what is a good choice for a career path with a secure future? Include information from graphs or tables to support your choice.*

Exercise 7.1 Preparing to Write

Work with a partner. Discuss the questions.

1 Is it important to have a college degree? Why or why not?

2 College tuition in the United States is very expensive. Do you think the benefits of a degree outweigh the costs? Why or why not?

3 A founder of Netscape, an early Internet search company, has said that people who earn a degree in a non-technical field like literature will probably be working in a shoe store upon graduation. Do you agree or disagree? Why or why not?

Exercise 7.2 Focusing on Vocabulary

Read the sentences. Then match the words in bold to the definitions.

1 Steve Jobs, one of the **founders** of Apple Inc., said that quality was more important than quantity.

2 Business leaders **disputed** the government's claim that the number of jobs had grown.

3 The successful campaign against buying the corporation's products **illustrates** the power of the consumer.

4 There is some **ambiguity** in the law, so it is difficult to know if the company did anything wrong.

5 This new technology has the **potential** to change how students learn about science.

6 According to economists, the more you consume something, the more your enjoyment of it will **diminish**. In other words, you will never enjoy it as much as you do when you first buy it.

7 The consequences of the economic crash **extend** beyond the city to the whole country.

a _____ (v) to disagree with

b _____ (n) the state of being unclear or having more than one possible meaning

c _____ (n) people who establish an organization

d _____ (v) to decrease in size or importance

e _____ (v) to go further

f _____ (n) the possibility to develop and succeed

g _____ (n) an example that explains something

What Is the Value of a College Education?

Benjamin Franklin, one of the founding fathers of the United States, once said, "An investment in knowledge pays the best interest." These days, a college education is a significant investment, so it makes sense to consider carefully whether it is worth the time and money. In good economic times and bad, and in spite of
5 its rising cost, the answer appears to be "yes." Figure 1, from the Organization for Economic Cooperation and Development (OECD), shows that around the world the number of people getting a college education is rising steadily.

A college education has a broad and positive impact. People with a college degree are by far the most likely to enter and remain in the labor force. In OECD
10 countries, average participation in the labor force for those who never completed high school is about 59%. The OECD reports that for those with a high school degree, the figure is about 76%, and for college graduates, it is about 84%. They also state that college graduates earn more than those with only a high school degree. In the United States, a new high school graduate earned on average
15 less than $30,000 per year in 2017, whereas those with a college degree made over $52,000. Over a lifetime, that difference adds up to about a million dollars. Figure 2 **illustrates** that the impact of a college degree on income in selected OECD countries can be dramatic.

The consequences of getting—or not getting—a college education **extend**
20 beyond income. There is a strong association between education and health. Chronic[1] diseases, such as heart disease and diabetes, pose the greatest risks to public health in developed countries today. These diseases are caused, at least partly, by lifestyle choices, such as poor diet or smoking. In general, people with higher levels of education make healthier lifestyle choices and have greater access
25 to high-quality healthcare.

It is evident that a college degree provides an economic advantage, but not all degrees have the same earning power. Most analysts suggest that degrees in STEM fields (science, technology, engineering, and math) have the greatest **potential** impact on future income. In the United States, a college graduate with, for example,
30 a chemical engineering degree can expect to earn about $70,000 annually, whereas a graduate with a literature or art degree may be lucky to get $36,000 for an entry-level position. Marc Andreessen, the **founder** of the internet company Netscape, once declared that someone who studies a non-technical field like literature will probably end up "working in a shoe store."

Yet, technical knowledge alone may not be sufficient for success. Steve Jobs, one of the founders of Apple, famously claimed, "It's
35 technology married with liberal arts ... that yields the results that make our hearts sing." Other major employers in the technology field agree. Industry leaders say that employees from the liberal arts are often good at managing **ambiguity**, unlike engineers, who tend to see situations in black and white. Liberal arts graduates can see a problem from multiple perspectives.

It is interesting to note that the income gap between liberal arts and STEM graduates gradually **diminishes** as they continue in their careers. In fact, liberal arts degrees are quite common among the world's most highly paid workers. About one-third of the directors of Fortune 500
40 companies have a liberal arts background. Students, parents, politicians, and industry leaders may argue over which are the most valuable degrees, but the value of a college degree in general cannot be **disputed**.

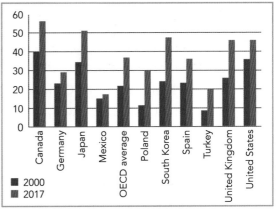

Figure 1 Percentage of Population (25–64) with a College Education
Source: Organization for Economic Cooperation and Development (OECD), Online Education Database, retrieved September 13, 2019, from https://stats. oecd.org/Index.aspx. See Digest of Education Statistics 2018, table 603.20.

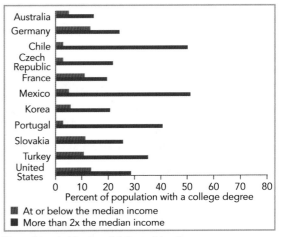

Figure 2 Level of Earnings Relative to Education
Source: OECD (2019), Education and earnings: Level of earnings relative to median earnings, by educational attainment, OEC.Stat, https://stats.oecd.org/ Index.aspx?DataSetCode=EAG_EARNINGS, accessed on August 1, 2019.

---

[1]**chronic** (adj) lasting for a long time, especially something bad

Exercise 7.3 Comprehension Check

Read the text on page 263. Work with a partner. Discuss the questions.

1 Summarize the main argument of the text.
2 What benefits of a college degree are mentioned in the text?
3 According to Figure 1, what three countries had the highest percentage of citizens with a college education?

Exercise 7.4 Noticing the Grammar and Writing

Work with a partner. Complete the tasks.

1 Underline the first sentence. Why does the writer use a quote to introduce the topic?
2 Find another quote in the text. How does the writer introduce the quote?
3 Look at Figure 1. What is the writer's purpose in using this graph?
4 Look at Figure 2. What is the writer's purpose in using this graph?
5 What is the source of the information in the graphs?

Understanding and Using Graphs and Tables

Information in academic texts is often presented through graphs and tables. Writers include these to support their ideas or argument. It is important to understand and interpret the information in your graphs and tables, and to draw inferences and conclusions for your reader.

Exercise 7.5 Applying the Skill

Work with a partner. Ask and answer the questions about the information in Table 1.

Table 1. The 100 Best Jobs in the U.S., with Median Salary

Rank	Job Title	Median Salary
1	Software Developer	$101,790
4	Dentist	$165,120
14	Surgeon	$208,000
28	IT Manager	$139,220
42	Lawyer	$119,250
62	Hairdresser	$24,850
66	Medical Assistant	$32,480
76	High School Teacher	$59,170
88	Massage Therapist	$39,990

Source: U.S. News and World Report 2018

1 What information does the table present?
2 What can you infer from the table?
3 In addition to salary, what other factors do you think make a job a "best job"?

My Writing

Argumentative Essays with Graphs or Tables as Support

In argumentative essays, writers present their position, reasons, and supporting evidence. Evidence used in graphs and tables should come from credible sources, such as educational or research institutions, government websites, and respected news organizations.

Exercise 7.6 Brainstorming Topics and Ideas

1 Work with a partner. Make a copy of the chart and complete it.

- Column 1: Write the names of three careers.
- Column 2: Write relevant information from the reading, Table 1, and other credible sources you find. Include the name of the source in parentheses.
- Column 3: Make notes about the career and the information you found.

Career	Information (Name of Source)	Notes

2 In your opinion, which of the careers is the best choice for a financially secure future? Why?

Using Reporting Verbs to Introduce Evidence

Writers use reporting verbs to introduce evidence. Reporting verbs also show readers how the writer feels about the evidence. **Neutral reporting verbs** show a more neutral feeling towards the evidence.

The report **said** that the number one skill employers are looking for is flexibility.

Strong reporting verbs show a strong feeling towards the evidence.

The report **asserted** that the number one skill employers are looking for is flexibility.

Neutral reporting verbs: *advise, accept, acknowledge, recognize, encourage, interpret, analyze, examine, investigate, consider, evaluate*

Strong reporting verbs: *argue, assert, convince, emphasize, indicate, persuade, refute, show, state, stress, support, warn*

Exercise 7.7 Applying the Skill

Use the information from Exercise 7.6 to write a paragraph that asserts which career would best lead to a secure future. Include a topic sentence, at least two reasons for your argument with supporting details and evidence, and a concluding sentence. Use at least one reporting verb to introduce evidence.

Indirect Questions; Indirect Imperatives, Requests, and Advice

Creative Problem Solving

1 Grammar in the Real World

ACADEMIC WRITING

Argumentative writing using graphs and tables for support

A When you have to solve a problem, what strategies do you use? Read the article about brainstorming. Would you prefer traditional brainstorming or "brainwriting"?

B Comprehension Check **Answer the questions.**

1 What are the four rules of brainstorming?

2 Why does Michalko believe that brainwriting may be more productive than brainstorming?

3 According to the writer, who can use brainstorming?

C Notice **Find the sentences in the article and complete them.**

1 First, he told participants _____ other people's ideas.

2 Therefore, he asked participants _____ even unusual ideas.

What are the forms of the missing verbs?

BRAINSTORMING
as a Problem-Solving Tool

There is more than one way to solve a problem. One method many people use is brainstorming. Brainstorming is an activity designed to produce a number of ideas in a short time. Alex Osborn
5 invented the word in 1939. In his book *Unlocking Your Creative Power*, Osborn said that the word *brainstorm* means using the brain to solve a problem creatively. Although he **said that groups should brainstorm** in a particular way, variations
10 on his technique have also become popular.

Osborn's original brainstorming method had four rules. First, he **told participants not to judge** other people's ideas. Second, he welcomed all ideas, even wild ideas. Osborn said that crazy
15 ideas could get people thinking along new lines and could lead to effective solutions. Therefore, he **asked participants to shout out** even unusual ideas. Third, Osborn **asked group members to produce** a large number of ideas. He thought that
20 the group would find a few really good ideas if

many different ones were available. Finally, Osborn **asked the brainstorming group if they could improve** the ideas that had been suggested.

One alternative to brainstorming is
25 brainwriting. Brainwriting is a silent version of brainstorming. With brainwriting, participants write down their ideas instead of shouting them out. In his book *Thinkertoys*, creativity expert Michael Michalko suggests that brainwriting may be more
30 productive than traditional brainstorming. This is because people often think of additional ideas as they write. He also asserts that this method is better for quieter individuals because they do not have to express their ideas out loud.

35 Brainstorming and brainwriting are flexible methods. Anyone can use them because they do not require a lot of training or expensive materials. These processes are all effective tools for creative problem solving in professional, academic, and
40 personal situations.

Creative Problem Solving **267**

2 Indirect Questions

Grammar Presentation

Indirect questions tell what other people have asked. There are two kinds of indirect questions: *Yes/No* questions and information questions.	He asked, *"Are your jobs satisfying?"* He asked *if our jobs were satisfying.* The director asked, *"Which technique do you prefer?"* The director asked *us which technique we preferred.*

2.1 Forming Indirect Questions

A	Use *asked* in the reporting clause and *if* to introduce an indirect *Yes/No* question.	*"Will we start attending brainstorming sessions?"* Mia **asked**. Mia **asked if** we will/would start attending brainstorming sessions.
	Use *asked* in the reporting clause and the same *wh-* word to introduce an indirect information question.	**"When** will the training begin?" our manager **asked**. Our manager **asked when** the training will/would begin.
B	Use statement word order in the indirect question.	He asked if **Rita was** one of our most productive employees.
C	After *ask*, you can use a direct object. The direct object can be a noun or pronoun.	She **asked the students** if they understood. She **asked me** when I wanted to leave the company.

Grammar Application

Exercise 2.1 Forming Indirect Questions

Read the interview between Joanna and Dr. Martin, a critical thinking expert. Then rewrite each of Joanna's questions as an indirect question.

Joanna	Dr. Martin, why is creative thinking in the business world so important?
Dr. Martin	Companies need very creative people to help design and market new products.
5 Joanna	Why will creative thinking be even more important in the future?
Dr. Martin	Competition is getting stronger. You have to be creative to stay competitive.
Joanna	What techniques have worked to get people to think creatively?
Dr. Martin	One technique that really works is to move the body. I tell people who are sitting at a desk to move into the conference room or take a walk outside.

Joanna	How does moving promote creativity?
Dr. Martin	Moving stimulates the brain.
Joanna	Are there any other ideas like this?
Dr. Martin	Of course. Try putting colorful pictures on the wall. Never try to be creative in an empty room.
Joanna	Do objects and colors stimulate creative thinking?
Dr. Martin	They definitely do.

15

1 What did Joanna ask Dr. Martin about creative thinking in the business world?

Joanna asked Dr. Martin why creative thinking in the business
world was important.

2 What did Joanna ask Dr. Martin about the future?

_____

3 What did Joanna ask about creative techniques?

_____

4 What did Joanna ask about moving?

_____

5 What did Joanna ask about other ideas?

_____

6 What did Joanna ask about stimulating creative thinking?

_____

Exercise 2.2 More Forming Indirect Questions

Read the conversation about a company's creativity exercises. Then rewrite each of Ahmet's questions as an indirect question.

Ahmet	How was your creativity session yesterday?
Irina	It was fun, and we had some really good ideas, too.
Ahmet	Was the session here?
Irina	Yes, it was here.
Ahmet	Who was your leader?
Irina	It was Dr. Martin, a creativity expert. She gave us a problem to solve. Then she gave us large pieces of white paper and markers in a lot of different colors.
Ahmet	What did you do with the paper and the markers?
Irina	We drew pictures of things that we wanted to say, that is, the solutions we had for the problem.
Ahmet	Interesting. How long were you drawing pictures?

5

10

Irina	We did that for about an hour. Then we had a thing called "incubation." We stopped working, had lunch, and then watched a TV show!
Ahmet	Why did you watch TV in the office?

15 | Irina | The idea was to forget about everything and then come back to the problem. When we went back to work, we then found the best solution. |
|---|---|

1 What did Ahmet ask Irina about yesterday?

   He asked her how her creativity session was.

2 What did Ahmet ask Irina about the location?

3 What did Ahmet ask Irina about the leader?

4 What did Ahmet ask Irina about the paper and the markers?

5 What else did Ahmet ask Irina about the activity with the paper and markers?

6 What did Ahmet ask Irina about watching TV in the office?

Exercise 2.3 Using Indirect Questions

Group Work **Ask and answer the questions about creativity with two students. Then share your answers with the whole class.**

- What are some situations in which people have to be creative?

- Why is creativity difficult for some people?

- When you have to be creative, do you have any techniques to stimulate your thinking? What are they?

3 Indirect Imperatives, Requests, and Advice

Grammar Presentation

Imperatives, requests, and advice are usually made indirect with an infinitive.	*"Please sit down."* He asked us **to sit down.** *"Would you please turn off your phones?"* He asked us **to turn off** our phones.

3.1 Indirect Imperatives, Requests, and Advice

A Use an infinitive in indirect imperatives. Use *not* + infinitive in negative indirect imperatives. You can use *tell* or *say*.	*"Don't make a lot of noise,"* said Mr. Jung. Mr. Jung <u>said</u> **not to make** a lot of noise.
Use an infinitive in indirect requests. You can use *ask, tell,* or *say*.	*"Please turn off your phones,"* said Mr. Cho. Mr. Cho <u>told</u> us **to turn off** our phones.
Use an infinitive to report advice given with modals such as *should*. Use *not* + infinitive to report advice with *should not*. You can use *tell* or *say*.	*"You shouldn't reject any ideas,"* Carl said. Carl <u>told</u> us not to reject any ideas.
B Always use an object after *tell*.	Ms. Ali **told** <u>us</u> to work quietly. NOT *Ms. Ali told to work quietly.*
Use a pronoun or noun after *ask* to show the person who is the object of the request.	Sam **asked** <u>her</u> to share her ideas with the group.

Grammar Application

Exercise 3.1 Indirect Imperatives and Requests

Read the directions that a trainer gave to a group of employees. Then rewrite the steps with infinitives and the words in parentheses.

1 "Get into groups of three or four."
2 "Don't get into a group with someone you usually work with."
3 "Cut out pictures from magazines that show your ideal working environment."
4 "Don't criticize your group members' choices."
5 "Present your picture to the other groups."
6 "Comment on the other groups' pictures, but don't criticize people's choices."
7 "Discuss the emotions that the pictures suggest."

I attended a problem-solving session with Dr. Martin yesterday. The goal was to help us get along better with each other. She helped us a great deal. Here's what she did:

1 (First / she / tell) *First, she told us to get into groups of three or four.*
2 (Then / she / say) _____
3 (She / tell) _____
4 (Dr. Martin / say) _____
5 (Then / she / tell) _____
6 (After that / she / say) _____
7 (Finally / Dr. Martin / say) _____

Listen to the marriage counseling session. Then answer the questions. Use the words in parentheses and *ask*, *say*, or *tell*.

1 What did the therapist tell the husband and wife to do?

   The therapist told them to take a pad
   of paper and a pencil.
   (take a pad of paper and a pencil)

2 What did the husband ask?

   _____

   _____
   (take a different pencil)

3 What did the wife ask?

   _____
   (use her own pen)

4 What did the therapist say?

   _____
   (write for 15 minutes without stopping)

5 What did the therapist tell the clients?

   _____
   (not look at each other's writing during the activity)

6 What did the therapist say?

   _____
   (not talk to each other)

7 What did the therapist tell the clients?

   _____
   (be prepared to read their descriptions to each other)

8 What did the husband ask?

   _____
   (have a little more time to write)

Exercise 3.3 Indirect Advice

A Over to You Think of some good and bad advice you or people you know have received. What was the advice? Write six sentences.

Good Advice

My father's doctor told him not to eat meat and to exercise more.

1 _____

2 _____

3 _____

Bad Advice

Economists told Americans in 2015 to buy real estate because prices would increase.

4 _____

5 _____

6 _____

B Group Work **Compare your answers with your group members. Discuss why the advice was good or bad. Take notes on your group members' answers.**

A *My father's doctor told him not to eat meat and to exercise more. This was good advice because it helped him to get into better shape.*

B *Many economists told their clients to buy real estate because prices would increase. This was bad advice because real estate prices went down.*

4 Avoid Common Mistakes ⚠

1 **Use infinitives in indirect imperatives.**

to

The leader asked us ~~that we~~ write for 5 minutes about the topic.

2 **In indirect *Yes/No* questions, remember to use an *if* clause.**

if   wanted

He asked me ~~did I want~~ to be the group leader.

3 **Remember to use an object pronoun or noun after *tell*.**

them

I told∧my ideas, and we ended up using two of them in the project.

Editing Task

Find and correct the mistakes in the paragraph about a brainstorming session.

if   wanted

When my psychology professor asked our class ~~did we want~~ to try brainstorming

as part of our next group project, I had no idea that the experience would be so

challenging or successful. First, when we started, one of our members asked many

unimportant questions. When the team leader asked her that she asks the questions

5   later, that person began complaining. Then the team leader asked the person did she

want to be the group leader. The rest of us told this was a bad idea, and there was

an argument. A different problem arose when we met the second time. The leader

asked one student that he takes electronic notes, but he forgot. As a result, when we

met the third time, the leader had to tell the information again. She asked me that

10   I write the notes this time, and I did. Aside from these minor problems, the group

generated a lot of ideas and finally came up with a successful proposal for a project.

So, if someone asked me do I want to work as a group again, I would say yes because

even though it is hard to work as a group, the outcome can be better.

5 Academic Writing

Argumentative Writing Using Graphs and Tables for Support

Brainstorm > Organize > Write > Edit

In Unit 17, you analyzed an essay with graphs and brainstormed ideas for the prompt below. In this unit (18), you will focus on incorporating information from graphs into your writing, and you will write a thesis statement and body paragraphs for your essay.

> *Using what you know about the job market, what is a good choice for a career path with a secure future? Include information from graphs or tables to support your choice.*

Analyzing Information in Graphs and Other Visuals

Academic writing involves including evidence. Evidence includes direct or indirect speech from experts, survey and research results, and visuals, such as graphs, tables, diagrams, and charts. The most common types of these visuals are bar graphs, line graphs, and pie charts. It is important to connect the information in the visual with the information in the text.

Exercise 5.1 Applying the Skill

1 Work with a partner. Look at the bar graph that ranks the most important interpersonal skills for workplace success. Take turns explaining each of the skills listed.

2 Think about the career you are going to write about. Which skills are critical for that career? Rank the skills that are important for that career. Explain your rankings to your partner.

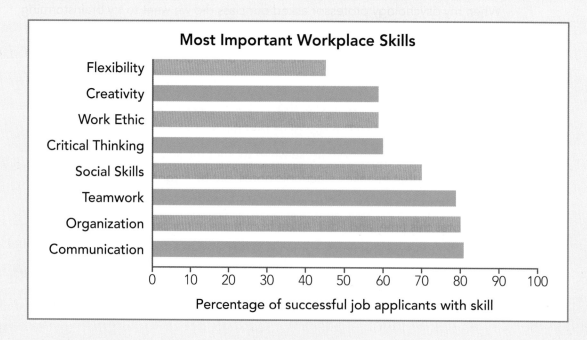

Most Important Workplace Skills

Percentage of successful job applicants with skill

Making and Evaluating Claims

In an argumentative essay, a writer makes a claim and then provides support for that claim. The claim is delivered in the thesis statement. Use the following criteria to evaluate the effectiveness of a thesis statement:

- Does my thesis statement make a claim that my readers can argue about?
- Does it give readers an idea of what my essay will be about?
- Is the claim specific enough to be effectively supported in a short essay?

Exercise 5.2 Applying the Skill

Work with a partner. Read three possible thesis statements for an essay about the importance of problem-solving in the workplace. Evaluate each one using the criteria you learned.

1 Brainstorming is one of the most popular tools when solving workplace problems.
2 According to the graph, being able to solve problems is the top skill for employers.
3 Brainstorming is an effective technique when solving problems because it gives everyone an opportunity to share their ideas.

Adding Indirect Advice from Experts

To strengthen their claims, writers often include indirect advice from experts. Indirect advice often appears directly after the writer's idea.

Exercise 5.3 Applying the Skill

Read the first two sentences of a paragraph about brainwriting. Underline the writer's claim. Circle the source and expert's name. Highlight the indirect advice.

Brainwriting is the most effective type of brainstorming. In his book, *Thinkertoys*, creativity expert Michael Michalko suggests that brainwriting may be more productive than traditional brainstorming because people think of additional ideas as they write.

My Writing

Exercise 5.4 Organizing Your Claims and Evidence

Work in a small group. Review your paragraph from My Writing in Unit 17. Discuss the questions.

1 What career did you choose to write about? Why?
2 What evidence do you have to support your claim? What could you add to strengthen it?
3 How could you better connect the evidence to your ideas?

Exercise 5.5 Writing Body Paragraphs

Write a thesis statement and two body paragraphs for your essay. Include a graph, table, or indirect advice as support.

The Passive (1)

English as a Global Language

1 Grammar in the Real World

ACADEMIC
WRITING

Argumentative
writing using
graphs and tables
for support

A Should everyone speak English? Why or why not? Read the article on the use of English around the world. Why is English important to learn?

B Comprehension Check Answer the questions.

1 Where is English being spoken?

2 When do people around the world speak English?

3 What might be some disadvantages of English being a global language?

C Notice Match the sentences in A with the sentences in B that mean the same thing.

	A		B
_____ 1	International companies **ask** their employees to learn English for their jobs.	a	How **is** English **used** by nonnative speakers?
_____ 2	In addition, English **dominates** the Internet.	b	Employees of international companies **are** often **asked** to learn English for their jobs.
_____ 3	How do nonnative speakers **use** English?	c	In addition, the Internet **is dominated** by English.

Look at the forms of the verbs in bold in each of the matched sentences. How are the verbs in column B different from the verbs in column A?

ENGLISH IS SPOKEN HERE

An Italian businesswoman in Russia speaks English in meetings. Teenagers from Argentina, Turkey, and Japan chat online – in English. Learning English is clearly important in today's world. David
5 Crystal, a linguist[1] who studies the English language, believes that English has become a global language, although it is not an official language in many countries. According to Crystal, no other language **has been spoken** in so many countries and by so
10 many speakers. Currently, over 360 million people speak English as a first language around the world, and approximately one billion speak it as a second language. This means that there are more nonnative speakers of English than native speakers. How **is**
15 English **used** by nonnative speakers? Employees of international companies **are** often **asked** to learn English for their jobs. In addition, the Internet **is dominated**[2] by English. Some experts say that more than half of the information on the Internet is
20 in English. Also, English **has** long **been viewed** as a common language among travelers from different countries. The use of English worldwide appears to have clear benefits for everyone.

Does this increase in the use of English worldwide
25 have any disadvantages? Some say that cultures may lose some of their identity if people use English instead of their native languages. For example, much of a culture's identity **is reflected** in its music and literature. Would these songs and stories be
30 as effective in English? Others say that the English language itself could change. In fact, this is happening now. When English **is spoken** by a group of people whose native language is not English, words from the native language **are** sometimes **mixed in**, and
35 the pronunciation of words is different from British or American English. This means that dialects[3] and different forms of English **are being spoken** in various areas around the world. Sociologists **are** currently **studying** this phenomenon. The loss of
40 cultural identity and the creation of varieties of English are two areas of interest for sociologists and linguists.

English **is being used** worldwide more and more, and for many people, learning it is necessary for their personal and professional lives. There are obvious
45 advantages to learning English. The disadvantages remain unclear. It is clear that varieties of English will continue to evolve. How will this affect how English is **taught**? In the future, will greater numbers of people have to decide which variety of English they learn?

---

[1]**linguist:** someone who studies languages and their structures

[2]**dominate:** control a place or person, want to be in charge, or be the most important person or thing

[3]**dialect:** a local variety of language that differs in its pronunciation and word usage

2 Active vs. Passive Sentences

Grammar Presentation

| A passive sentence and an active sentence have similar meanings, but the focus of the sentences is different. In the passive sentence, the focus is on the action or on the person or thing receiving the action. | The president **asked** <u>the employees</u> to speak English. (active)

 The employees **were asked** to speak English. (passive) |

2.1 Passive Sentences with *By* + Agent

A In active sentences, the agent (or doer of the action) is in subject position. In passive sentences, the object of the active sentence becomes the subject. The word *by* comes before the agent.	AGENT OBJECT *People* **spoke** *English at the meeting.* (active) *English* **was spoken** <u>by people</u> *at the meeting.* (passive)
B The agent is not always necessary.	*English* **was spoken** *at the meeting.* (We assume people were doing the speaking.)
C Use the *by* + agent phrase if the agent is important or if the meaning of the sentence would be unclear without it.	*The Internet* **is dominated** <u>by English</u>. NOT ~~The Internet is dominated.~~ (By who or what?)

2.2 Present and Past Forms of the Passive

A For the simple present form of the passive, use the present form of *be* + the past participle of the main verb.	*Some international companies* **ask** *their employees to learn English.* (active) *Employees* **are asked** *to learn English by some international companies.* (passive)
B For the present perfect form of the passive, use *has/have* + *been* + the past participle of the main verb.	*The company* **has told** *the employees to speak English.* (active) *The employees* **have been told** *to speak English.* (passive)
C For the present progressive form of the passive, use the present form of *be* + *being* + the past participle of the main verb.	*These days, people around the world* **are speaking** *many dialects of English.* (active) *These days, many dialects of English* **are being spoken** *by people around the world.* (passive)

2.2 Present and Past Forms of the Passive (continued)

D For the simple past form of the passive, use the past form of *be* + the past participle of the main verb. This form is the most common.	*Years ago, people did not consider English a global language.* (active) *Years ago, English was not considered a global language.* (passive)
E For the past progressive form of the passive, use the past form of *be* + *being* + the past participle of the main verb. This form is rare.	*Ten years ago, fewer people were using English online.* (active) *Ten years ago, English was being used by fewer people online.* (passive)
F In passive sentences, do not use a form of *do* in questions and negative statements in the simple present and simple past.	*Do most travelers speak English?* (active) *Is English spoken by most travelers?* (passive) *Turkish teenagers didn't use English to chat online two decades ago.* (active) *English wasn't used by Turkish teenagers to chat online two decades ago.* (passive)

🌐 Research shows that the simple present, present perfect, and simple past forms of the passive are much more frequent than the present progressive, past progressive, and past perfect forms of the passive.

⯈⯈ Irregular Verbs: See page A1.
⯈⯈ Passive Forms: See page A12.

🌐 DATA FROM THE REAL WORLD

Research shows that in academic writing, these are the most common verbs used in the passive:	*analyze, calculate, carry out, collect, determine, expect, find, measure, observe, obtain, prepare, see, set, show, test,* and *use*

Grammar Application

Exercise 2.1 Active and Passive Sentences

A Complete the online interview with a reporter from BusinessTimes Online and the CEO of an international company. Circle the correct verb forms.

Reporter	I would like to ask some questions about your use of English here at BR Corporation. **Do people speak English /** (**Is English spoken**) by most executives?
CEO	Yes, most executives **speak / are spoken** English at this branch.

Reporter	Do only executives speak English? I mean, do lower level employees **use / are used** English here, too?
	(3)
CEO	No, English **isn't used / doesn't use** by them much.
	(4)
Reporter	Why is English necessary for some employees?
CEO	English **is needed / needs** by executives who travel. Also, we
	(5)
	are expected / expect them to read technical documents in English.
	(6)
Reporter	**Does BR Corporation support / Is BR Corporation supported** English
	(7)
	language learning?
CEO	Yes, BR Corporation **is offered / offers** onsite English courses.
	(8)
Reporter	**Are the courses taught / Do the courses teach** by native English speakers?
	(9)
CEO	Yes, native speakers **are conducted / conduct** all of our English classes.
	(10)
Reporter	Thank you for speaking with me today.

B Pair Work Which sentences in A are in the passive? Rewrite them as active sentences.
Do most executives speak English?

C Group Work Rewrite the active sentences in A as passive sentences. In which sentences is the *by* + agent phrase necessary? Share your answers with the group.

Exercise 2.2 Present Forms of the Passive

Complete the article about foreign-language teaching. Use the simple present or present perfect form of the passive with the verbs in parentheses. Sometimes more than one answer is possible.

English _has been taught_ (teach) in many countries all over the world for years.
         (1)
It _____ currently _____ (speak), at least to some degree, by
   (2)   (2)
one–quarter of the world's population. Schools in the United States also recognize the

importance of learning other languages. For some time, languages other than English

_____ (include) in these schools' programs. Recently, a growing number of
        (3)
languages has become available. Which languages _____ (offered) by U.S.
                                                          (4)
high schools nowadays? The results may surprise you.

French is one of the most popular foreign languages for high school students.

It _____ (teach) in most U.S. high schools for many years. Arabic
       (5)
is becoming more and more popular. In fact, Arabic _____ (offer) at many
                                                            (6)

Massachusetts public schools these days. Chinese is also beginning to gain popularity.

An increase in the number of students learning Chinese _____
(7)

(report) for several years in various states across the country. It _____
(8)

(estimate) that more than 200,000 U.S. school children are now enrolled in

Mandarin Chinese classes.

Exercise 2.3 Past Forms of the Passive

A Read the active sentences about language. First underline the object in each sentence. Then rewrite the sentences as passive sentences. Sometimes more than one answer is possible.

1 At one time, many people used Latin as a global language.

   At one time, Latin was used as a global language by many people.

2 The ancient Romans spoke Latin.

   _____

3 Ancient Roman authors wrote many important manuscripts.

   _____

4 For many centuries, the Romans conquered neighboring nations.

   _____

5 These conquered groups spoke versions of Latin.

   _____

6 Conquered people from Britain to Africa used Latin.

   _____

7 People were still speaking Latin after the Roman Empire fell.

   _____

8 Scholars and scientists were using Latin until the eighteenth century.

   _____

B Read the sentences in A again. In which sentences are the agents not important? Discuss the reasons for your answers with a partner. Then rewrite these sentences in the passive without the agent.

   A *In the first sentence,* many people *isn't important because we know that only people use language.*

   B *You're right. The sentence could be* At one time, Latin was used as a global language.

3 Verbs and Objects with the Passive

Grammar Presentation

Transitive verbs (verbs that take an object) can occur in the passive.
Intransitive verbs (verbs that do not take an object) cannot occur in the passive.

Someone *saw* her at the conference. (transitive)
She *was seen* at the conference.
I *fell* asleep. (intransitive)

3.1 Transitive and Intransitive Verbs

A Some common transitive verbs that occur in the passive are *call, concern, do, expect, find, give, know, left, lose, make, put, see, take,* and *use.*

Improvement of your language skills *is expected.*
I *was given* a new English textbook.
The reasons for his success *were not known.*

B *Born* is the past participle of *bear. Born* is used almost exclusively in the passive.

I *was born* in a small town.
Where *were* you *born?*

C Some common intransitive verbs, which have no passive form, include *appear, arrive, come, die, fall, go, happen, live, look, occur, sit, smile, stay, wait,* and *walk.*

When *did* your symptoms first *appear?*
NOT ~~When were your symptoms first appeared?~~
Globalization of some languages *happens* over time.
NOT ~~Globalization of some languages is happened over time.~~

3.2 Passive Forms with Direct and Indirect Objects

Some verbs, such as *give, offer, show,* and *tell,* can have two objects: a direct and an indirect object. In passive sentences, either the direct object or the indirect object can become the subject. Use *to* before an indirect object that is not in subject position.

| INDIRECT OBJ | DIRECT OBJ |
The team gave the manager the report.
The manager *was given* the report by the team.
The report *was given* to the manager by the team.

Grammar Application

Read the sentences about "dead" languages. Underline
the verb in each sentence. If the sentence can occur in the
passive, write the passive sentence on the line. Do not use an
agent. Write ✗ if a passive form is not possible.

1 People in Ancient Rome spoke Latin.
   Latin was spoken in Ancient Rome.

2 People don't use Latin for everyday communication today.
   _____

3 Some languages die.
   _____

4 This occurred with Dalmatian.
   _____

5 People spoke Dalmatian in Croatia. _____

6 Dalmatian speakers lived in coastal towns of Croatia. _____

7 Groups in different regions developed dialects of Dalmatian.
   _____

8 Native speakers didn't record the grammar of Dalmatian.
   _____

A Over to You **Answer the questions about a language you know. Use the underlined
verbs in your answers. Use passive sentences when possible. Use the indirect object as the
subject of the passive sentence when possible. Write sentences that are true for you.**

1 What is a computer <u>called</u> in this language?
   A computer is called "bilgisayar" in Turkish.

2 What English words are <u>used</u> in this language?
   _____

3 Do any other foreign words <u>occur</u> in this language? If so, what are they?
   _____

4 Is this language <u>spoken</u> by more people or fewer people than it was 50 years ago?
   _____

5 What advice is frequently <u>given</u> by teachers to people learning this language?
   _____

6 Do speakers of this language <u>tell</u> their children traditional stories?
   _____

B Group Work **Share your sentences with your group members.**

A Read the sentences about Esperanto, a language that was created as a global language. Underline the agents.

1 The first book about Esperanto was published by <u>a company</u> in 1887.
2 Esperanto was invented by L. L. Zamenhof.
3 Esperanto was created by its inventors to be a very easy language to learn.
4 The grammar was designed by Zamenhof to be simple and clear.
5 It is spoken by about 10,000 people.
6 It is being used by people in about 115 countries.
7 It has not been recognized as an official language by any country.
8 The language is used by some international travelers.

B Pair Work Read the sentences in A again. Circle the direct objects. Compare your answers with a partner.

4 Reasons for Using the Passive

Grammar Presentation

The passive is used to describe processes and to report news events. The agent is not important. The focus is on the action or on the person or thing receiving the action.	*First, the students were shown a video in English.* *A "dead" language has been brought back to life in one community.*

4.1 Reasons for Using the Passive

A Use the passive to describe a process or a result. Common verbs to describe a process or a result are *compare, develop, examine, make, measure, study,* and *test.*	*First, the information was studied.* *Then recommendations were made.* (process) *Therefore, English was made the official language of the company in 2010.* (result)
B Use the passive when you don't know who performed the action. You can also use the passive to avoid directly blaming or criticizing someone.	*The report was poorly written.* (We don't know, or we don't want to say, who wrote the report.)
C Use the passive to report news events.	*Recommendations for the teaching of languages were published today.*

Grammar Application

A Listen to a report on a language study of English as a Second Language (ESL) students. Then complete the answers to the questions. Use the passive and the words in parentheses.

1 How many groups of students were there? (put into)

The students *were put into two groups* _____.

2 What was the assignment at the beginning of the semester? (give)

Students in each group _____.

3 What did group 1 study? (teach)

Group 1 _____.

4 What did group 2 study? (teach)

Students in group 2 _____.

5 Who read the essays? (read)

The first and final essays _____.

6 What did the judges do with all of the final essays? (put)

All of the final essays from group 1 and group 2 _____

_____.

7 How did the judges rate all the final essays? (rate)

The essays _____.

8 What rating did the essays produced by group 1 receive? (give)

Most of the final essays produced by group 1 _____.

9 What did the results seem to indicate? (include)

ESL students' writing improves when grammar and writing instruction

_____.

B Listen again and check your answers.

Read the sentences about preserving two Native American languages. Then rewrite each sentence in the passive. Do not use an agent. Sometimes more than one answer is possible.

1 In 2009 in Minnesota, the legislature established a volunteer group to preserve Native American languages.

In 2009 in Minnesota, a volunteer group was established to preserve Native American languages.

2 The legislature recognized the importance of preserving the Native American languages.

The importance of preserving the Native American languages was recognized.

3 The volunteer group collected data on the use of the Ojibwe and Dakota languages.

Data on the use of the Ojibwe and Dakota languages was collected

4 In Minnesota, many Native American people no longer spoke the Ojibwe and Dakota languages.

~~In Minnesota,~~ the Ojibwe and Dakota languages were no longer spoken. in Minnesota.

5 The volunteer group developed a strategy to teach the Ojibwe and Dakota languages in schools.

A strategy was developed to teach the Ojibwe and Dakota languages in schools.

6 The group is developing teacher-training programs.

Teacher-training programs are being developed.

7 In 2011, a nonprofit business released software for teaching the Ojibwe language.

In 2011, software for teaching the Ojibwe language was released.

8 The preservation of the languages will strengthen the Native Americans' cultural identities.

The Native American's cultural identities will be strengthened.

Read each classroom scenario and pretend you are the teacher. Then write passive statements to avoid directly blaming or criticizing someone. Use the underlined sentences in your answers. Sometimes more than one answer is possible.

1 Someone stole some valuable equipment from the classroom. You think that someone in the class is responsible, but you aren't sure. You tell the class:

Some valuable equipment was stolen from the classroom.

2 One student's essay contained plagiarized material. The student copied some material in his essay from the Internet. You tell the student:

Some material was copied from the Internet. in the essay.

3 A hacker broke into the school's e-mail system last night. No one knows who is responsible, but you must inform the students. You tell the class:

The school's e-mail system was broken last night. (handwritten)

4 A student hands in the second draft of an essay. You see a lot of grammar mistakes. The student did not edit the paper carefully. You tell the student:

The paper was not ~~edit~~ edited carefully. (handwritten, with "into" above)

5 Avoid Common Mistakes ⚠

1 **Remember to use a form of _be_ in passive sentences.**
  _is_
  English ∧ spoken at most airports.

2 **Always use the past participle form of the verb in passive sentences.**
  translated
  The words have been ~~translating~~ into Spanish, Arabic, Chinese, and Urdu.

3 **Do not use the passive form when the subject is the doer of the action.**
  studying
  I have been ~~studied~~ English for five years.
  Most students have ~~been~~ used an English dictionary.

4 **With questions, remember to put _be_ before the subject.**
  was
  Why ∧ he ~~was~~ given an award?

Editing Task

(handwritten: Mary might have been being examined by the doctor.)

Find and correct the mistakes in the paragraphs about English spelling.

    Even good writers will tell you that English spelling has ~~been~~ confused them at one time or another. The same sound _is_ spelled many different ways. For example, the words _lazy_ and _busy_ are pronounc~~ing~~ _ed_ with a /z/ sound, but they are not consistent in their spelling because of strange rules that are ~~being~~ related to the vowels.

5 Why English _is_ written this way? English is an ancient language that contains old spelling rules. Also, other languages have ~~been~~ contributed many words to English.

    Some experts who have ~~been~~ studied the English language for years would like to see English spelling simplified. They ask important questions: Why _is_ so much time ~~is~~ wasted on spelling lessons? Why is literacy lower in English-speaking countries than

10 in countries with simplified spelling? They point to the fact that many other languages _were_ simplified successfully. They suggest that in places such as Sweden, France, and Indonesia, changes to the written form have helped make learning ~~to~~ read easier.

6 Academic Writing

Argumentative Writing Using Graphs and Tables for Support

Brainstorm > Organize > **Write** > Edit

In Unit 18, you wrote the first draft of your thesis statement and body paragraphs for the prompt below. In this unit (19), you will focus on the introductory paragraph and then complete the first draft of your essay.

> *Using what you know about the job market, what is a good choice for a career path with a secure future? Include information from graphs or tables to support your choice.*

Making a Logical Appeal in the Introductory Paragraph

In an argumentative essay, writers try to create a connection with readers from the beginning that will persuade them to agree with the essay's thesis or possibly to take some action. Writers do this by making a logical appeal. A hook, such as a surprising statistic, interesting story, or powerful quote, can help make a strong logical appeal.

Exercise 6.1 Understanding the Skill

Read two possible introductory paragraphs (a-b) for an essay about the importance of learning English. Work with a partner. Discuss the questions.

a   English is everywhere. When people can speak English, they are able to travel anywhere, watch movies, and listen to music. English is a world language. People who speak and understand English have more opportunities than those who do not. Experts say that the number of people who speak English is growing every day. People should learn English.

b   Diana, who lives in Chile, chats with Hiro, who lives in Japan. Marc works for Amazon customer service and lives in Spain. Hoda takes classes from an American university while she is living in Iran. What do all these people have in common? They are communicating in English. Our world is growing smaller, and English is becoming a world language. More people are using English for work, school, and entertainment. Learning English opens up new opportunities, and can make a person a more marketable professional.

1 What kind of hook does each paragraph use?
2 What background information is included in each paragraph?
3 Which introduction makes the most successful logical appeal to you? Why?

My Writing

Exercise 6.2 Applying the Skill

Use your work in My Writing in Units 17 and 18 to answer the questions.

1 What is your thesis statement?
2 What is the main idea of each body paragraph?
3 Using the information in 1–2, what logical appeal can you make to your reader?
4 Write the introductory paragraph of your essay.

Using Active and Passive Voice to Discuss Visuals

When writers discuss figures (graphs, charts, diagrams), they use specific words and phrases, sometimes in the passive voice.

To introduce a trend by discussing a figure, the active voice is usually preferred.

English is now spoken by over 360 million people. Figure 1 *shows* where these speakers live.

Use the passive to focus on the information, not the *who* or the *where*.

Speakers of English, who do not reside in an English speaking country, learn English in a number of ways. The most common ways *are presented* in Figure 2.

The following verbs are frequently used to discuss figures in academic writing:
demonstrate, depict, display, illustrate, indicate, portray, present, reveal, show

Exercise 6.3 Applying the Skill

Work with a partner. Complete the tasks.

1 Review the body paragraphs of your essay. Identify where you included a figure.
2 How did you introduce it? Did you use a frequently used verb?
3 Revise your paragraphs if necessary.

Exercise 6.4 Writing Your Essay

Use your work in My Writing in Units 18 and 19 to write the first complete draft of your essay. Include:

- An introductory paragraph with your thesis statement
- 2-3 body paragraphs with information from graphs or tables for support
- A concluding paragraph that summarizes your thesis and reasons, and that includes a final thought, recommendation, or prediction

Food Safety

1 Grammar in the Real World

ACADEMIC WRITING

Argumentative writing using graphs and tables for support

A What do you know about genetically modified food? Read the article about genetically modified food. What are some genetically modified foods?

B Comprehension Check **Answer the questions.**

1 What are genetically modified foods?

2 What are some advantages of genetically modified foods?

3 What are some concerns about genetically modified foods?

C Notice **Find the sentences in the article and complete them.**

1 For example, those in favor of GM foods believe that crops _____ to resist insects.

2 Opponents insist that the problem of world hunger _____ by producing more food.

3 However, _____ extra care _____ until the long-term risks are known?

What verb comes after modals in passive verb forms?

GENETICALLY Modified Food

Genetically modified[1] (GM) foods come from plants that **have been changed** in a laboratory. This technology alters the genes[2] of the plants. It was developed so that food could have specific, desirable
5 traits. For example, the first GM crop in the United States consisted of tomatoes that were genetically changed to stay firmer longer.

Many people have strong opinions about the potential[3] benefits and risks of GM agriculture.
10 For example, those in favor of GM foods believe that crops **should be designed** to resist insects. They point to the example of sweet corn. They say that sweet corn **used to be destroyed** by pests. This created serious problems. Farmers lost money. Crops **got damaged**
15 and **could not be eaten**. Therefore, they say that a great benefit **can be found** in GM sweet corn, which has been modified to resist insects that cause damage. People who oppose GM foods see the issue differently. They cite[4] a study that links GM corn to organ[5] damage
20 in rats. They claim that the safety of these crops has not been tested adequately.[6]

GM supporters see GM soybeans as another beneficial crop. These crops are not harmed by a powerful weed-killing chemical. This chemical kills
25 weeds the first time it is applied, so farmers use less of it. Supporters say that this improves air and water quality since fewer pollutants enter the environment. Critics argue that the weeds are no longer affected by the weed killer, and new "superweeds" are growing.
30 Therefore, farmers have to use more chemicals to save their crops.

Finally, those in favor of GM foods say that better control of pests and weeds has made it possible for GM crops to produce more food in a shorter time.
35 They believe this increased production will help feed a world population which is expected to grow to 9 billion by 2050. Opponents insist that the problem of world hunger **will not be solved** by producing more food. They argue that farmers grow enough food now
40 and that global hunger is a result of unequal food distribution, not the result of a food shortage.[7]

Clearly, there are pros and cons to this debate. GM foods seem to have the potential to benefit the world. However, **should** extra care **be taken** until the long-
45 term risks are known?

---

[1]**modify:** change something in order to improve it

[2]**gene:** a code that controls the development of particular characteristics in a plant or animal

[3]**potential:** possible but not yet achieved

[4]**cite:** mention something as an example or proof of something else

[5]**organ:** a vital part of the body, like the heart, lungs, and kidneys

[6]**adequately:** good enough but not very good

[7]**shortage:** a lack of something needed

2 The Passive with *Be Going To* and Modals

Grammar Presentation

You can use the passive with *be going to* and modals.	GM foods **will replace** natural foods. (active) Natural foods **will be replaced** by GM foods. (passive)

2.1 Forming the Passive with *Be Going To* and Modals

A For the passive with *be going* to, use *be going to* + *be* + the past participle of the main verb. *Not* comes before *be going to* in the negative form.	Only natural foods **are going to be served** in our house. The food **is not going to be eaten** immediately. **Is** more GM food **going to be grown** in the future?
B For the passive with modals, use a modal + *be* + the past participle of the main verb. *Not* follows the modal in the negative form.	People **could be harmed** by GM food. People **must be informed**. Food **should not be eaten** if it isn't fresh. **Will** questions about GM food **be answered** by scientists?

▸▸ Passive Forms: See page A12.

Grammar Application

Exercise 2.1 The Passive with *Will* and *Be Going To*

Complete the interview about plans for a food conference. Circle the passive form of the verbs.

> **Reporter** A conference called **The Future of Food** will hold /(will be held) at
> Bay City Tech next week. Issues concerning the food industry
> (1)
> **will be discussed / will discuss** by experts from a variety of fields.
> (2)
> We interviewed two participants, Dr. Fred Bell, a biologist, and Deniz
> Martin, the president of the Traditional Food Society. First, what major
> issues **are going to address / are going to be addressed** at next week's
> (3)
> conference?
>
> **Dr. Bell** Policies on food aid **are going to debate / are going to be debated** in
> (4)
> one session.
>
> **Reporter** What are the issues there?

Dr. Bell Well, GM plants **are going to be promoted/are going to promote**
(5)
as the main solution to hunger in poor nations.

Reporter World hunger is a serious problem. What's your opinion as a biologist?
Will the situation **improve/be improved** by GM plants?
(6)

Dr. Bell No, the problem of world hunger **will not solve/will not be solved** by GM
(7)
crops, in my opinion.

Reporter Don't some experts believe that GM food will help increase crop production?

Dr. Bell In my opinion, crop production **will not be increased/will not increase** by
(8)
GM plants. In fact, there is no proof of this so far.

Reporter Ms. Martin, what Traditional Food Society issues
will be presented/will present at the conference?
(9)

Ms. Martin The issue of sustainable food production – growing food without
harming people or the environment – **will address/will be addressed** .
(10)
For example, ways to improve organic farming methods
will be demonstrated/will demonstrate .
(11)

Reporter Thank you both for your time.

Exercise 2.2 The Passive with Modals

A Read the facts that a student collected for a report on pesticides.[1] Rewrite the facts as passive sentences. Sometimes more than one answer is possible.

1 Pesticides can harm humans, animals, and the environment.
Humans, animals, and the environment can be harmed by pesticides.

2 Pesticides can cause air pollution.
Air pollution can be caused by pesticides.

3 In the United States, scientists can find pesticides in many streams.
In the United States, pesticides can be found in many streams.

4 Pesticides may have harmed some farm animals.
Some farm animals may have been harmed by pesticides.

5 Pesticides may have affected meat from farm animals.
Meat from farm animals may have been affected by pesticides.

6 Pesticides in water could affect fish.
Fish could be affected by pesticides in water.

7 In some cases, pesticides can affect humans.
In some cases, humans can be affected by pesticides.

[1]**pesticide:** a weed-killing chemical

B Pair Work Compare your sentences with a partner.

Exercise 2.3 More Passive with Modals

Complete the web article about a government recall. Rewrite the steps as passive sentences with modals. Use the indirect object as the subject of the passive sentence when possible. Sometimes more than one answer is possible.

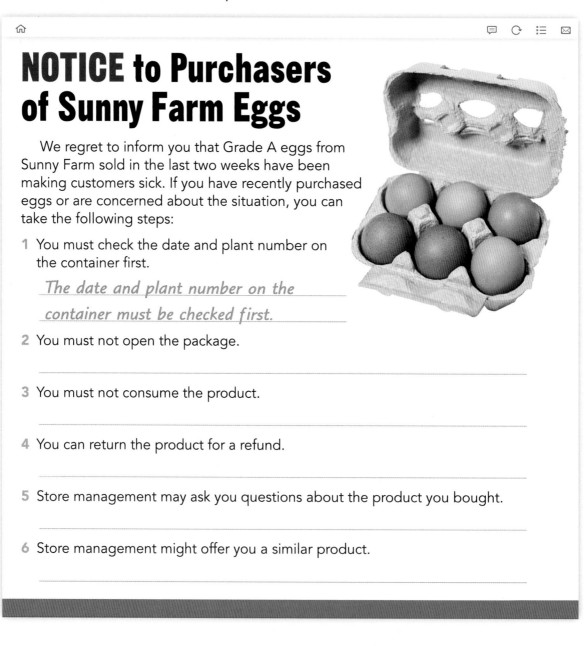

NOTICE to Purchasers of Sunny Farm Eggs

We regret to inform you that Grade A eggs from Sunny Farm sold in the last two weeks have been making customers sick. If you have recently purchased eggs or are concerned about the situation, you can take the following steps:

1 You must check the date and plant number on the container first.

   The date and plant number on the
   container must be checked first.

2 You must not open the package.

_____

3 You must not consume the product.

_____

4 You can return the product for a refund.

_____

5 Store management may ask you questions about the product you bought.

_____

6 Store management might offer you a similar product.

_____

Group Work **Discuss the questions about GM food. Use passive sentences with modals.**

- Should food be genetically modified? Why or why not?

- In your opinion, can people be harmed by eating genetically modified food? If yes, in what ways?

- Should genetically modified food be labeled in the United States? Why or why not?

A *In my opinion, food should not be genetically modified because we don't know the dangers.*

B *I disagree. I think food should be genetically modified because it's the best way to end world hunger.*

3 Get Passives

get is not academic

Grammar Presentation

Passive sentences with *get* instead of *be* are more informal and are often used to express stronger emotions.	*The storm destroyed the crops.* (active) *The crops got destroyed by the storm.* (passive)

3.1 Forming *Get* Passives

A For the *get* passive, use a form of *get* + the past participle of the main verb.	*He is getting transferred to the research department.* *Our orange trees got damaged last night.*
B For negative statements and questions in the simple present and simple past, use a form of *do* + *get* + the past participle of the main verb.	*In my opinion, food doesn't get inspected carefully enough.* *Did your crops get damaged in the hurricane?*

3.2 Using *Get* Passives

We often use *get* passives to talk about negative situations or situations we think are beyond our control.	*Some food companies are getting fined for using unsafe equipment.*

The *get* passive is more common in speaking than in general writing. In formal academic writing, the *get* passive is very infrequent.

speaking	▬▬▬▬▬▬▬▬▬▬
general writing	▬▬▬▬▬
formal academic writing	▬▬

Say: "She *got arrested and charged* with murder."
Write: She *was arrested and charged* with murder.

🖱 Grammar Application

Exercise 3.1 *Get* Passives

Complete the interview about food contamination. Write *get* passives with the words in parentheses. If there is a line through the agent, do not use it in the passive.

Alternative **REVIEW**

Interviewer There's been another case of contaminated[1]
lettuce. How does this happen? An anonymous
lettuce grower agreed to be interviewed if we did
not mention his name. So, I hear

you're getting investigated by the FDA
(1 the FDA[2] is investigating you)

for problems with food safety. What happened?

Grower Our lettuce is ~~getting~~ got contaminated .
(2 ~~Something~~ contaminated our lettuce)

Interviewer Did the lettuce get recalled by the FDA ?
(3 Did the FDA recall the lettuce)

Grower Yes, it got recalled .
(4 ~~The FDA~~ recalled it)

Interviewer What happened, exactly?

Grower I'm not sure. As you know, our produce gets picked
(5 ~~workers~~ pick our produce)

right here on the farm. It also gets packed here.
(6 ~~Workers~~ also pack it)

It sometimes gets mishandled . This can cause contamination.
(7 ~~Workers~~ sometimes mishandle it)

[1]**contaminated:** less pure and potentially harmful | [2]**FDA:** Food and Drug Administration, a U.S. government agency

Interviewer	Don't you have strict procedures?

Grower   Yes, but it's been very hot lately. Working conditions have been difficult.

Perhaps _the workers got distracted_ .
(8 ~~something~~ distracted the workers)

Interviewer   _Doesn't your produce get checked_ before it goes to
(9 Doesn't ~~someone~~ check your produce)

the stores?

Grower   No, _it doesn't get inspected_ . That's our responsibility,
(10 ~~people~~ don't inspect it)

and my company is very sorry that we didn't catch it.

Interviewer   I see. Well, thank you very much for agreeing to be interviewed.

Exercise 3.2 More *Get* Passives

A Over to You **Look at the following statements about food safety. Check (✓) the statements you agree with.**

☐ **1** When a restaurant gets inspected, the results should be posted on the restaurant's front door.

☐ **2** Food recalls get publicized too much. This hurts farmers, and a lot of perfectly good food gets thrown away.

☐ **3** If a supermarket sells spoiled food, the manager should get fired.

☐ **4** If a restaurant gets temporarily shut down for food safety problems, no one should ever eat there again.

☐ **5** All foreign fruit and vegetables should get inspected before entering the country.

B Group Work **Compare your answers with your group members. Discuss your reasons. Use *get* passives.**

A *I think that when a restaurant gets inspected, the results should be posted on the restaurant's front door.*

B *I disagree. If a restaurant gets inspected and receives a low rating, it's bad for business.*

4 Passive Gerunds and Infinitives

Grammar Presentation

Gerunds and infinitives can occur in the passive.	*Some people worry about genetically modified food* **harming** *them.* (active)
	Some people worry about **being harmed** *by genetically modified food.* (passive)
	Consumers should expect food companies **to give** *them accurate information about their food.* (active)
	Consumers should expect **to be given** *accurate information about their food.* (passive)

4.1 Forming Passive Gerunds

A To form passive gerunds, use *being* + the past participle of the main verb.	*Consumers are afraid of food companies* **harming** *them.* (active)
	Consumers are afraid of **being harmed** *by food companies.* (passive)
B Common verbs that are followed by passive gerunds include *avoid, consider, dislike, enjoy, like, miss, quit,* and *remember.*	*I* <u>remember</u> **being given** *information about GM foods in the supermarket.*
C Common verbs + prepositions that are followed by passive gerunds include *complain about, keep on, succeed in,* and *worry about.*	*The restaurant* <u>worried about</u> **being closed** *by the food inspectors.*
D Common adjectives + prepositions that are followed by passive gerunds include *afraid of, aware of, concerned about, content with, interested in, tired of,* and *worried about.*	*The company was* <u>interested in</u> **being seen** *as a socially responsible company.*

▶ Verbs Followed by Gerunds Only: See page A7.
▶ Verbs Followed by Gerunds or Infinitives: See page A7.
▶ Verbs + Prepositions: See page A9.
▶ Adjectives + Prepositions: See page A10.

4.2 Forming Passive Infinitives

A To form passive infinitives, use *to be* + the past participle of the main verb.	*Food companies are not likely **to solve** the problem of world hunger.* (active) *The problem of world hunger is not likely **to be solved** by food companies.* (passive)
B Common verbs followed by passive infinitives include *ask, expect, hope, manage, refuse, seem,* and *want.*	*The manager of the restaurant <u>expected</u> **to be told** that the restaurant passed the inspection.*

▶▶ Verbs Followed by Infinitives Only: See page A7.
▶▶ Verbs Followed by Gerunds or Infinitives: See page A7.

Grammar Application

Exercise 4.1 Passive Gerunds and Infinitives

Complete the sentences about restaurant food safety. Circle the correct passive forms of the verbs.

1 Customers at Corner Café recently complained about (being)/ to be served undercooked food.

2 The manager of the café was concerned about to be / being inspected.

3 The owners were afraid of to be / being told they must close the cafe if the problems were not corrected.

4 The owners expected being / to be cited by the county food safety bureau.

5 The staff hoped to be / being paid for the time that the restaurant was closed.

6 The manager was not happy about being / to be told to close the restaurant.

Exercise 4.2 More Passive Gerunds and Infinitives

A Listen to an interview with consumers about food labeling. Write the passive gerund or infinitive forms you hear.

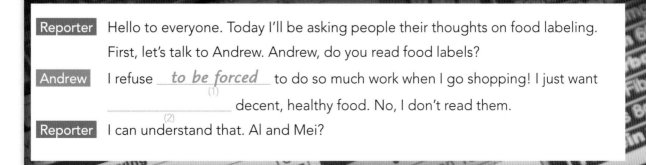

Reporter	Hello to everyone. Today I'll be asking people their thoughts on food labeling. First, let's talk to Andrew. Andrew, do you read food labels?
Andrew	I refuse ___*to be forced*___ to do so much work when I go shopping! I just want (1) _____ decent, healthy food. No, I don't read them. (2)
Reporter	I can understand that. Al and Mei?

Al	We expect _____ the truth by food companies,
	(3)
	but we know labels aren't always accurate.
Mei	You have to inform yourself. All consumers have to start _____
	(4)
	better _____ , so we always read them.
	(4)
Reporter	OK. And you, Roxana, do you read food labels?
Roxana	Yes, because I'm a pretty informed consumer. I'm not too concerned
	about _____ by food companies, but I'm not
	(5)
	interested in _____ , either!
	(6)
Reporter	Thank you, Roxana. And finally, Jessica. What do you think?
Jessica	It's sometimes easy _____ by product labeling, so I
	(7)
	don't read them much because they don't matter. Take the word
	natural, for example. You expect it _____ for food that
	(8)
	has few or no artificial ingredients. However, the word *natural* can be
	used for genetically modified food products.
Reporter	Thanks to you all. It appears that consumers are tired of
	_____ by food companies.
	(9)

B Over to You **Complete the sentences about food labeling with passive gerunds or infinitives and the verbs in the box. Write sentences that are true for you.**

confuse	give	lie to	tell
do	inform	sell	use

1 I'm tired of *being confused by food labels* _____ .

2 I expect _____ .

3 I'm (not) concerned about _____ .

4 I hope _____ .

5 It's (not) easy _____ .

C Pair Work **Compare your answers with a partner.**

A *I'm tired of being confused by food labels. I don't want to be told something is "organic" when it really isn't.*

B *Well, I know what you mean, but actually, I'm tired of being told to eat organic and healthy food all the time. Why can't I enjoy a candy bar once in a while?*

5 Avoid Common Mistakes ⚠

1 **In passive sentences, use a past participle after *be*, not the base form of the verb.**

produced
Unintended side effects can be ~~produce~~ by new technologies.

2 **Don't forget to use *be* + the past participle to express a passive meaning.**

be caused
An allergic reaction can ~~cause~~ by many different kinds of foods.

Editing Task

Find and correct seven more mistakes in the paragraph about some GM food concerns.

made
It is certain that many advances in technology will be ~~make~~ in the twenty-first century. Although many of these advances will improve our future, others may do as much harm as good. GM foods are one example. Currently, many new foods are creating by scientists. For instance, many people suffer from food allergies. Certain

5 GM foods may help avoid this problem; the food's DNA has been change so that the food no longer causes allergic reactions. Also, one day, the world's growing population may be feed with GM foods that grow quickly. This will make it possible for more food to be produce. These new foods can be use to feed more people. However, GM foods have another side. Because these foods have not existed very

10 long, scientists do not know all their effects. For example, some people fear that cancer can cause by GM foods. This is especially troubling because GM foods might not mark as such, so consumers may not know what they are buying. When they develop new foods, scientists should be aware of the concerns that consumers have. In my view, we should be careful with any new technology.

6 Academic Writing

Argumentative Writing Using Graphs and Tables for Support

Brainstorm > Organize > Write > Edit

In Unit 19, you wrote the first draft of your essay to answer the prompt below. In this unit (20), you will review, revise, and edit your essay.

> *Using what you know about the job market, what is a good choice for a career path with a secure future? Include information from graphs or tables to support your choice.*

My Writing

Using the Passive Voice in Academic Writing

Academic writers often use the passive voice to avoid repetition or when the focus is on a process or action rather than who did the process or action. However, in academic writing it is important to avoid using *get* passives.

Exercise 6.1 Applying the Skill

Review the essay you wrote in My Writing in Unit 19.
- Find at least one place to use the passive voice to avoid repetition.
- Find at least one place to use the passive voice to focus is on a process or action rather than who did the process or action.
- Edit any sentences in which you used a *get* passive.

Exercise 6.2 Revising Your Ideas

1 Work with a partner. Use the questions to give feedback on your partner's essay.

- Which of your partner's ideas seem strongest to you?
- Which of your partner's ideas need to be explained more clearly?
- What could your partner add or remove to make the essay stronger and easier to understand?

2 Use the feedback from your partner to revise the ideas and content of your essay.

Exercise 6.3 Editing Your Writing

1 Use the checklist to review and edit your essay.

Did you answer the writing prompt completely?	
Did you organize your essay correctly?	
Does your introduction make a successful logical appeal?	
Does your thesis statement make a claim that people could argue about?	
Do your body paragraphs have topic sentences that connect to your thesis statement and support your claim?	
Did you include and analyze at least one graph or other visual?	
Did you use reporting verbs to introduce evidence?	
Did you add indirect advice from an expert?	

Exercise 6.4 Editing Your Grammar

Use the checklist to review and edit the grammar in your essay.

Did you use direct and indirect speech correctly?	
Did you include indirect advice correctly?	
Did you use active and passive voice correctly?	
Did you avoid *get* passives?	
Did you avoid the common mistakes on pages 261, 273, 287 and 301?	

Exercise 6.5 Writing Your Final Draft

Apply the feedback and edits from Exercises 6.2 to 6.4 to write the final draft of your essay.

Subject Relative Clauses (Adjective Clauses with Subject Relative Pronouns)

Alternative Energy Sources

1 Grammar in the Real World

ACADEMIC WRITING

Expository writing

A What are some alternative sources of energy (other than oil or coal)? Read the article about one type of alternative energy. Is "people power" an efficient energy source? Why or why not?

B Comprehension Check **Answer the questions.**

1 What are some ways that people can make energy?
2 How can "people power" help the environment?
3 What are some problems with people power?

C Notice **Find the sentences in the article and complete them. Then draw an arrow from each missing word to the word that it refers to.**

1 Professional athletes, _____whose_____ **exercise routines** can last for several hours, could help power a house!

2 This heat, _____which_____ **is sent** to a nearby building, cuts the energy bill by 25 percent.

3 However, people _____who_____ **support** green energy are confident that this technology will catch on in the near future.

Look at the words in bold that follow the words you wrote. What parts of speech are the words in bold?

EXERCISING for ELECTRICITY

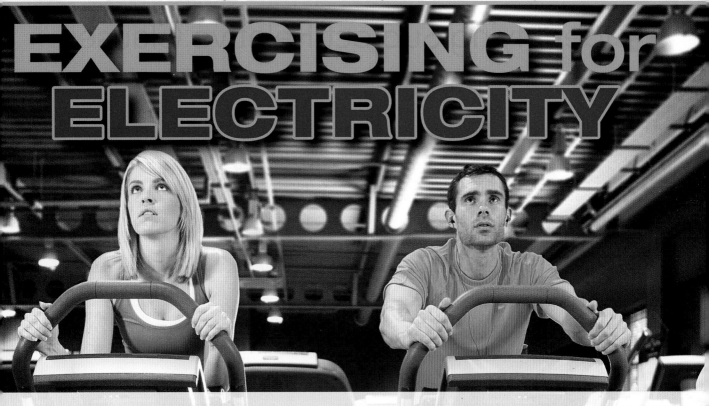

Much of the world's energy comes from sources like oil and coal, **which cannot be replaced when used up.** Renewable sources – water, wind, and the sun – are better for the environment. However, these alternative sources of energy have not always been sufficiently explored for political and economic reasons. People **who care about the environment** are looking for more alternative sources that might appeal to people who make decisions about these things. One source **that is becoming popular** uses energy **that is generated by humans**, sometimes called "people power."

With people power, people create electricity through exercise. People exercise in green gyms, **which contain special treadmills**. These machines convert human energy into electricity that helps run the lights and air-conditioning. People power also helps prevent air pollution. Someone **who exercises for one hour** can feel good about the fact that he or she is helping prevent carbon dioxide from going into the air. Professional athletes, **whose exercise routines can last for several hours,** could help power a house!

Exercise is not the only way people can make energy. One company has created surfaces **which are powered by humans.** People dance or walk on special dance floors and sidewalks. This movement generates electricity, **which can light up the dance floor or power street lamps.** Body heat is used for power, too. One system in Sweden gathers the body heat from commuters in a train station. This heat, **which is sent to a nearby building,** cuts the energy bill by 25 percent.

People power is not perfect, though. Large gyms need a lot of energy to run. People power, **which only generates a part of the total electricity needed,** does not lower the gym's electric bill much. Also, the use of this technology is moving slowly. Business leaders, **who must focus on making a profit,** do not always want to be the first to create new products. They are afraid to spend money on technology **which might not be successful.** However, people **who support green energy** are confident that this technology will catch on in the near future.

People power is not a major energy source yet, but it could be soon. Meanwhile, this "green energy" encourages people to exercise, and it makes people more aware of the environment. It is one kind of technology **that helps people and the planet** at the same time.

2 Identifying Subject Relative Clauses

Grammar Presentation

Relative clauses modify – define, describe, identify, or give more information about – nouns. In a subject relative clause, the relative pronoun is the subject of the clause. An identifying relative clause gives essential information about the noun it modifies.	SUBJECT *I go to a gym. **The gym** creates its own electricity.* RELATIVE PRONOUN *I go to a gym **that** creates its own electricity.*

2.1 Forming Identifying Subject Relative Clauses

A The subject of an identifying subject relative clause is the relative pronoun. The relative pronoun refers to the noun before it. Use *who* or *that* for people, and *which* or *that* for things.	NOUN RELATIVE PRONOUN *Nowadays, people often drive cars **that** don't use a lot of gas.*
Do not add a second subject to the clauses.	*People **that exercise** can use special machines to create electricity.* NOT *People that ~~they~~ exercise can use special machines to create electricity.*
B The information in an identifying subject relative clause is essential. Do not add a comma before this type of clause.	*People **who care about the environment** often recycle their garbage.* (The relative clause tells which people.) *The school uses the electricity **that comes from the exercise machines in the gym**.* (The relative clause tells which electricity.)
C The verb in the relative clause agrees with the noun that the relative pronoun modifies.	SINGULAR NOUN SINGULAR VERB *Someone **that supports** the environment recycles.* PLURAL NOUN PLURAL VERB *Many people **that support** the environment recycle.*

▸▸ Relative Clauses: See page A13.

2.2 Using Identifying Subject Relative Clauses

A	Use an identifying relative clause to give essential information about a noun. These clauses are also called restrictive subject clauses.	*People power is a kind of energy.* (What kind of energy? What is important about it?) *People power is a kind of energy **that creates electricity**.* (The relative clause gives essential information.)	
B	Use an identifying relative clause in definitions, especially with words such as *anyone, people, someone,* or *something*.	*Green energy is something **which doesn't hurt the environment.*** *Environmentalists are people **who care about the environment**.*	

Grammar Application

Exercise 2.1 Subject Relative Pronouns

A Complete the article about people power. Use *who* or *which* and the simple present form of the verbs in parentheses.

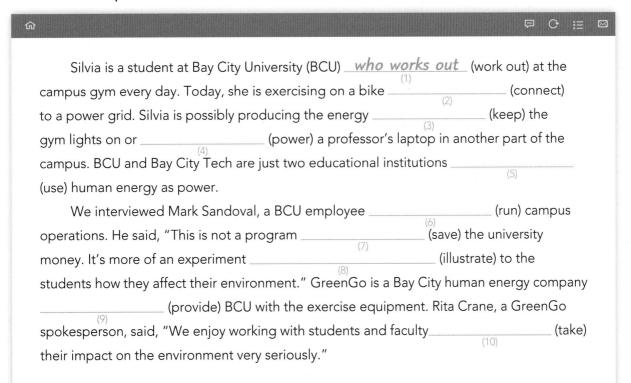

Silvia is a student at Bay City University (BCU) _who works out_ (work out) at the
(1)
campus gym every day. Today, she is exercising on a bike _____ (connect)
(2)
to a power grid. Silvia is possibly producing the energy _____ (keep) the
(3)
gym lights on or _____ (power) a professor's laptop in another part of the
(4)
campus. BCU and Bay City Tech are just two educational institutions _____
(5)
(use) human energy as power.

We interviewed Mark Sandoval, a BCU employee _____ (run) campus
(6)
operations. He said, "This is not a program _____ (save) the university
(7)
money. It's more of an experiment _____ (illustrate) to the
(8)
students how they affect their environment." GreenGo is a Bay City human energy company
_____ (provide) BCU with the exercise equipment. Rita Crane, a GreenGo
(9)
spokesperson, said, "We enjoy working with students and faculty_____ (take)
(10)
their impact on the environment very seriously."

B Listen to the article and check your answers.

A Complete the energy definitions with *who* or *that* and the correct form of the verbs in parentheses. Sometimes more than one answer is possible.

1 Geothermal energy is heat __*that comes*__ (come) from inside the earth.

2 Renewable energy is something _that doesn't disappear_ (not/disappear).

3 Ecologists are people _who study_ (study) the relationship between organisms and the environment.

4 A green politician is someone _who puts_ (put) environmental issues ahead of other issues.

5 A sustainable engineer is anyone _who designs_ (design) objects to protect the environment.

B Complete the energy definitions with subject relative pronouns and the words in the box.

> chemicals/trap/heat in the atmosphere
> fuel/come/from vegetable oil or animal fat
> people/be/part of a political group focused
>   on good environmental policy
> someone/work/to protect the environment
> structures/not have/a large negative
>   impact on the environment
>
> a type of energy/come/from human
>   exercise
> a type of energy/use/the sun as its source
> a vehicle/use/two sources of power
>   to run

1 Biodiesel is a kind of *fuel that/which comes from vegetable oil or animal fat* .

2 A conservationist is _____ .

3 "Greens" are _____ .

4 Greenhouse gases are _____ .

5 A hybrid car is _____ .

6 Solar energy is _____ .

7 People power is _____ .

8 Green buildings are _____ .

A Combine the sentences from an alternative energy company's advertisement. Use *who*, *that*, or *which* in subject relative clauses. Sometimes more than one answer is possible.

1 GreenGo is a company. It develops renewable energy systems.

   GreenGo is a company that/which develops renewable energy systems.

2 GreenGo developed a technology. The technology turns exercise machines into power generators.

   GreenGo developed a technology that/which turns exercise machines into power generators.

3 GreenGo builds machines like exercise bikes. These exercise bikes let exercisers generate electricity from their workouts.

GreenGo builds machines like exercise bikes that/which let exercisers generate electricity from their workouts.

4 The electricity connects to a power grid. The power grid covers a large geographic area.

The electricity connects to a power grid that/which covers a large geographic area.

5 Sachiko Hanley is the woman. The woman invented this technology.

Sachiko Hanley is the woman who/that invented this technology.

6 Many GreenGo clients are colleges and other institutions. The institutions have on-site gyms.

Many GreenGo clients are colleges and other institutions that/which have on-site gyms.

7 GreenGo provides an energy source. The energy source is good for the environment.

GreenGo provides an energy source that/which is good for the environment.

8 "We are proud to work with institutions. They have the same environmental goals that we do."

"We are proud to work with institutions which/that have the same environment goals that we do."

B In each of the sentences you wrote in A, underline the subject relative clause and draw an arrow from the relative pronoun to the noun in the main clause it refers to.

GreenGo is a company that develops renewable energy systems.

3 Nonidentifying Subject Relative Clauses

Grammar Presentation

Nonidentifying subject relative clauses have the same form as identifying clauses. Unlike identifying clauses, nonidentifying clauses provide additional, not essential, information about the nouns they modify.	*Biodiesel fuel, **which often comes from plants,** is an economical source of energy.* (Where the fuel comes from is extra information. It is not essential information about *Biodiesel fuel*.)

3.1 Forming Nonidentifying Subject Relative Clauses

A Like identifying subject relative clauses, the subject of a nonidentifying subject relative clause is the relative pronoun. The relative pronoun refers to the noun before it.

Use *who* for people and *which* for things. Do not use *that* in a nonidentifying clause.

*People power, **which** is a way to create energy, is popular.*

NOT *People power, ~~that~~ is a way to create energy, is popular.*

B Use commas before and after the nonidentifying subject relative clause. The commas indicate that the information is not essential to the meaning of the noun. It is extra information.

*Hybrid cars, **which are better for the environment**, use less gas.*

3.2 Using Nonidentifying Subject Relative Clauses

A Use a nonidentifying subject relative clause to give nonessential information about a noun. These clauses are also called nonrestrictive clauses.

*People power, **which is a way to create energy**, is popular with environmentalists.*

B Nonidentifying relative clauses are more common in writing and formal speaking than in informal speaking.

3.3 Identifying vs. Nonidentifying Subject Relative Clauses

A Identifying relative clauses provide essential information about the noun. The information in the clause identifies or distinguishes the noun.

*Renewable energy **that comes directly from the sun** is called solar energy.* (The information identifies a particular type of renewable energy – not all types of renewable energy.)

*My sister **who lives in Maine** loves being outside.* (The information distinguishes this sister from the other or others; it implies there is more than one sister.)

B Nonidentifying clauses give extra information about a noun. The information is not essential. In speaking, use a short pause before and after the clause. In writing, separate the clause between commas.

*Renewable energy, **which releases fewer greenhouse gases**, is becoming more popular.* (The information does not identify the type of renewable energy; it gives more information about it.)

*My sister, **who lives in Maine**, loves being outside.* (The information is extra, not essential; it also implies the speaker has only one sister.)

Grammar Application

Exercise 3.1 Identifying or Nonidentifying?

A Read the news report on building affordable green homes in New Orleans. Underline the relative clauses. Label each of the relative clauses *I* (for identifying) or *NI* (for nonidentifying).

As the environment changes, hurricanes and other severe storms have become a serious problem in the United States and Latin America. Hurricanes, <u>which primarily attack</u> ^{NI} <u>southern and southeastern parts of the United States</u>, have been increasing in severity. The hurricane <u>that did the most damage in recent history</u> ^I was Hurricane Katrina. Since
5 then, a great number of Americans, including many celebrities, have helped the people of New Orleans rebuild their homes.

The celebrity <u>who is best known for building homes in New Orleans</u> ^I is Brad Pitt. Pitt, <u>who created a foundation called Make It Right</u> ^{NI}, helps build new "green" homes in New Orleans. The goals of this foundation are admirable. Make It Right volunteers, <u>who work for</u> ^{NI}
10 <u>free</u>, want to build 150 new green homes in the Lower 9th Ward.

The foundation is not simply providing new homes. Make It Right homes have many features <u>which are environmentally sound</u> ^I. For example, Make It Right homes have metal roofs <u>which absorb heat and keep them cool</u> ^I. It is possible that Make It Right homes will inspire new home builders not only in New Orleans but around the world as well.

B Pair Work **Compare your answers with a partner. Discuss the reason for each of your answers.**

The relative clause which primarily attack southern and southeastern parts of the United States *is nonidentifying, because it is not essential to understanding the sentence. You can say* Hurricanes have been increasing in severity, *and the idea is complete.*

Exercise 3.2 Nonidentifying Subject Relative Clauses

Combine the facts and the additional information about green architecture. Use nonidentifying relative clauses.

1 **Fact:** Green architecture is becoming more common.

   Additional Information: Green architecture considers both design and the environment.

   Green architecture, which considers both design and the environment, is becoming more common.

2 **Fact:** The Turning Torso building uses only renewable energy.
   Additional Information: The Turning Torso building is located in Malmö, Sweden.

   The Turning Torso building, which is located in Malmö, Sweden, uses ~.

3 Fact: The Turning Torso building was inspired by a sculpture of a twisting human being.

Additional Information: The Turning Torso building is the tallest building in Sweden.

> The Turning Torso, which is the tallest building in Sweden, was inspired by ~.

4 Fact: The Burj al-Taqa will be a wind- and solar-powered green skyscraper.

Additional Information: The Burj al-Taqa will be in Dubai.

> The Burj al-Taqa, which will be in Dubai, will be a wind- ~

5 Fact: Eckhard Gerber has also designed a green building in Riyadh.

Additional Information: Eckhard Gerber designed the Burj al-Taqa.

> Eckhard Gerber, who designed the Burj al-Taqa, has also ~.

6 Fact: Architect Eric Corey Freed believes that people will pay more for green buildings.

Additional Information: Eric Corey Freed has written several books on building green structures.

> Architect Eric Corey Freed, who has written several books on building green structures, believes that ~.

4 Subject Relative Clauses with *Whose*

Grammar Presentation

Subject relative clauses that begin with the pronoun *whose* show possession.	*In Sweden, there are train commuters. The commuters' body heat supplies energy for a building.*
	In Sweden, there are train commuters whose body heat supplies energy for a building.

4.1 Forming Relative Clauses with *Whose*

A The pronoun *whose* shows a possessive relationship between the noun before and after it.	*They are the scientists whose research has won awards.* (The research belongs to the scientists.)
	That is the product whose inventor attended this college. (The product is related to the inventor.)

4.1 Forming Relative Clauses with *Whose* *(continued)*

B The verb in the relative clause agrees with the noun following *whose*.

WHOSE + SINGULAR NOUN + SINGULAR VERB
He's the scientist whose newest idea is often quoted.

WHOSE + PLURAL NOUN + PLURAL VERB
He's the scientist whose ideas are often quoted.

4.2 Using Relative Clauses with *Whose*

Relative clauses with *whose* can be identifying or nonidentifying subject relative clauses.

IDENTIFYING RELATIVE CLAUSE
They are the journalists whose articles have explained green energy. (The information in the clause identifies which journalists.)

NONIDENTIFYING RELATIVE CLAUSE
Brad Pitt, whose movies are well known, gives a lot of money to environmental causes. (The information about his movies is not essential to identifying Brad Pitt.)

Grammar Application

Exercise 4.1 Subject Relative Clauses with *Whose*: Identifying or Nonidentifying?

A Read the article about a human-powered vehicle. Underline the subject relative clauses. Add commas when necessary.

Meet Charles Greenwood, the inventor of a new type of car. Greenwood, whose human-powered car can go up to 60 miles per hour, is an engineer. This inventor whose dream is to sell the cars to the public has also started a business to manufacture it. A car whose power source is human energy is obviously good for the environment. How does

5   it work? The car whose main power source is human-operated hand cranks[1] also runs with a battery. It's not expensive, either. The car – the HumanCar Imagine PS – will sell for about $15,000. A hybrid car whose selling price will only be about $15,000 should be very popular with energy-conscious consumers.

10   There are other benefits to a human-powered car. A car whose power source is human energy might also help drivers stay fit. In addition, owners expect to save money operating the HumanCar. The HumanCar whose main source of power is human-operated hand cranks gets the

15   equivalent of 100 miles to the gallon of gas in a regular car.

[1]**crank:** a handle or bar on a machine that you can turn to make another part turn

Alternative Energy Sources   313

B Pair Work Compare your answers with a partner. Discuss whether each subject relative clause is identifying or nonidentifying.

The relative clause whose human-power car can go up to 60 miles per hour *is nonidentifying because it is not necessary for identifying Greenwood.*

Exercise 4.2 *That, Who, or Whose?*

Complete the article about green awards. Use *that, who,* or *whose*. Sometimes more than one answer is possible.

AWARDS for Being Green

There are many organizations __*that*__ offer awards to companies __whose__ practices
               (1)   (2)
help the environment and society. Some organizations recognize the work of companies
__that__ focus on environmentally responsible practices. The Evergreen Award program
 (3)
honors companies __that/ich__ create environmentally friendly products. An award in 2010
                   (4)
went to Play Mart Inc., a maker of plastic playground equipment __whose__ products were
                                                  (5)
made from jugs and bottles from landfills.

The One Show is another awards organization, __whose/which__ Green Pencil award
                                             (6)
celebrates environmentally conscious advertising. In 2009, Häagen-Dazs received the
award for their advertisements __that__ raised awareness about the disappearance of
                                (7)
honeybees. Häagen-Dazs, __whose__ ice-cream is well known, also donates money to
                      (8)
research __that/ich__ studies honeybees. People __who (that__ buy certain flavors of
     (9)   (10)
Häagen-Dazs ice-cream help support this research.

Exercise 4.3 Subject Relative Clauses with *Whose*

Pair Work Answer the questions. Use subject relative clauses with *whose* in your sentences. Then compare your answers with a partner.

■ What are the benefits of human-powered vehicles and flying machines?

■ What are the disadvantages to these inventions?

A *I said, "A vehicle whose power source is human energy is good for the environment."*

B *I said, "A vehicle whose power source is human energy probably won't go very far or very fast."*

5 Avoid Common Mistakes ⚠

1 **Use *which* or *that* for things, not *who*.**

which/that

Scientists are looking for new energy sources ~~who~~ don't harm the environment.

2 **Use *who* or *that* for people, not *which*.**

who/that

Governments support researchers ~~which~~ are trying to develop alternative approaches to energy.

3 **Don't use *who's* when you mean *whose*.**

whose

An inventor ~~who's~~ innovative technology solves the energy crisis will help all of us.

4 **Don't include a second subject in the relative clause.**

A fuel that ~~it~~ is renewable will help solve the world's pollution problems.

Editing Task

Find and correct eight more mistakes in the paragraph about an alternative renewable energy source.

People think renewable energy only comes from water, wind, or the sun, but there

which/that

is another renewable energy source: biofuels. Biofuels are fuels ~~who~~ are derived from

whose

oils in plants. Farmers ~~who's~~ fields were once planted with food crops can now grow

which/that

energy on their land. The most commonly used example of this is ethanol, a biofuel ~~who~~

5 is usually made from corn and added to gasoline. However, ethanol has been criticized.

whose

Some critics say that the world, ~~who's~~ population continues to grow, needs all of its corn

for food production. Others have argued that it takes too much energy to produce corn

who/that

ethanol. Recently, scientists ~~which~~ do biofuels research have been working to overcome

these problems. For example, some scientists have produced a genetically modified

10 tobacco that ~~it~~ contains more oil than usual. Other scientists have produced genetically

modified tobacco plants that ~~they~~ produce a lot of oil. This oil can be made into ethanol.

In fact, some scientists have produced ethanol from inedible grass that ~~it~~ grows in the

who/that

wild. The scientists ~~which~~ made these inventions hope that biofuels will become an

important part of our renewable energy future.

6 Academic Writing

Expository Writing

Brainstorm > Organize > Write > Edit

In this writing cycle (Units 21-23), you will write an expository essay that answers the prompt below. In this unit (21), you will analyze a text, and then brainstorm and organize ideas about the topic.

> *Explain the advantages and disadvantages of three types of renewable energy and decide which would work best in your country or region.*

Exercise 6.1 Preparing to Read

Work with a partner. Discuss the questions.

1 What can we do to protect our natural resources like air and water?
2 What will happen if important resources that we use, like water, fresh food, and oil disappear?
3 What do you think the slogan, "Reduce, Reuse, Recycle" means?
4 What are some other things that you do to be "green"?

Exercise 6.2 Focusing on Vocabulary

Read the definitions. Complete the sentences with the correct form of the words in bold.

> **adopt** (v) to accept or begin to use something
>
> **alarming** (adj) causing worry or fear
>
> **catastrophic** (adj) causing sudden and very great harm or destruction
>
> **resistant** (adj) not wanting to accept something, especially change or new ideas
>
> **urgent** (adj) needing immediate attention
>
> **vital** (adj) necessary or extremely important for the success or continued existence of something

1 Finding solutions to climate change is a(n) _____ issue that must be addressed now.
2 Global warming is _____ to most people because the future of the planet is in danger.
3 Scientists warn us that not reducing our use of fossil fuels will have _____ effects on our environment and will likely lead to the extinction of many species.
4 Over one hundred United Nations delegates signed a document to _____ new environmental standards in order to slow down climate change.
5 Experts say that it is _____ to stop pollution caused by factories for the survival of certain plant and animal species.
6 Manufacturers are often _____ to using "green" production methods that cost more, so we need new laws that force them to do it.

Maintaining Our Natural Resources

The world's natural resources are being used at an **alarming** rate—not only fossil fuels such as coal, oil, and gas, but also water, wood, metals, and minerals. This has many potential consequences for the billions of people who live on Earth. In
5 recent years, both individuals and governments have become more interested in better management of the world's resources. An immediate way for individuals to improve the situation is for everyone to reduce, reuse, and recycle products. Alternative energy solutions, which are equally essential to our future, are
10 generally the responsibility of governments, though they are not always practical for various reasons.

Each of us must learn to use fewer natural resources on a daily basis. We can start by reducing the number of electrical items that we leave plugged in, using less water, and avoiding fossil fuel-powered transportation. In our homes, we can use only energy-saving light bulbs and install water meters. Parents need to train children from an
15 early age to turn off lights that they are not using. It is sometimes difficult to persuade people to use less energy and water or to waste less food, but an effective way to motivate people to **adopt** less-wasteful practices is to make these important commodities more expensive. As a result, many cities now tax carbon emissions, which is a step in the right direction.

Another effective way to help the environment is by encouraging people to reuse or restore old, unwanted
20 objects. When people reuse, they reduce waste. Additionally, items like glass bottles can be cleaned and reused without having to be broken and remade. Reusing objects is an efficient process that consumes less energy than recycling. It does, however, often require a lot of planning and administration, which can increase costs. For example, there are concerns regarding reused medical equipment and food-storage items because of safety and hygiene issues. Still, the benefits of reusing many items are clear.

25 Most of us know that materials such as paper and plastic can be recycled into new products, but this process depends on individual and community action. It is true that sorting through used materials before recycling them can be a dirty job, and breaking up electronic equipment to recycle rare metals is time-consuming and potentially dangerous. However, as long as we understand the work and potential dangers involved, the necessity of recycling on a community scale is evident.

30 In recent years, a lot of attention has been paid to the dangers of relying on fossil fuels. For this reason, the use of alternatives to coal, oil, and gas are becoming more and more common. Alternative energy sources can be recovered or produced without emitting carbon dioxide and without contributing to global warming. They can decrease air pollution, which is better for our health, as it diminishes instances of asthma. They are often sustainable resources as well, which means they will not get used up.

35 There are many examples of alternative energy sources including hydropower, solar energy, biomass[1], and geothermal energy, though each has its limitations. Hydropower, which utilizes the power of moving water, is a good choice for places with waterfalls and rivers. Wind power is most productive in areas with sustained wind, like hilltops and open water. Places that receive constant sunlight during the day, like deserts, are the best candidates for solar energy. The burning of biomass can be used to create steam and is available everywhere, but only if
40 government or companies are willing to invest in it. Finally, geothermal energy, which uses the heat within the earth to produce electricity and heat buildings, is limited to countries like Iceland that are situated above this kind of energy source. Clearly, particular types of alternative energy may work best for particular regions. The other side of this reality is that some of these energy sources may not be available at all to some people because of where they live. However, these are not reasons for governments to do nothing.

45 Clearly, individuals, governments, and businesses must work together to avoid a **catastrophic** depletion of **vital** natural resources in the future, and **urgent** action is required now. Alternative energy production is certainly essential, but it can be expensive and time-consuming to install the required elements. Some developing areas of the world may simply be unable to pay for it. In other places, corporations and taxpayers may be **resistant** to it. The "reduce, reuse, recycle" strategy, at least for the present, seems to be a manageable one that can be
50 practiced by both individuals and organizations. People who may be resistant to the idea of changing their ways by "going green" need to see that it is crucial to do this for the future of the planet.

---

[1]**biomass (n)** dead plant and animal material suitable for using as fuel

Read the text on page 317. Work with a partner. Discuss the questions.

1 What is the writer's main idea?
2 What are two suggestions that the writer offers for using fewer natural resources on a daily basis?
3 What are three advantages of alternative energy sources?
4 What are two disadvantages of alternative energy sources?

Exercise 6.4 Noticing the Grammar and Writing

1 Highlight two examples of *that* in paragraph 2. How does the writer use these relative clauses?
2 Highlight two examples of *which* in paragraph 6. How does the writer use these relative clauses?
3 Look at paragraph 3. Circle the advantages. Underline the disadvantages. How is the paragraph organized?
4 Read the last sentence of paragraphs 2-7. How do they support the writer's main idea?

Organizing Ideas in a Table

A **table** is a graphic organizer that helps writers visualize and organize ideas, relationships, and concepts before writing. Tables are especially helpful when examining the advantages, disadvantages, and other characteristics of multiple items.

Exercise 6.4 Applying the Skill

1 Use information from the reading on page 317 to complete the table.

	What are the benefits?	What are the drawbacks?	Is it effective for my country? What is the impact of producing it?
hydropower			
solar energy			
wind power			
biomass energy			
geothermal energy			

2 Compare your answers with a partner, and discuss the differences.

My Writing

Expository Essays

In expository essays, writers explain, illustrate, or clarify ideas about a topic. When you explain ideas, it is important to discuss both the advantages and disadvantages. This will help readers better understand your thesis.

Exercise 6.6 Brainstorming Topics and Ideas

Work with a partner. Complete the tasks.

1 Review the alternative energy sources you discussed in Exercise 6.4. Decide which three would work best in your country.

2 Complete the table below. Use ideas from the reading on page 317 to help you.

Rank	Type of Energy	Reason
1		
2		
3		

Using Relative Clauses to Add Information and Avoid Repetition

As you learned in this unit, relative clauses add information about nouns. Relative clauses are often formed by combining two sentences. When you combine two sentences with a relative clause, you avoid repetition, which makes your ideas clearer and more fluent. Look at these examples:

My university has solar panels. The **solar panels** were made in Germany.

My university has solar panels **that** were made in Germany.

In the first example, the term *solar panels* is repeated. Repeating a term or phrase can make your writing choppy. The second example flows better and is more concise.

Exercise 6.7 Writing a Paragraph

Write a paragraph about one of the alternative energy sources in Exercise 6.6. Include a topic sentence, at least two advantages and two disadvantages, and a concluding sentence. Use the grammar and writing skills you learned in this unit to improve your writing.

UNIT 22

Object Relative Clauses (Adjective Clauses with Object Relative Pronouns)

Biometrics

1 Grammar in the Real World

**ACADEMIC
WRITING**

Expository
writing

A What are some techniques that the police use to solve crimes? Read the article about how the police analyze evidence. What are some modern techniques for analyzing evidence?

B Comprehension Check **Answer the questions.**

1 What are some types of forensic evidence?
2 What is one way that police can identify someone?
3 Why can forensic evidence sometimes be inaccurate?

C Notice **Match the first part of the sentence from the article on the left with the second part on the right.**

A	B
1 The victim shows the police the room __b__	a **that** thieves leave behind.
2 Traditional forensic techniques include collecting and analyzing evidence __c__ __a__	b in **which** the theft occurred.
3 This evidence includes dust, hair, or fibers __a__ __c__	c **that** police find at the crime scene.

Do the words in B in bold act as the subjects or objects of the clauses they are in?

FORENSICS | An Imperfect Science

Someone steals a painting from a private home. The victim shows the police the room **in which the theft occurred**. Police collect clothing fibers and dirt left on the carpet. Experts then use the fibers and dirt to identify the thief. The thief is caught, and the art is returned. The use of scientific tests to investigate crimes like this one is called forensics. Traditional forensic techniques include collecting and analyzing evidence **that police find at the crime scene**. This evidence includes dust, hair, or fibers **that thieves leave behind**. Police sometimes use dogs to investigate a crime. Scents **that dogs are trained to recognize** include the scents of people, drugs, and explosives. Police also look for fingerprints, **which they often find on hard surfaces**. Unfortunately, fingerprints are often incomplete. However, new techniques use computer programs to help police identify suspects or missing people. Computer programs can produce a list of matches for partial fingerprints. This kind of list, **which police use to narrow a large field of suspects**, helps investigators work efficiently.

In addition, new technology is being used to analyze other evidence. New video cameras can
25 automatically identify a face **whose image police have on film**. Police can compare the faces of suspects to the image of the criminal and find the actual person more quickly. There is also a new way **in which police can identify someone who may be
30 a "missing person."**[1] This new technology compares a digital image of the person's iris[2] with the irises of people who are listed as missing in a database.

Forensic evidence **that police collect** is not always accurate. For example, fiber matching is inconclusive.[3]
35 Currently, fibers **that investigators analyze** can only be matched to a type of cloth. The fibers may not be from clothes **that the suspect owns**. Another concern is that there are no strict training standards for forensic dogs. Therefore, agencies like the FBI have only a few
40 dog teams **whose work they trust.**

Combining technology with traditional methods is changing the way **that criminal investigations are done.** Forensic science is not perfect, but it is still an important tool in investigations.

---

[1]**missing person:** someone who has disappeared

[2]**iris:** the colored part of the eye

[3]**inconclusive:** not leading to a definite result or decision; uncertain

2 Identifying Object Relative Clauses

Grammar Presentation

In an object relative clause, the relative pronoun is the object of the clause. An identifying object relative clause gives essential information about the noun it modifies.	OBJECT *Evidence is sometimes inaccurate. Police collect <u>this evidence</u>.* RELATIVE PRONOUN *Evidence <u>that</u> police collect is sometimes inaccurate.*

2.1 Forming Identifying Object Relative Clauses

A The object relative pronoun follows the noun it replaces and comes at the beginning of the relative clause. In an object relative clause, the relative pronoun is the object of the clause.	*Humans aren't aware of <u>smells</u>. A dog can recognize <u>smells</u>.* NOUN RELATIVE PRONOUN *Humans aren't aware of smells <u>that</u> a dog can recognize.*
B Use the relative pronouns *who*, *that*, or *whom* with people. Use *which* or *that* for things.	*Detectives are <u>people</u> **who/that/whom** I respect tremendously.*
These pronouns are frequently omitted in speaking, but not in formal writing.	*Forensic evidence is something <u>which/that</u> police count on.* (in writing) *Forensic evidence is something police count on.* (in speaking)
When referring to people, *that* is more common than *who*. The pronoun *whom* is very formal and is much less common than *that* or *who* in conversation.	least formal *Detective Paula Cho is a person **that** I admire very much.* *Detective Paula Cho is a person **who** I admire very much.* *Detective Paula Cho is a person **whom** I admire very much.* most formal
C Use *whose* + a noun to show possession. *Whose* cannot be omitted.	*The person <u>whose car</u> **the thieves stole** was a friend of mine.*

▶▶ Relative Clauses: See page A13.

2.2 Using Identifying Subject Relative Clauses

Use an identifying relative clause to give essential information that defines or identifies the noun it modifies.	*Evidence **that criminals leave at the crime scene** is called forensic evidence.* (*That criminals leave at the crime scene* identifies the evidence.)

Grammar Application

Complete the sentences about forensic technology. Use *who* or *which* and the verbs in parentheses.

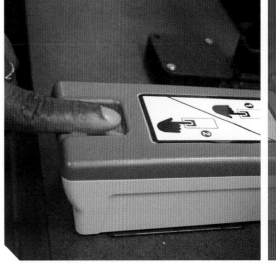

1 *Biometrics* refers to the techniques __*which*__ people __*use*__ (use) to identify individuals by their physical or behavioral characteristics.

2 Biometric information _____ experts _____ (analyze) includes DNA, fingerprints, eyes, and voice patterns.

3 People _____ the police _____ (suspect) of a crime can be excluded with the use of biometrics.

4 Biometric technology can match fingerprints with ones _____ the police _____ (have) on file.

5 One type of biometric technology _____ people _____ (utilize) for security is the fingerprint scanner.

6 For example, people _____ Disney World _____ (admit) to the park must have their fingerprints scanned.

7 The fingerprint scanners _____ Disney World _____ (use) help to stop people from entering the park without a proper ticket.

Complete the web interview about forensic technology. Rewrite the sentence pairs in parentheses as single sentences with object relative clauses. Sometimes more than one answer is possible.

> ⌂   💬 ↻ ☰ ✉
>
> **Reporter**   I understand that our police department has some new forensic technology.
>
> **Mayor**   *Yes, it has a new system that it uses to analyze DNA.*
>   (1 Yes, it has a new system. It uses the system to analyze DNA.)
>
> **Reporter**   What does it look like?
>
> **Mayor**   _____
>   (2 It's a hand-held device. Officers bring it to the crime scene.)
>
>   _____
>   (3 It helps the police to analyze data. They find the data at the scene.)
>
> **Reporter**   I understand that not everyone is happy about this device.
>
> **Mayor**   _____
>   (4 The device has privacy issues. Some people are concerned about these privacy issues.)

Reporter	Why is this a concern?
Mayor	

(5 Well, the DNA might get the person in trouble. The device collected this DNA.)

(6 For example, many people have health issues. They want to keep these issues private.)

Reporter	Oh, I see. This is certainly a lot to think about. Thank you for the interview.

Exercise 2.3 Sentence Combining

A Rewrite the reporter's notes on local crimes. Use identifying object relative clauses with the relative pronouns in parentheses.

Recent Crime Reports

1 A man was arrested for theft. Police raided his house last night. (whose)

A man *whose house police raided last night was arrested for theft* .

2 The detectives made their report. The police sent the detectives to the crime scene. (whom)

The detectives whom the police sent to the crime scene made their report .

3 Several valuable items had been stolen. The police recovered the items. (that)

Several valuable items that the police recovered had been stolen .

4 The man has not been identified. Burglars invaded the man's home. (whose)

The man whose home burglars invaded has not been identified .

5 Detectives have visited the house. The thief broke into the house yesterday. (which)

Detectives have visited the house which the thief broke into yesterday .

6 The man is in good condition. A car hit him last night. (that)

The man that a car hit last night is in good condition .

B Pair Work In which sentences in A can you omit the pronoun? Discuss the answer with a partner. Then rewrite the sentences with the pronoun omitted.

3 Nonidentifying Object Relative Clauses

Grammar Presentation

Nonidentifying object relative clauses have the same form as identifying clauses. Unlike identifying clauses, nonidentifying clauses provide additional, not essential, information about the nouns they modify.	*Evidence from crimes, **which we call forensic evidence**, can help police solve cases.* (*Which we call forensic evidence* is extra information. It is not essential to understanding *Evidence from crimes*.)

3.1 Forming Nonidentifying Object Relative Clauses

A Use *who* or *whom* for people. Use *which* for things. Use *whose* for possessive people and things.	*The Sherlock Holmes stories were written by the Scottish author Arthur Conan Doyle, **who/whom many people think was English**.*
Do not use *that* in nonidentifying relative clauses.	*Forensic science, **which Sherlock Holmes used**, has been recognized as science since the 1800s.* NOT *Forensic science, ~~that~~ Sherlock Holmes used, has been recognized as science since the 1800s.*
Do not omit the relative pronoun in nonidentifying object clauses.	*The character Sherlock Holmes, **who Arthur Conan Doyle created**, was a fictional detective.* NOT *The character Sherlock Holmes, ~~Arthur Conan Doyle created~~, was a fictional detective.*
B Use commas before and after the nonidentifying object relative clause.	*Arthur Conan Doyle, **whose medical clinic not many patients attended**, had time to write his stories.*

Grammar Application

Exercise 3.1 Nonidentifying Object Relative Clauses

Read part of a presentation on a forensic science program. Underline the nonidentifying clauses. Add commas.

Forensic science, which many of you know about from popular TV shows, has become a popular career. Forensic science courses, which many colleges are offering today, prepare students for careers in crime scene investigation. The University of Central Florida (UCF), which I attended, has a forensic science program. Your area of
5 specialization, which you choose during your time here, depends on your interests and skills. The area that I chose was forensic biochemistry because I wanted to study

odontology. Forensic odontology, which the police use to analyze teeth, is challenging and fascinating. Forensic analysis which focuses on chemistry and analysis of different kinds of evidence is also available. Introduction to Forensic Science which you take

10 after other preliminary courses will help you decide on the area of specialty. I wish you all the best of luck!

Exercise 3.2 Using Nonidentifying Object Relative Clauses

Read the sentences about a TV show that popularizes forensics. Combine the sentences with nonidentifying object relative clauses. Add commas when necessary.

1 NCIS: Naval Criminal Investigative Service is an American TV series. Donald Bellisario and Don McGill created it.

NCIS: Naval Criminal Investigative Service, _which Donald Bellisario and Don McGill created, is an American TV series._ .

2 The program became a hit in 2011. CBS first showed it in 2003.
The program _, which CBS first showed in 2003, became a hit in 2011_

3 NCIS has been on the air for many years. The entertainment industry has awarded it several awards.
NCIS _, which the entertainment industry has awarded several awards, has been on the air for many years_ .

4 The program is shown in Australia, New Zealand, Canada, the UK, and Poland. Over 22 million people watched season 10.
The program _, which over 22 million people watched season 10, is shown ~_

5 "NCIS Theme" is the show's theme tune. CBS records first released it in 2009.
"NCIS Theme," _which CBS records first released in 2009, is the_ . _show's theme tune_ .

6 NCIS: The Game was popular. CBS released it in 2010.
NCIS: The Game _, which CBS released in 2010, was popular_ .

4 Object Relative Clauses as Objects of Prepositions

Grammar Presentation

The relative pronouns in object relative clauses can be the object of prepositions.	OBJ. OF PREP. There's the police officer. I spoke to _her_. RELATIVE PRONOUN There's the police officer **to whom I spoke**. There's the police officer **who I spoke to**.

4.1 Object Relative Clauses as Objects of Prepositions

A The prepositions in object relative clauses can come at the end of the clause in informal speaking and writing.	The police examined the chair that/which I was sitting <u>on</u>. The witness, who/whom I spoke <u>to</u> yesterday, will appear in court.
In identifying relative clauses, use the relative pronouns *who*, *that*, or *whom* for people and *that* or *which* for things. You can also omit the relative pronoun.	*IDENTIFYING RELATIVE CLAUSE* The police examined the chair (that/which) I was sitting <u>on</u>. The police officer (who/that/whom) I met <u>with</u> was robbed.
In nonidentifying relative clauses, use the relative pronouns *who* or *whom* for people and *which* for things. You cannot omit the relative pronoun.	*NONIDENTIFYING RELATIVE CLAUSE* The door, which I entered through, was broken during the crime. The witness, <u>who/whom</u> I spoke to yesterday, will appear in court. NOT The witness, ~~I spoke to yesterday~~, will appear in court.
B In more formal spoken and especially in written English, the preposition comes before the relative pronouns *whom* or *which*. Do not use *that* or *who*.	The police examined the chair <u>on which</u> I was sitting. NOT The police examined the chair on ~~that~~ I was sitting. The witness, <u>with whom</u> I spoke yesterday, will appear in court. NOT The witness, with ~~who/that~~ I spoke yesterday, will appear in court.
You cannot omit the relative pronoun.	NOT The police examined the chair ~~on I was sitting~~. NOT The witness, ~~with I spoke yesterday~~, will appear in court.

Grammar Application

Exercise 4.1 Prepositions and Object Relative Clauses

A Listen to a detective describe a crime scene. Complete the sentences with the words you hear.

I arrived at the crime scene at 11:00 a.m. The crime had taken place in a

restaurant. The room __*that*__ the crime occurred ___*in*___ was the kitchen.
          (1)   (1)

The back door was open. The back wall was covered in graffiti. I found a spray can

under a table. The spray can, _____ I found fingerprints _____ , matched
                (2)   (2)

the color of the graffiti. I asked the kitchen staff to talk to me as a group. The group,

_____ the chef was the only one missing, was very nervous. I learned that the
       (3)

chef had a lot of enemies. I spoke to a cleaning person _____ the chef had argued
                                         (4)

_____ last week. I also interviewed several waitresses _____ the chef had
(4)   (5)
gone out _____ . One waitress showed me the chef's locker, _____ I found
               (5)   (6)
more spray cans _____ .
                        (6)

B Listen again and check your answers.

A Combine the sentences from a crime scene investigator. Use identifying object relative
clauses with a preposition at the end of the clause. Sometimes more than one answer
is possible.

1 The room was the office. I found broken furniture in it.

The room _which/that I found broken furniture in_ was the office.

2 I found fibers on the floor. The broken furniture was lying on the floor.

I found fibers on the floor _which / that the broken furniture was lying on_

3 The neighbors said they heard nothing. I spoke to them.

The neighbors _who /that I spoke to_ said they heard nothing.
              whom

4 The house was unlocked. The crime took place in it.

The house _which / that the crime took place in_ was unlocked.

5 There were fingerprints on the door. The criminal entered through it.

There were fingerprints on the door _which /that the criminal entered through_ .

6 The lab matched the fingerprints immediately. I sent the evidence to it.

The lab _which /that I sent the evidence_ matched the fingerprints immediately.
                                      _to_

B Rewrite your answers in A as formal sentences.

1 _The room in which I found broken furniture was the office._

2 _on which_

3 _to whom_

4 _in which_

5 _through which_

6 _to which_

5 Avoid Common Mistakes ⚠

1 **Use *who/whom/that*, not *which*, for people and *which/that* for things.**

who/whom/that
The investigator is someone ~~which~~ he respects.

that/which
NCIS is a crime show ~~who~~ I watch.

2 **Remember to omit the object pronoun after the verb in object relative clauses.**

The evidence that the police found ~~it~~ was used to find the suspect.

3 **Do not use a comma before an identifying object relative clause.**

The TV crime program⸏ that people thought was the most popular⸏ worked closely with the police to develop its stories.

4 **Do not use *what* in relative clauses.**

The crime ~~what~~ I am talking about happened yesterday.

Editing Task

Find and correct six more mistakes in the paragraphs about eyewitness testimony.

A victim who police have taken ~~her~~ to the police station gives testimony. She

who/whom/that/ø
looks at a man in a police lineup and says, "That's the person ~~which~~ I saw in my car."

During the trial, the woman gives her testimony in front of the jury, and the jury makes a

decision. Soon, the man goes to jail. However, it is possible the woman whose testimony

that/which/ø
5 was used is wrong. Researchers now claim that the eyewitness stories ~~what~~ courts often

rely on are not always reliable.

that/which
Psychologists have conducted experiments ~~who~~ revealed some surprising results.

They played a crime-scene video for participants and then asked the participants to

remember details. Results showed that participants often described events⸏ which

10 they knew nothing about and had not seen in the video. Similarly, the suspect ~~what~~

participants chose out of a police lineup was rarely the actual criminal.

Psychologists who courts have hired ~~them~~ have testified that eyewitness testimony

is not as accurate as was once assumed. As such, psychologists have developed new

rules to guide the use of eyewitness testimony.

6 Academic Writing

Expository Writing

Brainstorm > Organize > Write > Edit

In Unit 21, you analyzed an essay and used a table to brainstorm and organize ideas for the prompt below. In this unit (22), you will develop your ideas, learn ways to make your writing clearer and more coherent, and write the first draft of your expository essay.

> Explain the advantages and disadvantages of three types of renewable energy and decide which would work best in your country or region.

Introducing Advantages and Disadvantages

You can use a range of phrases that introduce advantages and disadvantages of ideas or solutions to problems.

One major advantage of … is …	The most serious disadvantage of … is …
The most obvious advantages of … are …	A distinct disadvantage of … is …
Another apparent advantage of … is …	One other potential disadvantage of … is …

When a criminal leaves hair at the scene of a crime, the police can use it to find the criminal. This **is one major advantage of** forensic science.

A **distinct disadvantage of** forensic science is that evidence is not always useful. For example, fingerprints may be incomplete.

Exercise 6.1 Understanding the Skill

Work with a partner. Use the prompts to create sentences. Use phrases from the skill box to introduce advantages and disadvantages.

1 advantage, eyewitness, identify criminal
2 disadvantage, eyewitness, misidentify criminal
3 advantage, study, chemistry and forensics
4 disadvantage, study, chemistry and forensics

Exercise 6.2 Applying the Skill

Look at your paragraph from My Writing in Unit 21. Identify the sentences in which you have listed an advantage or disadvantage. Rewrite the sentences with phrases you have learned.

Building Coherence

It is important to make the relationship between different ideas in a text clear to your reader. The ideas should flow in a logical way. This is called **coherence**, and it makes your writing easier to follow. For example, if you are referring back to an idea already presented, the reader should understand that clearly. Use the following to build coherence in your writing.

- Pronouns that refer back to an idea already introduced: *they, them, it, one*, etc.
- Conjunctions and connectors: *however, therefore, in contrast, although*, etc.
- Determiners: *this, that, these, those*, etc.
- Transition words and phrases: *for example, in the same way*, etc.

Exercise 6.3 Applying the Skill

Complete the paragraph with words from the box. You will not use all the words.

For example	However	That	Them	They	Those

Many students are interested in studying forensic science due to the large number of programs that feature it. (1)_____, *Forensic Cops* is a popular TV show that follows crime scene investigators in Los Angeles. (2)_____ are employed by a police department and help conduct the investigation. (3)_____, the forensic team does not physically find the criminal. (4)_____ job is for the police team.

My Writing

Ordering Ideas in an Essay

Writers often present several ideas related to the main topic in an expository essay. The most important or useful idea generally comes last to leave the readers with a powerful idea. Therefore, when writing about your energy sources, put the energy source that is most likely to be successful in your country at the end.

Exercise 6.4 Planning Your Essay

Work in a small group. Complete the tasks.

1 Compare your paragraphs from My Writing in Unit 21. Which energy sources are the most popular? Why?
2 Discuss the advantages and disadvantages of each source you listed in the brainstorming table on page 319. Revise and edit your ideas based on your discussion.
3 Order the energy sources you are going to write about. Put the most important one last.

Exercise 6.5 Writing Your First Draft

Review your notes. Write an introductory paragraph and three body paragraphs. Use the grammar and writing skills you learned in this unit to improve your writing.

UNIT 23

Relative Clauses with *Where* and *When*; Reduced Relative Clauses

Millennials

1 Grammar in the Real World

A Do you know anyone born after 1995? Some studies suggest that individuals born during this time have similar traits, such as a high level of independence. Read the article about Generation Z, a term for these individuals. How might these people be different from other, older people in the workplace?

B Comprehension Check **Answer the questions.**

1 When was Generation Z born?
2 Why are Gen Zers so hard-working and entrepreneurial?
3 Why is Generation Z so comfortable with technology?

C Notice **Read the sentences. What words could you add to the words in bold to make them relative clauses? Are the new clauses subject or object relative clauses?**

1 David Stillman, *who is* **a Generation Z expert**, believes this is the result of the way they were raised.

2 **Gen Zers** *who work* **working a regular job** often have their own income-generating projects on the side.

Generation Z in the Workplace

Generation Z, **also known as iGen or Gen Zers**, are people born between 1995 and 2012. There are over 65 million of them in the United States alone, **where they are now entering the workplace**. It is hard to generalize about such a large group, but these young workers often share certain traits.

This group is hard-working, pragmatic, and entrepreneurial. David Stillman, **a Generation Z expert**, believes this is the result of the way they were raised. They were raised at a time **when many parents lost their jobs in the Great Recession**. Therefore iGen values job security more than previous generations.

In the workplace, their entrepreneurial spirit shows up in several ways. Gen Zers are willing to work very hard, and they prefer to work alone. They also expect to be able to spend time on their own projects at work. **Gen Zers working a regular job** often have their own income-generating projects on the side. These "side hustles" include selling things online and providing services via social media.

Generation Z, **raised in the era of YouTube, social media, and smartphones**, are the first real digital natives. They have never known life without Wi-Fi. They are totally comfortable with technology in the workplace. They are multi-tasking experts. They can watch an online video, comment on Instragram, and listen to music at the same time.

However, their work habits can sometimes serve as distractions. Working on their own side projects can cause moments of inattentiveness, **during which serious errors can occur**. Some members of Generation Z are known for being distracted on the job. Older colleagues may find this trait annoying.

This generation of employees will use technology and their own entrepreneurial spirit to make the workplace more efficient. They want to work hard and succeed. Generation Z is ambitious, independent, and tech savvy. These are the traits **already helping them** succeed in workplaces around the country.

2 Relative Clauses with *Where* and *When*

Grammar Presentation

The adverbs *where* and *when* can be used in relative clauses. *Where* is used to modify nouns of place, and *when* is used to modify nouns of time. In these cases, we call these words relative adverbs.

*The computer lab is a place **where many young students feel comfortable**.*

*Night is a time **when many students study for exams**.*

2.1 Relative Clauses with *Where*

A Use *where* in relative clauses to modify a noun referring to a place.

Common nouns include *area*, *country*, *house*, *place*, and *room*.

*This is the only <u>area</u> **where you can find Wi-Fi outside of the office**.*

*The United States is a <u>country</u> **where a lot of research on young people is done**.*

*The office is a <u>place</u> **where workers often compete**.*

B Do not use a preposition before *where*. Use *which* instead. The use of preposition + *which* is common <u>in academic writing.</u>

*It's a city <u>**in which**</u> you can find Wi-Fi almost everywhere.*

NOT *It's a city in where you can find Wi-Fi almost everywhere.*

▸▸ Relative Clauses: See page A13.

2.2 Relative Clauses with *When*

A Use *when* in relative clauses to modify a noun referring to a time.

Common nouns include *day*, *moment*, *period*, *season*, *time*, and *year*.

*The <u>day</u> **when you graduate** is the <u>day</u> **when you will need to find a job**.*

*Spring is the <u>time</u> **when most students graduate**.*

*The late 1990s and early 2000s are the years **when many young people in the workforce were born**.*

B Do not use a preposition before *when*. Use *which* instead. The use of preposition + *which* is very formal.

*Summer is the time <u>**during which**</u> many jobs become available.*

NOT *Summer is the time during when many jobs become available.*

*The day <u>**on which**</u> you start your new job will be very busy.*

NOT *The day on when you start your new job will be very busy.*

2.2 Relative Clauses with *When* (continued)

C You can omit the relative adverb *when* in identifying relative clauses.	*Ricardo remembered the moment he met his boss.* = *Ricardo remembered the moment when he met his boss.*

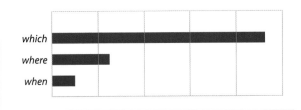

DATA FROM THE REAL WORLD

Research shows that in writing, nonidentifying relative clauses with *where* and *when* are much less common than nonidentifying relative clauses with *which*. Clauses with *when* are the least common and are used in rather formal writing.

⌨ Grammar Application

Exercise 2.1 Object Relative Clauses with *Where* and *When*

Complete the sentences about Generation Z. Circle the correct words. Note Ø means no relative adverb.

1 Gen Zers believe America is a place **(where)/ when** anyone can be successful.

2 They were born at a time in **(which)/ where** technology was a part of everyday life.

3 They had childhoods **when / (in)** which everyone had a smartphone.

4 They are entering the workplace during a period **(when)/ which** Wi-Fi.

5 They expect a work environment **Ø / (where)** people can work independently.

6 They grew up during a period **(when)/ where** the Great Recession was an issue.

7 The day **(Ø)/ where** they graduate from school is a time of both joy and anxiety.

Exercise 2.2 More Object Relative Clauses with *Where* and *When*

A Listen to an interview with a Millennial who is helping to change the world in a positive way. Circle the answers to the questions.

1 Where did Sean go?

   a (To Haiti)   **b** To Florida

2 When did Sean go?

   a After a rainstorm   **b** After an earthquake

3 Why did Sean go?

    a To help people   **b** To take a break from school

4 What did he do there?

    a Work in a large city to   **b** Work in small towns
       give basic medical care   to give basic medical care

B **Listen again. Complete the interview with the words you hear.**

Interviewer   Some people think that members of the Millennial generation only think about themselves, but there are a lot of young people who are making a difference. They are helping others and trying to make the world a better place. One of these young people is Sean Green. Sean is a medical student in Florida. He went to Haiti at a time ___*in which*___ they needed him the most.
                                                     (1)
    Sean, tell us your story.

Sean   Sure, I'd be happy to. I went to Haiti at a time _____ many
                                                        (2)
    people were suffering – right after the 2010 earthquake.

Interviewer   Why did you go?

Sean   Haiti is a place _____ there aren't enough doctors. I'm in
                                         (3)
    medical school now. So it seemed like a good opportunity for me to get experience and to help people as well.

Interviewer   What did you do there?

Sean   I worked in small towns _____ the earthquake destroyed
                                        (4)
    the homes of many people. I lived in a town _____ a lot of
                                          (5)
    people were hurt, and helped give basic medical care. It was the season
    _____ there is a lot of rain. There was mud everywhere. It was a
                   (6)
    challenge to keep things clean.

Interviewer   Tell us a little about the people you worked with.

Sean   The people in the town _____ I worked gave us a lot of help.
                                   (7)
    They were very friendly and welcoming. It was an amazing experience.

Interviewer   Thank you for your time, Sean.

C **Listen again and check your answers.**

Exercise 2.3 Relative Clauses with *When*

Look at the information in the chart. It shows three important generations in the United States and the major events or influences in their lifetimes. Then write sentences about the years in parentheses. Use relative clauses with *when, in which,* and *during which.* Sometimes more than one answer is possible.

	Name of Generation	Years Born	Important Lifetime Events or Influences
	Baby Boomers	1946–1964	President Kennedy dies, 1963 Vietnam War ends, 1975
	Generation X (Gen Xers)	1965–1981	The Berlin Wall falls, 1989
	Millennials	1980–2000	The Great Recession occurs, 2007–2009

1 (1946–1964)

  The years 1946–1964 are the years when the Baby Boomers were born.

2 (1963)

_____

3 (1975)

_____

4 (1965–1981)

_____

5 (1989)

_____

6 (1980–2000)

_____

7 (2007)

_____

3 Reduced Relative Clauses

Grammar Presentation

Relative clauses with *be* can often be reduced to phrases. There are three types of reduced relative clauses: participle phrases, prepositional phrases, and appositives.

RELATIVE CLAUSE

The expert who is giving tomorrow's talk on Generation Z is very well known.

REDUCED RELATIVE CLAUSE

The expert giving tomorrow's talk on Generation Z is very well known.

3.1 Forming Reduced Relative Clauses

A Reduce a subject relative clause by omitting the relative pronoun (*that, which, who*) and *be*.	*My brother, a Gen Zer, likes a fast-paced environment.* = *My brother, who is a Gen Zer, likes a fast-paced environment.*
B Do not shorten a subject relative clause with *be* + a single adjective. Instead, move the adjective before the modified noun.	*I know a lot of people who are self-confident.* *I know a lot of self-confident people.* NOT *I know a lot of people self-confident.*
C Do not reduce object relative clauses.	*Our new assistant, who I am meeting tomorrow, is a Gen Zer.* NOT *Our new assistant, meeting tomorrow, is a Gen Zer.*

3.2 Reduced Relative Clauses with Participle Phrases

A Participle phrases are a reduced form of relative clauses with a verb that includes a form of *be*.	*Students concerned with the environment should get involved in environmental groups on campus.* = *Students who are concerned with the environment should get involved in environmental groups on campus.*
B This verb can be in the form of verb + *-ing* (present participle) or the past participle form. This includes progressive verbs and passive verbs.	VERB + -ING *He is the person designing the best software.* PAST PARTICIPLE *She did the things not expected of her.* *This is the intern known to be the hardest working.*

3.3 Reduced Relative Clauses with Prepositional Phrases

A You can omit the relative pronoun and the verb *be* when they are followed by a prepositional phrase in identifying relative clauses.	PREP. PHRASE *The computers in our classroom are fast.* = *The computers that are in our classroom are fast.*
B An adjective can also come before the prepositional phrase.	ADJ. + PREP. PHRASE *Young workers low in self-esteem are unusual.*

3.4 Reduced Relative Clauses with Appositives

A You can omit the relative pronoun and the verb *be* when they are followed by a noun phrase in nonidentifying relative clauses. This is called an appositive.	*Jan Smith, an expert on Generation Z, will be speaking at noon today.* = *Jan Smith, who is an expert on Generation Z, will be speaking at noon today.*
Often the position of the modified noun and the appositive is interchangeable.	*An expert on Generation Z, Jan Smith, will be speaking at noon today.*
B Appositives begin and end with commas.	*Résumés, brief documents that summarize an applicant's work background, are necessary for all job applications.*
In academic writing, appositives often occur in parentheses, instead of commas.	*Résumés (brief documents that summarize an applicant's work background) are necessary for all job applications.*

Grammar Application

Exercise 3.1 Reducing Relative Clauses

A Read the sentences about different generations. Check (✓) the sentences that can be reduced.

- ☑ **1** Young people who are entering the workforce are different from other generations.

- ☐ **2** In general, Millennials, who attentive parents raised, are confident workers.

- ☑ **3** Gen Zers ~~who are~~ in the workforce tend to be independent and hard-working.

- ☑ **4** Generation X, which is another large group in the workforce, does not tend to equate age with respect.

□ 5 Baby Boomers who work with Millennials often think they do not show enough respect.

☑ 6 Baby Boomers, who are loyal employees, have started to retire from their jobs.

☒ 7 Millennials, who were hurt by the recession, still tend to be optimistic.

☑ 8 Baby Boomers who were graduating from college in the 1960s lived in prosperous times.

☑ 9 Most Millennials who are not attending school say they intend to go back.

☑ 10 Many Gen Zers ~~who are~~ in the office also have side jobs.

□ 11 Gen Zers that dress casually at work sometimes upset older workers.

B Rewrite the sentences in A with reduced relative clauses. If a sentence cannot be reduced, write **✗**.

1 *Young people entering the workforce are different from other generations.*

2 X

3 X

4 Generation X, another large group in ~ ,

5 X

6 Baby Boomers, loyal employees, ~

✗ Millennials hurt by the recession, ~

8 Baby Boomers graduating from college ~

9 Most Millennials not attending school ~

10 X

11 X

C Pair Work **Compare your answers with a partner. Discuss what kind of reduced relative clause each sentence is. If a sentence couldn't be reduced, say why not.**

A *The reduced relative clause in number 1 is a participle phrase, so it can be reduced.*

B *That's right, but the relative clause in 2 can't be reduced because it is an object relative clause.*

Exercise 3.2 Relative Clauses with *Be* + Prepositional Phrases and *Be* + Adjectives + Prepositional Phrases

Combine the sentences from a company website about the type of employees it seeks. Use relative clauses. Then rewrite the sentences using reduced relative clauses.

1 People are at JP Corporation. They represent every generation.

People *who are at JP Corporation* represent every generation.

People at JP Corporation represent every generation.

2 People are good with technology. They have an advantage here.

People _____ have an advantage here.

_____

3 Workers are familiar with soical media. They will be able to use these skills here.

Workers _____ will be able to use these skills here.

_____

4 Employees are good at multitasking. They will enjoy our fast-paced environment.

Employees _____ will enjoy our fast-paced environment.

_____

5 Employees are high in self-esteem. They do well here.

Employees _____ do well here.

_____

6 People are interested in advancement. They will find it here.

People _____ will find it here.

_____

7 Employees are in our training programs. They appreciate learning new skills.

Employees _____ appreciate learning new skills.

_____

8 People are accustomed to a dynamic environment. They will be happy here.

People _____ will be happy here.

_____

Read the advice for managers who work with Generation Z. Rewrite the sentences that you can shorten. If you can't shorten the sentence, write **X**.

1 Managers should encourage Gen Zers who are hard-working.

   Managers should encourage hard-working Gen Zers.

2 Workers who are Generation Z seek independence from their managers.

3 Even Gen Zers who are confident appreciate feedback.

4 Gen Zers appreciate work schedules that are flexible.

5 Employees who are Generation Z want their managers to listen to them.

6 It's important to provide challenges for Gen Zers who are successful.

7 Managers must not underestimate GenZers who are self-educated.

8 Managers who are Millenials might expect Gen Zers to work 9 to 5.

9 Employees who are Gen Zers sometimes need less direction than older workers.

10 Gen Zers who are unemployed don't always have a lot of experience in job interviews.

Pair Work **With a partner, discuss the work styles of people at your school, such as students, teachers, and administrators. Write five sentences with relative clauses. Then write shortened versions without relative clauses. Use the words in the box or your own ideas.**

appreciate feedback	are family oriented	enjoy team work
appreciate work-life balance	are self-assured	have a "can-do" attitude

Students who are at this school tend to have a "can-do" attitude.
Students at this school tend to have a "can-do" attitude.

4 Avoid Common Mistakes ⚠

1 **Do not use a preposition before *when*.**

There was a period ~~in~~ when people did not change jobs often.

2 **In clauses with *where*, remember to use a subject.**

         he
The place where ⌄works is very busy.

3 **When shortening relative clauses to appositives, be sure to omit both the pronoun and *be*.**

My mother, ~~is~~ an office manager, often works late.

Editing Task

Find and correct eight more mistakes in the paragraphs about the separation between younger and older technology users.

Digital Natives vs. Digital Immigrants

    There was a time ~~in~~ when my mother always complained about my use of technology. She did not understand why I had to constantly text friends and go online. My mother, ~~is~~ a digital immigrant, grew up without a lot of tech gadgets. As a result, she is uncomfortable using technology at the office where works. On the other hand, my
5 brothers and I, ~~are~~ all digital natives, are happy to use technology all the time.

    Digital natives, ~~are~~ lifelong technology users, use mobile devices instinctively. These people do not remember a time in when they were not connected to the Internet. In fact, they find it annoying when they go to places where cannot connect to the Internet. Digital immigrants, in contrast, remember a time in when there was no Internet.
10 As a result, some of them see the Internet as useful but not essential. In addition, digital immigrants sometimes find it difficult to figure out how to use technology. For example, when my mother first began uploading information, she had to call someone for help. Lately, however, my mother has found a social media site where often goes in her free time to stay in touch with friends and family members.

5 Academic Writing

Expository Writing

Brainstorm > Organize > **Write** > **Edit**

In Unit 22, you learned how to make your writing clearer and more coherent, and you wrote your introduction and body paragraphs for the prompt below. In this unit (23), you will write the conclusion, and then you will revise and edit your essay.

> *Explain the advantages and disadvantages of three types of renewable energy and decide which would work best in your country.*

My Writing

Concluding Paragraphs

Concluding paragraphs restate the writer's main ideas and leave the reader with a final thought. The first sentence, or topic sentence, should summarize your thesis. Do not repeat your thesis exactly; instead, restate it. The end of your conclusion should leave the reader with a final thought, recommendation, or call to action.

Exercise 5.1 Applying the Skill

Review your paragraphs from My Writing in Unit 22. Complete the tasks.

1 Write your thesis statement. _____

_____

2 Restate your thesis. _____

_____

3 What three renewable energy sources did you discuss? _____

4 What source did you think would work best for your country? _____

5 What do you want your readers to do or think about in your conclusion? ____

_____

Exercise 5.2 Writing Your Conclusion

Use the information in Exercise 5.1 to write your conclusion. Add it to the rest of your essay.

Exercise 5.3 Revising Your Ideas

1 Work with a partner. Use the questions to give feedback on your partner's essay.
   - Which of your partner's ideas seem strongest to you?
   - Which of your partner's ideas needs to be explained more clearly?
   - What could your partner add or remove to make the ideas easier to understand?

2 Use the feedback from your partner to revise the ideas and content of your essay.

Exercise 5.4 Editing Your Writing

Use the checklist to review and edit your essay.

Did you answer the prompt completely?	
Did you organize your essay correctly?	
Did you use relative clauses to add information and avoid repetition?	
Did you use academic phrases to introduce advantages and disadvantages?	
Did you use several methods to build coherence in your essay?	
Did you put your ideas in a logical order that leaves your reader with a strong understanding of your thesis?	
Did you summarize your thesis and main points, and offer your readers a final thought, recommendation, or call to action in your concluding paragraph?	

Exercise 5.5 Editing Your Grammar

Use the checklist below to review and edit the grammar in your essay.

Did you use relative clauses to avoid repetition and make your writing clearer and more concise?	
Did you use identifying subject relative clauses to help identify or clarify any nouns you discussed?	
Did you use relative clauses to provide background information or to add information?	
Did you form reduced relative clauses correctly?	
Did you avoid the common mistakes in the charts on pages 315, 329, and 343?	

Exercise 5.6 Writing Your Final Draft

Apply the feedback and edits from Exercises 5.3 to 5.5 to write the final draft of your essay.

1 Grammar in the Real World

ACADEMIC
WRITING

Argumentative
writing

A Do all the news sources you read (websites, magazines, newspapers, etc.) have similar viewpoints about current topics and issues? Read the article about the news media in the United States. What is the writer's view of the media?

B Comprehension Check **Answer the questions.**

1 How do some political analysts describe the behavior of Americans toward media?

2 What is an example of how media sources reinforce someone's political views?

3 Why might people become even more isolated in their beliefs in the future?

C Notice **Read the sentences from the article. Which sentence describes a present situation? Which sentence describes a future situation?**

1 On the other hand, if people mostly disagree with the president's policies, they often choose to watch news shows that criticize the president.

2 If predictions of increased Internet use are correct, people will likely become even more isolated in their beliefs.

The Influence of **MEDIA** on Public Opinion

The media[1] provide news from a wide of sources with a variety of viewpoints. Some sources provide a more balanced look at the issues than others. These more balanced news sources offer
5 a deeper understanding of the issues without the influence of the views of political parties. This unbiased[2] view of the news may appear to align[3] with the values of Americans, but is it, in fact, what Americans really want? Some political analysts
10 claim that many Americans tend to read, watch, and listen to the news media that reflect their own views. **If people surround themselves with media that reflect only their beliefs,** they may not be exposed to opposing ideas. The media, in
15 this case, are not informing people, but reinforcing that their view of the world is right.

One example of this occurs during an economic crisis. **If people watch certain TV news stations,** they will hear mostly positive things
20 about the president's solutions. **If they support the president's policies,** they may also choose to read online news pages with a similar view. These websites likely explain how the crisis was caused by politicians from the opposing party.
25 **If those people read only these websites,** they might be convinced that the crisis was the fault of the opposing party. They might conclude that the president was doing a wonderful job. On the other hand, **if people mostly disagree with the**
30 **president's policies,** they often choose to watch news shows that criticize the president. They might also visit websites and read blogs that do not support the president's policies. **When they rely only on these news sources,** they come to a
35 different conclusion. They are convinced that the president is failing.

If predictions of increased Internet use are correct, people will likely become even more isolated in their beliefs. This is because links in
40 blogs and web pages will connect people with information that supports only their views. How might this affect politics in the future? **If we don't address this issue today,** could the isolation of beliefs become problematic in our political future?

---

[1]**media:** newspapers, magazines, television, and radio, considered as a group

[2]**unbiased:** not influenced by personal opinion

[3]**align:** agree with and support something or someone

2 Present Real Conditionals

Grammar Presentation

Present real conditionals describe situations that are possible now and their results. They describe general truths, facts, and habits.

If people share beliefs, they often get along better. I usually believe something when I read it in a good newspaper.

2.1 Forming Present Real Conditionals

A Use an *if* clause to describe a possible situation. The *if* clause is the condition. The main clause describes the result. It expresses what happens when the condition exists.

IF CLAUSE (CONDITION)   MAIN CLAUSE (RESULT)
If I like a reporter, I read her articles.

Use the simple present in the *if* clause and in the main clause.

If I have time in the morning, I read the newspaper.

B You can use *when* or *whenever* in the *if* clause. The meaning does not change.

When you trust people, you tend to believe them.
= If you trust people, you tend to believe them.

C You can put the *if* clause or the main clause first, but the punctuation is different. If the *if* clause is first, a comma follows it. If the main clause is first, do not use a comma. Usually the *if* clause comes first.

IF CLAUSE   MAIN CLAUSE
If you control the media, you control public opinion.

MAIN CLAUSE   IF CLAUSE
You control public opinion if you control the media.

D You can use conditionals in questions. Use question word order only in the main clause.

IF CLAUSE   MAIN CLAUSE
If you see something on the news, do you always believe it?

▶▶ Conditionals: See page A14.

2.2 Using Present Real Conditionals

A Use present real conditionals to describe:
Facts and general truths
Habits and routines

If a website is popular, people talk about it.
I always read the news online if I wake up early.

B You can emphasize the result by putting the *if* clause first and using *then* to introduce the main clause. Using *then* is more common in speaking.

If you only read one news website, then you never get the full story.

Grammar Application

Exercise 2.1 Present Real Conditionals for Habits and Routines

Complete the article about news habits. Use present real conditionals with the verbs in parentheses. Add commas when necessary.

CITY VOICES: The News and You

City Voices talked to several area residents. Here's what they had to say.

"When I _____ *am* _____ (be) in the car, I _____ (listen) to the radio.
            (1)   (2)

My husband _____ (watch) the comedy news shows if he _____
                  (3)   (4)

(stay) up late." – Alexa, 28, office manager

"If a friend _____ (text) me about something interesting I generally
                    (5)

_____ (check) out other websites to find out more information." – Su Ho, 32, engineer
      (6)

Exercise 2.2 Present Real Conditionals for Facts, General Truths, Habits, and Routines

Complete the interview with a foreign correspondent. Use the conditions and results in the chart.

Condition	Result
1 I hear about a story	I get on the phone
2 I hear about a good story	I try to go beyond the basic facts
3 I feel like I'm getting emotionally involved in a story	I drop it
4 A story is important	Many people talk about it
5 My editor calls and tells me to investigate a story	I move quickly

CAREERS MAGAZINE

Careers Today, we are talking to our foreign correspondent, Mercedes Rivera.
Ms. Rivera, how do you get a story?

Mercedes If *I hear about a story, I get on the phone* . I make
                                    (1)
appointments to interview people connected with the story.

Careers	What makes your reporting special?
Mercedes	If _____ . I look
	(2)
	at all the details to give both sides of the story.
Careers	How do you avoid bias?
Mercedes	If _____ . I give
	(3)
	it to another reporter.
Careers	What is difficult about your job?
Mercedes	There's a certain amount of pressure. _____
	(4)
	when _____ . I have to work fast in the digital
	(4)
	age. _____ if _____ .
	(5) (5)
Careers	Well, thank you for talking to us today, Ms. Rivera.

Exercise 2.3 Emphasizing the Result in Present Real Conditionals

A Read the tips on how to detect bias in the media. Then rewrite the tips as present real conditionals with the words in parentheses and *probably (not) be*. Emphasize the result by using *then*.

How to Detect BIAS in the MEDIA

To detect bias in the media, be aware of the following conditions. These conditions often indicate bias.

1 A newspaper, website, or TV station ignores important stories.
2 A newspaper prints sensational headlines.
3 A newspaper prints an important story in the back of the newspaper.
4 A magazine prints an unflattering[1] photo of a politician.
5 A reporter uses words with negative connotations[2] instead of neutral terms.

[1]**unflattering:** making someone look less attractive or seem worse than they usually do
[2]**connotation:** a feeling or idea that is suggested by a word in addition to its basic meaning

1 (impartial) _If a newspaper, website, or TV station ignores important_
   stories, then it probably isn't impartial.

2 (accurate) _____

   _____

3 (balanced) _____

_____

4 (biased) _____

_____

5 (fair) _____

_____

B Pair Work Discuss other ways that the media show that they are biased or fair. Write two sentences using *if* clauses and the expressions with *probably (not) be* in A.

Exercise 2.4 Present Real Conditionals

A Over to You Answer the questions with information that is true for you. Write present real conditionals on a separate piece of paper. Use the phrases in the box or your own ideas.

get the news online	pay attention to the news
know a story is accurate	read a newspaper
listen to news on the radio	watch TV news

■ Do you pay attention to the news?

■ How do you get the news?

■ How do you know a news story is accurate?

If there's a big story in the news, I watch one of the TV news channels, but I don't pay attention to the news much in general.

B Pair Work Interview your partner. Ask and answer the questions in A. Do not look at your sentences when you answer. Look at your partner.

3 Future Real Conditionals

Grammar Presentation

Future real conditionals describe possible situations in the future and the likely results.	*If you don't like a politician*, you won't like his or her policies.

3.1 Forming Future Real Conditionals

A Use the simple present in the *if* clause and a future verb form in the main clause.	*If you arrive early tomorrow at the debate*, you will get a good seat.

3.1 Forming Future Real Conditionals (continued)

B Use a comma after the *if* clause only when it begins the sentence.	*We will have a more balanced view if we read a variety of news websites.* *If Sandra doesn't agree with a politician's ideas, she will not vote for him.*

3.2 Using Future Real Conditionals

A Use future real conditionals to describe: Plans Predictions	*If the TV media don't cover the debate tonight, I'll read about it online.* *If you read this article, you won't be disappointed.*
B Use *even if* when you believe the result will not change. *Even if* means "whether or not."	*Some people will believe the news <u>even if</u> it isn't true.* (The news may or may not be true. Some people will believe it either way.)
Use *unless* to state a negative condition more strongly. It often has the same meaning as *if . . . not*.	*Unless a reporter interviews many people, she won't find out the truth.* *= If a reporter does <u>not</u> interview many people, she won't find out the truth.*
C When an *if* clause has many results, use the *if* clause only once.	*If people believe everything they hear, they won't know the truth. <u>They will be easily fooled.</u>* NOT *If people believe everything they hear, they won't know the truth. ~~If people believe everything they hear,~~ they will be easily fooled.*

Grammar Application

Exercise 3.1 Future Real Conditionals for Predictions

Complete the sentences about being well informed about political viewpoints. Circle the correct verb forms. Add commas when necessary.

1 If a person (studies)/ will study history, she understands /(will understand) political issues better.

2 You **are / will be** a better critical thinker if you **listen / will listen** to opposing viewpoints.

3 You **become / will become** a more informed voter if you **understand / will understand** the issues.

4 You **make / will make** better choices in future elections if you **learn / will learn** about the candidates' voting records.

5 If a person **learns / will learn** about economics he **makes / will make** wiser financial decisions.

6 If people <u>get/will get</u> the news from several sources they <u>have/will have</u> a more complete picture of an issue.

A A newspaper is having financial difficulties. Write future real conditionals with the information in the chart.

Proposals	Predictions and Plans
1 fire 10 reporters	be able to stay in business
2 stop home deliveries	lose money
3 charge for online access	increase revenue
4 not find new advertisers	not make more money
5 put more articles online	attract new readers

1 *If we fire 10 reporters, we'll be able to stay in business.*

2 _____

3 _____

4 _____

5 _____

B Read what members of the staff have to say about the proposals in A. Circle the correct meaning for each opinion.

1 Even if we fire 10 reporters, we won't be able to stay in business.

   a Firing reporters will help.   (**b** Firing reporters won't help.)

2 Unless we fire 20 reporters, we'll go out of business.

   a Firing reporters will help.   **b** Firing reporters won't help.

3 Unless we charge for online access, we won't increase revenue.

   a Charging will help.   **b** Charging won't help.

4 Even if we stop home deliveries, we'll lose money.

   a Stopping home deliveries will help.   **b** Stopping home deliveries won't help.

5 Even if we find new advertisers, we won't make more money.

   a Finding new advertisers will help.   **b** Finding new advertisers won't help.

6 Unless we put more articles online, we won't attract new readers.

   a Putting more articles online will help.   **b** Putting more articles online won't help.

Over to You **Complete the sentences about being informed. Write two or more results for the conditions. Don't repeat the *if* clauses for the second or third results. Write sentences that are true for you.**

1 If people stop reading newspapers, *newspapers will go out of business. Many reporters will be unemployed.*

2 If people get only one source of news, _____

_____

3 If you only listen to people you agree with, _____

_____

4 If you are not an informed voter, _____

_____

4 Real Conditionals with Modals, Modal-like Expressions, and Imperatives

Grammar Presentation

Modals, modal-like expressions, and imperatives can be used in the main clause of real conditionals.	*If I watch a lot of TV, I may become more aware of political issues.* *If you have finished reading the paper, put it in the recycling container.*

4.1 Forming Real Conditionals with Modals, Modal-like Expressions, and Imperatives

A In present and future real conditionals with modals and modal-like expressions, use a present form of the verb in the *if* clause. Use a present or future modal or modal-like expression in the main clause.	*If you **haven't heard** the news yet, you* <u>*should read*</u> *the newspaper.* *If you **are planning** to vote, you* <u>*have to register*</u>. *She* <u>*might learn*</u> *more about politics if she **subscribes** to that political magazine.*
B In present and future real conditionals, you can use the imperative in the main clause.	*If you are at home tonight at 7:00 p.m.,* <u>*watch*</u> *the president's speech.*

▸ Modals and Modal-like Expressions: See page A3.

Grammar Application

Complete the sentences about being an involved citizen. Use the words in parentheses.

1 If people don't vote, _they must not be interested in politics_ .
   (be interested in politics / not / must)

2 If you haven't registered to vote yet, _____ .
   (do it today / should)

3 People _____ if they want to become involved in their community.
   (volunteer / ought to)

4 People _____ if they enjoy teaching.
   (tutor children / can)

5 If you want to become informed, _____ .
   (watch the news / have to)

6 If people participate in elections, _____ .
   (influence the outcome / might)

7 If you aren't happy, _____ .
   (change things / could)

8 People _____ if they have not already tried to find solutions to community problems.
   (complain / not / should)

Pair Work **Answer the questions about how you think people can be better citizens. Write real conditionals and share them with a partner. Use _you_ in the _if_ clause and an imperative in the main clause. Use the phrases in the box or your own ideas.**

be aware of bias in the media	study both sides of an issue
research alternative news sources	volunteer

- What should people do if they want to become better informed?

- What should people do if they want to become better citizens?

If you want to become better informed, research alternative news sources.

A Listen to an interview about how to be an informed voter. As you listen, complete the chart. Check (✓) *Do* if this is something an informed voter should do. Check (✓) *Don't* if this is something an informed voter should not do.

Action	Do	Don't
1 register early	✓	
2 visit campaign headquarters		
3 visit candidates' websites		
4 rely on campaign ads		
5 pay attention to what media sources say		
6 be influenced by other people's opinions		

B Listen to the interview again. As you listen, complete the sentences with the words you hear.

1 If you _aren't registered_ to vote, _register_ early so you don't miss the deadline.

2 If you _____ to be an informed voter, _____ the local campaign headquarters for the candidates of both parties.

3 If you _____ to make the right choice, you _____ also _____ the websites of all the candidates.

4 _____ campaign ads for information about the candidates or the issues if you _____ to be an informed voter.

5 _____ attention to what media sources say about a candidate, either, if you _____ the truth.

6 Finally, _____ other people's opinions influence your vote if you _____ to make good choices.

5 Avoid Common Mistakes ⚠

1 **In future real conditionals, use the simple present in the *if* clause.**

has
If my son ~~will have~~ time, he will buy tickets for the show.

2 **Remember that *if* clauses are followed by a comma when they start a sentence.**

If I get the time off work and the weather looks good ͮ I will join you.

3 **Remember to use *if*, not *when*, to describe possible future conditions.**

if
We will cancel the speech ~~when~~ it rains tomorrow.

4 **In questions with *if* clauses, remember to use question word order in the main clause.**

should
If I don't have a signal, what I ~~should~~ do?

Editing Task

Find and correct the mistakes in the paragraphs about the advantages of a campus blog.

should
If incoming students want to learn what this college is like, where they ~~should~~ look?
If they visit the college website they can learn about sports and campus events. However,
incoming freshmen might want a more personal perspective. They may not have the time to
attend lectures and other events, or they may want some anonymity. I have decided to start a
5 blog that provides an alternative source of information and help.

    When I want the blog to be successful at helping students, I will need to provide
practical suggestions. For example, one concern may be, "If I want to meet people with
similar interests, what I can do?" I will tell that person places where he or she can post
requests on the school website and how to write his or her requests. I will also include ways to
10 safely respond to queries.

    In addition, if a student will have a problem with a professor, I will write about it in my
blog and provide possible ways to solve it. If people want to add advice, how they can do so?
They can share advice by commenting. If professors want to comment, they can, too.

    I will not try to write like a journalist and give a lot of facts. If students will want facts,
15 they can go to the college website. In contrast, I will give them personal advice that will help
them with everyday problems. If students want real answers to their problems they should try
my blog.

6 Academic Writing

Argumentative Writing

Brainstorm > Organize > Write > Edit

In this writing cycle (Units 24-25), you are going to write an argumentative essay for the prompt below. In this unit (24), you will learn to build support for arguments and to develop unified paragraphs. You will then brainstorm and organize ideas, and write body paragraphs.

> *Research an aging but culturally or historically important building in your city or country. What do you think should be done with it and why?*

Exercise 6.1 Preparing to Write

Work with a partner. Discuss the questions.

1 What responsibility do we have to preserve historic buildings?

2 What are some ways that people express their disagreement with decisions to tear down important buildings?

3 How might the media influence people's opinions on this type of issue? Give an example.

Exercise 6.2 Focusing on Vocabulary

Read the sentences and choose the best definitions for the words in bold.

1 The beautiful old train station closed in 1990 and has been **vacant** since then.
   a busy   b ugly   c empty

2 Historic buildings that are converted to apartments often have high rent and are not **affordable** for working or middle class families.
   a not expensive   b average   c small but comfortable

3 The athletic **facility** at the university has a new ice-skating rink.
   a a building for a special purpose   b a field   c a place where people can meet

4 Despite the extra tax money, the government **maintains** that it has no money for public housing.
   a continues to claim   b finally understands   c deeply regrets

5 If the ancient buildings are allowed to **deteriorate** any more, the government will not be able to restore them as a historical site for tourists.
   a grow worse   b stabilize   c strengthen

6 The old school is now a museum and is **prospering** as part of a growing art community.
   a building   b doing well   c being optimistic

Dear Members of the County Board:

Tusing County Hospital (TCH), which has been standing **vacant** for more than ten years, has become an eyesore in our neighborhood. In spite of the fact that the government has spent millions of dollars studying the best use for the site,
5 we are still waiting for action. Let's stop trying to figure out how to save this out-of-date pile of bricks. Our neighborhood is expanding and **prospering**. If the board shows some leadership by adopting a proposal that embraces the future, it will not be seen as clinging to the past but rather as moving forward.

It has been argued that it would be cheaper to reuse the old building than
10 to tear it down and build a new one. Almost ten years ago, experts estimated that if the TCH building were saved it would cost more than 150 million dollars. This figure may have been true then, but over the last decade, the building has **deteriorated** considerably, which would no doubt add to the cost of any renovation[1] carried out today. Our experts agree that if the county decides to update this one hundred-year-old building to meet modern safety standards, it will actually be more expensive than starting from scratch.
15 What this neighborhood really needs is an up-to-date, green structure that will provide much-needed housing and retail space. If it is accepted, our proposal will replace the decaying hospital building with a hotel, apartments (including 15% **affordable** housing), and space for stores, restaurants, and medical offices. Just as important, construction of these structures, and the businesses that will be located in them, will provide good jobs for people in the community. How much longer do we have to wait for our leaders
20 to make the right decision for the future of our neighborhood? Please tear down TCH!

Respectfully yours,
New Neighborhood Group

Dear Tusing County Board:

Tusing County Hospital (TCH), which has welcomed patients and their families for almost a century, is a community landmark. The building is beautiful, but more beautiful than the structure itself is the statement it made to the city and the world. When it opened its doors in 1916, TCH offered an attractive,
5 modern **facility**, not just to the city's elite, but also to the poor. It sent the message that the poor are just as deserving of quality healthcare as the wealthy. People in the neighborhood called the hospital our Statue of Liberty. Let's make sure this site continues to serve all of our citizens by renovating it now.

Some opponents to our proposal have argued that renovation is too expensive, but a recent similar project demonstrated that this may not be the case. In fact, if we renovate, the cost will be about $25 per
10 square foot, which is less than even the most basic new construction, while also preserving the beauty of the original building. And, although it is often claimed that old buildings have a more significant environmental footprint compared with new construction, architect and sustainability expert Carl Elefante **maintains** that the greenest building is the one that is already built. New construction almost always has a
15 more serious environmental impact because it requires the use of all new materials.

If our group's proposal for renovation of the hospital is accepted, the site will continue to serve the community by providing affordable housing, medical clinics, a school, and a community center—resources that we badly need. However, if instead we allow developers[2] to take over the project, the guiding principle will be profit, not neighborhood preservation. The people who will benefit most will be the investors in the project,
20 not the people of our community. Please save the Tusing County Hospital building and our community!

Respectfully,
Citizens Neighborhood Coalition

[1]**renovation** (n) the repair of a building to bring it into good condition
[2]**developer** (n) an entrepreneur or company that buys land and builds on it

Media in the United States **359**

Read the texts on page 359. Work with a partner. Discuss the questions.

1 Which letter makes the argument that the hospital should be torn down?
2 What reasons does the letter give for its argument?
3 In addition to cost, why does the opposing letter argue that the hospital should not be torn down?

Exercise 6.4 Noticing the Grammar and Structure

Work with a partner. Complete the tasks.

1 Highlight all conditional sentences in the first letter. Choose one conditional sentence. Explain how the writer uses the form to persuade his or her readers.
2 Underline an opposing argument in each letter. How does each writer refute the opposing argument?
3 What kind of support do the coalitions use to strengthen their arguments?

Building Support for an Argument

When writers make an argument, they need to decide which facts are relevant and will support it. It is also important to include relevant facts when presenting an opposing argument. However, those facts should weaken the opposing argument.

Argument: To be an informed citizen, people need to get their news from a variety of sources.

Relevant fact to support the argument: Based on recent research, only 20% our news organizations in the United States are considered neutral.

Opposing argument: Many people maintain that news organizations in the United States are unbiased, neutral reporters of the news.

Relevant fact that weakens the opposing argument: However, nearly 80% of news organizations endorse political candidates in elections. If you endorse a political candidate, you are essentially supporting a particular party, which is not neutral and unbiased.

Exercise 6.5 Applying the Skill

Read a thesis and some facts about the news media. Write *T* if the fact supports the thesis. Write *O* if the fact supports an opposing argument.

Thesis: News organizations should not publish paper newspapers.

1 People no longer get their news from newspapers. Sales fell 28% in three years. _____
2 Many people prefer the tactile experience of reading a paper newspaper. _____
3 Companies do not get the return on their advertisements in digital news articles as they do in paper newspapers. _____
4 Newspapers are not sustainable due to the natural resources involved in printing them. _____

Maintaining Paragraph Unity

Paragraph unity means that the entire paragraph focuses on the main idea. All the other sentences in the paragraph should provide relevant background information or support for the main idea.

Exercise 6.6 Applying the Skill

Read the paragraph. Cross out any irrelevant sentences to create paragraph unity.

Before you support a candidate, you need to research that person. What does that mean? First, it is important to look at different sources for different viewpoints of the candidate. Visit websites, read a variety of newspapers, and watch the his or her speeches and interviews. Search engines are useful tools. Next, it is extremely important not to believe everything you hear about the person, even if it comes from a friend. Fortunately, researching is not very difficult. Lastly, do not listen to his or her campaign ads, which are created to distract many voters.

My Writing

Exercise 6.7 Brainstorming and Organizing Ideas

Read the writing prompt on page 358. Choose a building to write about.

1 Use the questions to brainstorm ideas for your essay.

- What should be done with the building? Why?
- What relevant facts might support your argument?
- What is an opposing argument? What facts might weaken it?

2 Share and discuss your ideas with a partner. Use the feedback to edit your notes.

Exercise 6.8 Writing Body Paragraphs

1 Write a possible thesis statement for your argumentative essay.
2 Write the first draft of 2-3 body paragraphs. Include an opposing argument in the first body paragraph. Use the grammar in this unit correctly.

1 Grammar in the Real World

**ACADEMIC
WRITING**

Argumentative
writing

A Think of some natural disasters in recent history. Were there any positive effects or changes that resulted from the disasters? Read the article about Hurricane Katrina. What is one positive effect of Hurricane Katrina?

B Comprehension Check **Answer the questions.**

1 Why is Hurricane Katrina considered a catastrophe?

2 What did Paul Vallas do to improve New Orleans's schools?

3 What are charter schools?

C Notice **Read the sentences from the article. Underline the main clause in each sentence.**

1 If they found a strong school superintendent, they could hope for real change.

2 If you had been a public school student in New Orleans prior to 2005, you would have had little hope for the future of your education.

3 Vallas knew that if state exam scores improved, the charter schools would be considered a success.

4 If Katrina hadn't happened, the school might have been closed down.

Is the situation in each main clause real or imaginary?

HURRICANE KATRINA

In 2005, Hurricane Katrina devastated New Orleans, Louisiana. The storm killed over 1,800 people and caused over $75 billion in damages. Certainly, Katrina was a catastrophe.[1] **People**
5 **wish it had never happened.** Nonetheless, some say Katrina saved the city's schools from failure. In fact, U.S. Education Secretary, Arne Duncan, said, "I think the best thing that happened to the education system in New Orleans was
10 Hurricane Katrina." Although some people thought Duncan's comment was inappropriate, is it possible that the storm did the city a favor and helped its school system?

If you had been a public school student in
15 **New Orleans prior to 2005,** you would have had little hope for the future of your education. With low test scores and high dropout rates, the New Orleans School District was already in trouble when the hurricane struck. The storm
20 destroyed almost every school in the city. State legislators realized the hurricane was tragic. They also knew it provided a fresh start to rebuild the city's schools. **If they found a strong school superintendent,** they could hope for real change.

25 In 2007, Paul Vallas was hired to rescue the poverty stricken and low-performing district. He knew that in order to succeed, he would have to make drastic changes. He hired top teachers and modernized classrooms. Vallas also started
30 several charter schools. Charter schools are independently run public schools. They control their own academics and policies but must show the state how their students have improved. Vallas knew that **if state exam scores improved,** the
35 charter schools would be considered a success.

Vallas received national praise for his experiment with charter schools. Student scores on state tests went up every year that he worked for the district. The Sophie B. Wright Charter
40 School is a good example. It was a failing traditional school before the hurricane. **If Katrina hadn't happened,** the school might have been closed down. Instead, it became a successful charter school.

45 As for Duncan's comment about Katrina, **some wish he had used a better choice of words.** A number of educational experts disagree. They say that in the end, New Orleans schools are only successful because of the work that Vallas
50 did to rebuild the school system.

---

[1]**catastrophe:** a sudden event that causes great suffering or destruction

2 Present and Future Unreal Conditionals

Grammar Presentation

Present and future unreal conditionals describe imagined situations (situations that are not true).	*If children got better grades on their exams, parents wouldn't be so worried.*

2.1 Forming Present and Future Unreal Conditionals

A Use the simple past or the past progressive in the *if* clause. Use the modals *could*, *might*, or *would* in the main clause.	*If I studied every day*, I *could pass* all my tests. (But I don't study every day, so I can't pass all my tests.) *Parents wouldn't worry so much about their children's future if their children's grades were improving.* (But the children's grades aren't improving, so their parents are worried.)
B In formal language, use *were* for the verb *be* for all subjects, including *I*. In informal language, native speakers often use *was* for the subject pronouns *I*, *he*, *she*, and *it*.	*If I were better at math, I would become an engineer.* (formal) *If I was better at math, I would become an engineer.* (informal)

▶▶ Conditionals: See page A14.

2.2 Using Present and Future Unreal Conditionals

A The *if* clause describes an imagined condition (something that is not true at the time of speaking or writing). The main clause describes the predicted result or possible outcome.	*If all public schools worked well, parents wouldn't choose private schools.* (But some public schools don't work well, so parents choose private schools.)
B Use *would* in the main clause to express the predicted result. Use *could* or *might* in the main clause to express something that is possible or doable.	*If teachers gave students study guides, more students would pass their exams.* (Passing is a predicted result.) *If students studied more for exams, more of them could/might pass.* (Passing exams is doable.)
C Use *could* or the past progressive in the *if* clause to describe an imagined possible situation.	*If the city could hire more teachers, we would have smaller classes.* (But they can't hire more teachers, so we have large classes.) *We wouldn't feel hopeful if schools weren't improving.* (But schools are improving, so we do feel hopeful.)

2.2 Using Present and Future Unreal Conditionals (*continued*)

D Use time words to show present or future time.	*We wouldn't have a place to learn if our school closed <u>next year</u>.* *If classes were smaller <u>today</u>, students might be more motivated.*
E Use unreal conditionals with *If I were you* to give advice. Use *I would* in the main clause.	*<u>If I were you</u>, I'd study harder.* (My advice is to study harder.) *<u>I wouldn't</u> drop out of school <u>if I were you</u>.* (My advice is to stay in school.)

Grammar Application

Exercise 2.1 Present and Future Unreal Conditionals

Complete the sentences about natural disasters. Use present and future unreal conditionals. If you are writing a main clause, use the modals in parentheses.

1 Their house is damaged, so they have to build a new one.

If their house weren't damaged, _*they wouldn't have to build a new one*_ (wouldn't).

2 We don't have flood insurance, so we have to pay for water damage.

*If we had flood insurance* , we wouldn't have to pay for water damage.

3 There aren't earthquakes here, so we don't need earthquake insurance.

If there were earthquakes here, _____ (might).

4 There's a tsunami[1] warning, so they have to leave the beach.

_____ , they wouldn't have to leave the beach.

5 We don't have a first-aid kit, so we aren't prepared for an earthquake.

If we had a first-aid kit, _____ (would).

6 There's a tornado warning, so José is going into the basement.

_____ , José wouldn't go into the basement.

7 The fire alarm is ringing, so we have to leave the building.

If the fire alarm weren't ringing, _____ (might not).

8 Everyone is worrying about the storm, so we are leaving.

_____ , we wouldn't be leaving.

[1]**tsunami:** an extremely high wave of water that is caused by an earthquake

Complete the statements made by earthquake experts. Use present and future unreal conditionals with *could (not)* in the *if* clause and *would (not)* in the main clause.

Dr. Sarah Green:

1 The government can't repair old bridges. Therefore, people don't feel safe.

   If the government _could repair_ old bridges, people _would feel_ safe.

2 They can't build quake-proof bridges very quickly, so we aren't optimistic.

   If the government _____

   quake-proof bridges quickly, we

   _____ optimistic.

Dr. Joe Wu:

3 Certain regions can build quake-proof buildings. Therefore, they don't suffer a lot of damage.

   If certain regions _____ quake-proof buildings, they

   _____ a lot of damage.

Dr. Rafael Rodriguez:

4 Some countries often can't avoid contaminated water after an earthquake. Therefore, people get sick.

   If some countries _____ contaminated water after an

   earthquake, people _____ sick.

5 Engineers aren't able to improve the water systems in all places, so people are not healthy.

   If engineers _____ the water systems in all places, people

   _____ healthy.

A Over to You **Answer the questions with information that is true for you. Write your answers on a separate piece of paper. Use the ideas in the box or your own ideas. Write present and future unreal conditionals.**

basement	escape	exit	higher ground
emergency services	evacuate	find shelter	take cover

What would you do if:

- you knew a hurricane were coming?
- an earthquake struck?
- you were driving and heard a tornado warning on the radio?
- you were within a half mile of a wildfire?
- you were at the beach and got a tsunami warning?
- you were in a heat wave?

If I knew a hurricane were coming, I would evacuate the area immediately.

B Group Work **Brainstorm other answers to the questions in A. Share them with another group.**

Exercise 2.4 *If I Were You . . .* for Advice

A Complete the conversations. Write sentences that give advice. Use *If I were you* and the ideas in the box. Sometimes more than one answer is possible.

build a new one	leave immediately	not go to work
get earthquake insurance	leave the building	stay indoors

1 **A** The house was damaged in the hurricane. What should we do?

  B *If I were you, I'd build a new one.*

2 **A** I live in an earthquake zone. What should I do?

  B _____

3 **A** There's a blizzard warning for tomorrow. What should I do?

  B _____

4 **A** Forecasters are predicting a terrible heat wave for tomorrow. What should we do?

  B _____

5 **A** There's a wildfire three blocks from our house. What should we do?

  B _____

6 **A** The fire alarm is ringing. What should we do?

  B _____

B Pair Work **Take turns asking and answering the questions in A. Use your own ideas in your answers.**

3 Past Unreal Conditionals

Grammar Presentation

Past unreal conditionals express situations that were not true in the past. They describe something that was possible but did not happen.	*If I had stayed home from school, I would have missed the exam.* (But I went to school, so I didn't miss the exam.)

3.1 Forming Past Unreal Conditionals

A Use the past perfect in the *if* clause. Use *could have*, *may have*, *might have*, or *would have* and the past participle of the verb in the main clause.	*If the city had hired more teachers, the schools might have improved.* (But the city didn't hire more teachers, and the schools didn't improve.)
B The *if* clause typically comes before the main clause, but it may also follow the main clause.	*The schools might have improved if the city had hired more teachers.*

3.2 Using Past Unreal Conditionals

A The *if* clause expresses the past unreal condition (a situation that was untrue in the past). The main clause describes an imagined result.	*If the hurricane had missed our city, the schools wouldn't have received money from the government.* (But it didn't miss our city, so the schools have received money.)
B Use *would have* in the main clause to express a predicted result.	*If you had applied, you would have gotten the job.* (Getting the job was a predicted result.)
C Use *could have* or *might have* in the main clause to express something possible or doable.	*I could have/might have passed the test if I had studied harder.* (Passing the test was doable.)
D You can use past unreal conditionals to express regrets or sadness.	*If I hadn't quit school, I would have become an engineer.* (But I quit school, and I regret it.)
E Use *If I had been you* to give advice indirectly. Use *I would (not)* in the main clause. *Had* is often contracted (*'d*).	*If I'd been you, I wouldn't have quit school.*

Grammar Application

Exercise 3.1 Past Unreal Conditionals

Complete the interview with a scientist who studied Mount Vesuvius, a volcano that erupted[1] in 79 CE near Pompeii, Italy. Use past unreal conditionals with the verbs in parentheses.

Reporter Today, I'm talking to Dr. Adam Gannon.

Dr. Gannon, we are all fascinated by Vesuvius, I think, because it practically erased an ancient city.

Dr. Gannon That's correct. If Vesuvius
hadn't erupted (not/erupt), Pompeii
(1)
would not have disappeared
(2)
(not/would/disappear).

Reporter So, Pompeii _____ (would/survived) if Vesuvius
(3)
_____ (not/explode)?
(4)

Dr. Gannon Yes, that's correct. On the other hand, if ash
_____ (not/cover) the city, it
(5)
_____ (not/would/be preserved).
(6)

Reporter The volcano caused other great changes, too, didn't it?

Dr. Gannon Yes. In fact, it completely changed the direction of a nearby river. The Sarno
_____ (would/stay) in the same place if
(7)
Vesuvius _____ (not/change) the course of the
(8)
river. It was a very powerful eruption.

Reporter How do we know so much about the eruption of Vesuvius?

Dr. Gannon We have the writer Pliny the Younger to thank for that. If he and his uncle
_____ (not/be) near Pompeii that day, we
(9)
_____ (not/would/know) much about the
(10)
eruption of Vesuvius. But we still don't know everything.

Reporter Fascinating. Thank you, Dr. Gannon.

[1]**erupt:** throw out smoke, fire, and melted rocks

A Group Work **Look at the pictures and discuss these questions in groups: What does a volcanic eruption look like? What are some of the effects of a volcanic eruption?**

Mount St. Helens,
Washington State

landslide

ash cloud

B Listen to a man talk about his experience surviving the 1980 Mount St. Helens volcano eruption. Circle *T* if the statement is true. Circle *F* if the statement is false.

1 The speaker and his family were hiking on the mountain the day the volcano erupted. T (F)

2 Falling trees hit the speaker and his friends.   T   F

3 The speaker thinks it's possible that many people on the mountain survived.   T   F

4 The speaker's wife wasn't affected by the eruption.   T   F

5 The sideways eruption of Mount St. Helens caused a lot of damage.   T   F

6 Ten years after the eruption, the speaker returned to his campsite.   T   F

7 Scientists didn't learn anything from the eruption.   T   F

C Listen again and check your answers.

D Complete the statements about the story. Use the words in parentheses to write past unreal conditionals with possible or predicted results.

1 If we hadn't gone camping that day, we *might have avoided the disaster*
    (**possible:** avoid / the disaster).

2 If we hadn't been in a hole, falling trees _____ (**possible:** hit) us.

3 If people hadn't been on the mountain, they _____ (**predicted:** survive).

4 If his wife had been with him, the eruption _____ (**possible:** affect) her.

5 If Mount St. Helens hadn't been a sideways explosion, it _____
    (**predicted:** not / do) so much damage.

6 If the speaker and his friends hadn't returned to the mountain, they
    _____ (**predicted:** not / see) the site of the destruction.

7 If the eruption hadn't happened, scientists _____
    (**predicted:** not / learn) how quickly plant and animal life can return.

4 Wishes About the Present, Future, and Past

Grammar Presentation

Sentences with *wish* express a desire for something to be different, or feelings of sadness or regret.	*I wish (that) every child could have a better education.* (Unfortunately, not every child can have a better education.)

4.1 Wish in the Present, Future, and Past

A *Wish* is followed by a *that* clause. Use a past form of the verb in the *that* clause, similar to conditional sentences.

The word *that* is often omitted in informal speaking.

*There aren't enough teachers. We **wish that** we **could hire** more teachers.*

B Wishes about the present are followed by *that* clauses with verbs in the simple past or past progressive, or the modal *could*.

*I **wish (that)** we **had** more classrooms. (We don't have a lot of classrooms.)*
*I **wish (that)** my son **were doing** well in school. (My son is not doing well in school.)*
*Some people **wish (that)** they **could afford** to go to college. (They can't afford to go to college.)*

C Wishes about the future are followed by *that* clauses with *was/were going to* or the modals *could* or *would*.

*I **wish (that)** I **were going to have** time to meet you tonight. (I'm not going to have time to meet you.)*
*She **wishes (that)** she **could go** to class tonight, but she has to work. (She can't go to class tonight.)*
*We **wish (that)** the school **would build** a parking lot, but it's too costly. (The school will not build a parking lot.)*

D Wishes about the past are followed by *that* clauses with the verb in the past perfect.

*We **wish (that)** we **had had** more time to study for the test. (We didn't have enough time to study.)*

DATA FROM THE REAL WORLD

In academic writing, *wish* followed by a singular subject is more commonly followed by *were* than *was*.

Wish + singular subject + *were*					
Wish + singular subject + *was*					

*The president wishes the solution to the problem **were** simpler.* (more common in academic writing)

*The president wishes the solution to the problem **was** simpler.* (less common in academic writing)

Grammar Application

Exercise 4.1 Present and Future Wishes

Complete the sentences about a family's disaster. Write wishes in the present and future. Sometimes more than one answer is possible.

1 There isn't a lot of light. Ben *wishes (that) there was/were more light* .

2 We don't have enough bottled water. We _____ .

3 The roof is leaking. Mom _____ .

4 We are running out of batteries. Paul _____ .

5 The electricity doesn't work. Dad _____ .

6 The Internet isn't working. Sue _____ .

7 The furniture is going to be ruined. Grandma and Grandpa _____

_____ .

8 We can't go to a hotel. We _____ .

Exercise 4.2 Past Wishes

Read the sentences about some past disasters. Then write sentences about the speakers' wishes. Use past wish forms. Sometimes more than one answer is possible.

1 An architect: The 1906 earthquake destroyed a historic building. There wasn't enough money to rebuild it.

I wish the earthquake hadn't destroyed the building./I wish
there had been enough money to rebuild it.

2 A surfer: They closed my favorite beach after the storm. They didn't let people in to clean it up.

3 A historian: A flood destroyed the ancient city. There were no records of what life was like there.

4 A student: A hurricane destroyed my high school. We weren't able to attend graduation.

5 Avoid Common Mistakes ⚠

1 **When forming the present unreal conditional, use the past (not present) form of the verb after *if*.**

understood
If I ~~understand~~ my teacher, I would enjoy my class more.

2 **Remember to include a subject when forming an *if* clause.**

she
She would feel safer if ∧ could stay with us during the storm.

3 **When forming the past unreal conditional, use the past perfect form in the *if* clause.**

had not ruined
If the flood ~~did not ruin~~ his car, he would have arrived home safely.

4 **When making past unreal wishes, use the past perfect (not the simple past).**

had not moved
I wish I ~~did not move~~ to such a dangerous place.

Editing Task

Find and correct eight more mistakes in the story about Hurricane Ike.

        had
If Hurricane Ike ~~did~~ not come, we would have had an easier time. If the storm missed us, we would not have lived without electricity for two weeks. We would have been able to go to work and school. Our trees would look a lot better if had not been destroyed by the strong winds. For these reasons, some people wish that Hurricane

5 Ike never happened. However, I do not. If the storm did not come to Houston, we would not have learned many valuable lessons.

     First, we learned about our neighbors. We all came together to help each other before and after the storm. If I live in a different place, maybe I would not have gotten to know my neighbors in this way. Second, we learned good emergency survival skills.

10 If we had not learned to boardup our houses, might have been damaged. If another storm comes today, my house would be safe.

     Sometimes I wish that my family did not move to this city. However, I do not feel this way because of the hurricanes. The hurricanes have made our community stronger.

6 Academic Writing

Argumentative Writing

Brainstorm > Organize > Write > Edit

In Unit 24, you analyzed two letters and learned how to build support and unify paragraphs before brainstorming ideas and writing body paragraphs for the prompt below. In this unit (25), you will learn ways to integrate multiple sources to support your argument. You will then write, revise, and edit your essay.

> Research an aging but culturally or historically important building in your city or country. What do you think should be done with it and why?

Integrating Information from Multiple Sources

When you present an argument, you need to use facts to support your argument. Including facts from more than one credible source strengthens your argument and helps persuade your reader. When integrating multiple sources, it is necessary to show a connection between the sources in order to build coherence and improve the flow of your writing. Some common words and phrases you can use to connect multiple sources are: *in addition (to), another, like, likewise, similar (to), similarly, in the same way,* and *both.*

Natural disasters are caused by nature; however, human activity increases their frequency and intensity. **According to** *Agriculture Today*, when humans tear down trees, which leads to deforestation, our planet heats up, leading to global warming. **Similar to** *Agriculture Today*, Dr. Jonas Tomas notes that deforestation can have disastrous environmental consequences because it increases the risk of flooding.

Exercise 6.1 Applying the Skill

Work with a partner. Read the paragraphs and the source information. Then complete each paragraph by integrating the information from the two sources.

1   It is vital to reduce the number of deaths due to natural disasters have greatly increased over the last two decades. One effective strategy for saving lives in the future is to move people away from areas that are prone to natural disasters. _____

    _____

    _____

    (Source One) Dr. Ross, a professor in Geophysics, has found that the largest fault line in California is moving.

    (Source Two) The Center for Earthquake Studies has determined that an earthquake in this area could result in the death of hundreds of thousands of people.

2   Humans are directly responsible for the increasing number of number of hurricanes and the rising physical and economic costs. _____

_____

_____

Our planet is producing more energy, and 93% of this excess energy has been taken in by the oceans.

(Source One) According to the Meteorological Center, climate change, which has been a result of human behavior, is causing the increase. The waters of the Atlantic are warmer, and global warming has affected the circulation pattern.

(Source Two) Dr. Jonas holds global warming responsible for the increase.

Using Impersonal Statements

In most academic writing, when you state a position, there is no need to use phrases that mark it as your personal opinion such as *in my opinion, I think,* or *we should.* The reader understands that you are making a case based on your view of the subject.

Instead of writing a personal statement, express the same idea with an **impersonal statement**.

Personal statement: In my opinion, we need to take responsibility for the increase in natural disasters.

Impersonal statement: Humans need to take responsibility for the increase in natural disasters.

Exercise 6.2 Applying the Skill

Rewrite the sentences as impersonal statements. Compare your sentences with a partner's.

1 It is only my opinion, but I believe that city leaders did not act responsibly when they voted to allow construction on park land.

2 As far as I am concerned, it is always better to reuse and recycle the resources that we have instead of using up additional resources.

3 As I see it, a new convention center would be an incredible benefit for this city and its citizens, as it would provide both jobs and revenue.

4 It seems to me that by designating this neighborhood a historic area, we are telling all low-income homebuyers to stay away.

My Writing

Using Unreal Conditionals to Support Ideas

Writers use **unreal conditionals** to explain and illustrate their ideas using hypothetical situations. Showing readers what is likely to happen if a particular change is made can help persuade them to support the thesis of an argument. Look at the following examples.

It is still very difficult to predict many earthquakes and volcanic eruptions. **If more money had been spent on research before the Northridge earthquake, scientists might have been able to warn people of the approaching disaster**.

Last year's fire moved very slowly. **If it had moved faster, firefighters would not have stopped it so quickly**.

Exercise 6.3 Applying the Skill

Review the body paragraphs you wrote in My Writing in Unit 24. Add two unreal conditional sentences to support your ideas.

Exercise 6.4 Writing Your First Draft

Write an argumentative essay that answers the prompt on page 374.
- Write an introductory paragraph with a hook, background information, and your thesis statement.
- Revise your body paragraphs. Use impersonal statements to present your ideas. Integrate multiple sources and use unreal conditionals to support and strengthen your argument.
- Write a concluding paragraph with a final thought, recommendation, or call to action.

Exercise 6.5 Revising Your Ideas

1 Work with a partner. Use the questions to give feedback on your partner's essay.

- Which of your partner's ideas seem strongest to you?
- Which of your partner's ideas need to be explained more clearly?
- What could your partner add or remove to make the essay stronger and easier to understand?

2 Use the feedback from your partner to revise the ideas and content of your essay.

Exercise 6.6 Editing Your Writing

Use the checklist to review and edit your essay.

Did you answer the prompt completely?	
Does the introductory paragraph provide a good description of the building?	
Is your position definitely and clearly stated in your introduction?	
Does each paragraph include a topic sentence?	
Did you use relevant evidence to build support for your argument?	
Is each paragraph unified?	
Did you include and refute an opposing argument?	
Did you use multiple sources of support and integrate them coherently?	
Did you use impersonal statements to make your writing more academic?	

Exercise 6.7 Editing Your Grammar

Use the checklist to review and edit the grammar in your essay.

Did you use present or future real conditionals correctly?	
Did you use unreal conditional sentences to support important ideas?	
Did you use the correct verb forms in the main and *if* clauses of conditional sentences?	
Did you avoid the common mistakes in the charts on pages 357 and 373?	

Exercise 6.8 Writing Your Final Draft

Apply the feedback and edits from Exercises 6.5 to 6.7 to write the final draft of your essay.

26

Conjunctions

Globalization of Food

1 Grammar in the Real World

A Have you ever had fast food in a foreign country? Do you think the food looks and tastes the same everywhere that it is sold? Read the article about the globalization of fast-food chains. What do fast-food businesses do to their products to make customers happy?

B Comprehension Check **Answer the questions.**

1 What has Dunkin' Donuts done to succeed globally?

2 How has McDonald's changed its menu to attract vegetarians in India?

3 How is the United States affected by the globalization of fast food?

C Notice **Find the sentences in the article and complete them. What is the function of the missing words? Circle *a* or *b*.**

1 That is not surprising since sweet foods are popular with

Americans, _____ you might not be able to

find that donut in other countries.

a to add information

b to show a contrast

2 In Indonesia, they sell donuts filled _____ with

red bean paste _____ with lychee and orange.

a to emphasize additional negative information

b to emphasize surprising information

3 Adapting their products to local preferences is a way

to keep customers happy _____ to keep

business booming.

a to add information

b to show a contrast

The Globalization of FAST FOOD

Do you want a glazed[1] donut for breakfast? Go to your favorite Dunkin' Donuts in Arizona, New York, **or** almost anywhere in the United States **and** you will find it. That is not surprising since sweet foods are popular with Americans, **but** you might not be able to find that donut in other countries. Instead, in parts of Asia you might find green tea or mango mochi ring donuts. In Korea, they offer kimchi[2] croquettes, donuts filled with pickled[3] vegetables. In Singapore, you would find donuts filled with wasabi[4] cheese **and** seaweed cheese. The wasabi creates a very hot-tasting donut that appeals to people in Singapore. In Thailand, Dunkin' Donuts makes delicious Kai-yong donuts, a combination of glazed donut and shredded chicken that is topped with a spicy Thai chili paste. In Indonesia, they sell donuts filled **not only** with red bean paste **but also** with lychee[5] **and** orange. Thinking globally **but** acting locally has been one of the reasons for Dunkin' Donuts' success in over 32 countries **and** over 10,000 restaurants worldwide.

American fast-food chains, like Dunkin' Donuts, seem to be everywhere, **but** these days they are serving **both** food from their U.S. menus **and** food adapted to the tastes **and** customs of other cultures in other countries. McDonald's is another example. In India, there are many people who do not eat meat, **so** McDonald's in India serves only vegetarian burgers **and** prepares non-vegetarian (chicken and fish) meals in a separate area. McDonald's is one of the largest fast-food restaurants worldwide. More than one third of its 33,000 restaurants are located outside the United States. Adapting to local cultures is very important.

The globalization of the fast-food industry is happening with restaurants from all over the world. Pollo Campero, a fast-food restaurant that began in Guatemala in 1971, started adding stores in **both** Europe **and** the Middle East after expanding in Central America. In 2002, it opened its first restaurant in the United States **and** has been growing ever since. In order to appeal to health-conscious consumers in the United States, Pollo Campero decided to offer customers a choice: **either** a healthier, grilled chicken **or** a lightly fried chicken. Grilled **or** fried, the uniquely seasoned chicken has become popular with **both** immigrants from Latin American countries **and** Americans from other cultural backgrounds.

These days, more and more chain restaurants are selling their food in different countries. Adapting their products to local preferences is a way to keep customers happy **and** to keep business booming.[6] It appears to be a strategy for success.

---

[1]**glazed:** covered with a sweet, shiny coating made of sugar

[2]**kimchi:** a Korean dish of pickled vegetables

[3]**pickled:** preserved in a liquid containing salt or vinegar

[4]**wasabi:** a strong-tasting condiment

[5]**lychee:** a sweet, juicy fruit often found in Southeast Asia and other parts of Asia

[6]**boom:** grow rapidly, especially economically

Globalization of Food **379**

2 Connecting Words and Phrases with Conjunctions

Grammar Presentation

Conjunctions connect words and phrases.
Coordinating conjunctions include *and*, *but*, and *or*.
Correlative conjunctions include *both . . . and*, *neither . . . nor*, *either . . . or*, and *not only . . . but also*.

*I love pizza, hamburgers, **and** hot dogs.*
*I eat **not only** fast food **but also** healthy food.*

2.1 Coordinating Conjunctions

A Use coordinating conjunctions to link two or more nouns, gerunds, verbs, or adverbs. Use the same part of speech in linked words or phrases to create parallel structure. This makes speech and writing clearer.	*Have you ever eaten pizza with shrimp **or** olives?* (nouns) *I've been to fast-food restaurants in Asia, Europe, Africa, **and** North America.* (proper nouns) *I don't like cooking **or** baking.* (gerunds) *The meal is unhealthy **but** delicious.* (adjectives)
B Use *and* to add information.	*There are many vegetarians in India **and** the U.K.*
Use *but* to show a contrast.	*This food is cheap **but** very good.* (*But* contrasts the price of the food and the quality.)
Use *or* to connect related ideas or items in a negative statement or to show alternatives.	*I don't like hamburgers **or** pizza.* *Do you want to eat at a restaurant **or** at home?*
C When you connect three or more words or phrases, use a comma between each one. Put the conjunction before the last word or phrase.	*I select my food based on taste, nutritional value, **and** price.* *Would you like to have juice, milk, **or** water with your meal?*

2.2 Correlative Conjunctions

A Correlative conjunctions have two parts. They often emphasize equality between the words or phrases they connect.	*Both fried foods and grilled foods are served here.* *Fast food is neither delicious nor healthy.*

2.2 Correlative Conjunctions (continued)

B Use *both . . . and* to add information. When connecting two subjects, use a plural verb.	*Both* the food *and* the atmosphere <u>are</u> wonderful.
Use *either . . . or* to emphasize alternatives. The verb agrees in number with the noun that is closest to it.	*Either* potatoes *or* rice <u>is</u> fine with me. (Use a singular verb with *rice*.) *Either* rice *or* potatoes <u>are</u> fine with me. (Use a plural verb with *potatoes*.)
Use *not only . . . but also* to emphasize surprising information. The verb agrees in number with the noun that is closest to it.	*Not only* two drinks *but also* dessert <u>comes</u> with this entree. (Use a singular verb with *dessert*.) *Not only* dessert *but also* two drinks <u>come</u> with this entree. (Use a plural verb with *drinks*.)
Use *neither . . . nor* to emphasize additional information in negative statements. The verb agrees in number with the noun that is closest to it.	*Neither* my parents *nor* my brother <u>wants</u> to try eel. (Use a singular verb with *brother*.) *Neither* my brother *nor* my parents <u>want</u> to try eel. (Use a plural verb with *parents*.)

Grammar Application

Exercise 2.1 Coordinating Conjunctions

Combine the sentences about global food. Use the coordinating conjunctions in parentheses. Sometimes more than one answer is possible.

1 There's a Taco Bell in Iceland. There's a Taco Bell in India. (and)

   There's a Taco Bell in Iceland and in India.

2 Starbucks operates in Asia. It operates in Europe. It operates in Latin America. (and)

   _____

3 The U.S. branch doesn't have vegetarian burgers. It doesn't have lamb burgers. (or)

   _____

4 Would you prefer to try something unusual? Would you prefer to try something familiar? (or)

   _____

5 Vegans don't eat eggs. Vegans don't eat cheese. Vegans don't eat yogurt. (or)

   _____

6 The food is cheap. The food is very healthy. (but)

   _____

7 The coffee is expensive. The coffee is very popular. (but)

   _____

A Read the monthly sales report from Branch #345. Then complete the report to headquarters. Circle the correct correlative conjunctions.

Branch #345 – Shanghai, China – June

PRODUCTS

Frozen Yogurt and Smoothies	Drinks	Snacks
frozen yogurt: **55%** smoothies: **45%**	coffee: **50%** tea: **43%** mineral water: **5%** milkshakes: **2%**	chips: **59%** cookies: **41%**

FLAVORS OF FROZEN YOGURT AND SMOOTHIES

Western Flavors	chocolate: **3%**
	vanilla: **2%**
Asian Flavors	dragon fruit: **55%**
	lychee: **40%**

Report to Headquarters on Branch #345

This branch offers (**both**)/ neither Western (**and**)/ or Asian flavors. Asian flavors seem to be
(1)   (1)
more popular. For example, dragon fruit and lychee are the most popular flavors this month.

Most customers tend to choose **neither/either** dragon fruit **nor/or** lychee yogurt. Therefore,
(2)   (2)
please note that **both/neither** chocolate **and/nor** vanilla is selling well at this branch.
(3)   (3)

Neither/Not only frozen yogurt **nor/but also** smoothies are popular at this branch.
(4)   (4)
Either/Neither mineral water **or/nor** milkshakes sold well this month. The reason is that
(5)   (5)
most customers prefer **neither/either** coffee **nor/or** tea. **Both/Neither** coffee **and/nor**
(6)   (6)   (7)   (7)
tea are selling well. It is interesting to note that customers are buying snacks. Surprisingly,

neither/not only chips **nor/but also** cookies are selling well.
(8)   (8)

I recommend that we create more locally flavored products to offer at this location.

B Group Work In groups, choose a country that you know well. Discuss possible frozen yogurt flavors and types of drinks and snacks that you think would or would not sell well in this country. Then write five sentences about your choices with correlative conjunctions.

Both chocolate and vanilla would sell well in Mexico.

Exercise 2.3 More Correlative Conjunctions

Combine the sentences about the availability of items in a Latin American coffee chain's global locations. Use the correlative conjunctions in parentheses.

1 Milk is available in the United States. Juice is available in the United States. (both . . . and)

   Both milk and juice are available in the United States.

2 Tea is inexpensive in Egypt. Tea is very popular in Egypt. (both . . . and)

   Tea is both inexpensive and very popular in Egypt.

3 You can use your own mug at coffee shops in the U.K. You can use a store cup at coffee shops in the U.K. (either . . . or)

   You can use either your own mug or a store cup at coffee shops in the U.K.

4 Donuts are available in the United States. Muffins are available in the United States. (not only . . . but also)

   Not only donuts but also muffins are available in the United States.

5 Recycling is encouraged in China. Reusing cups is encouraged in China. (not only . . . but also)

   Not only recycling but also reusing cups is encouraged in China.

6 Generally, forks are not available in Chinese restaurants. Generally, knives are not available in Chinese restaurants. (neither . . . nor)

   Generally, neither forks nor knives are available in Chinese restaurants.

7 Hot dogs are not typically eaten for lunch in the Dominican Republic. Pizza is not typically eaten for lunch in the Dominican Republic. (neither . . . nor)

   Neither hot dogs nor Pizza is typically eaten for lunch in the Dominican Republic.

3 Connecting Sentences with Coordinating Conjunctions

Grammar Presentation

The coordinating conjunctions *and*, *but*, *or*, *so*, and *yet* can connect independent clauses.	Kevin doesn't eat meat, **but** he eats fish. Jennifer is a vegetarian, **so** we shouldn't put meat in the lasagna.

3.1 Connecting Sentences with *And*, *But*, and *Or*

A Use a comma before the coordinating conjunction when you connect two complete sentences. The comma implies a pause.	*Starbucks opened in 1971,* **and** *it has become an international success.* *The café sold muffins,* **but** *it did not sell sandwiches.* *Consumers liked the food,* **so** *sales were good.*
B When you connect sentences with the same subject with *and* or *or*, you do not need to repeat the subject. The result is a compound verb. Do not use a comma with compound verbs. If the modals or the auxiliary verbs are the same, you do not have to repeat the modals or auxiliaries.	CLAUSE, + AND + CLAUSE *We ate at that restaurant last week,* **and** *we really liked it.* VERB + AND + VERB *We ate at that restaurant last week* **and** *really liked it.* *Karen can ride with us,* **or** *she can meet us at the restaurant.* *Karen can ride with us* **or** *meet us at the restaurant.* *My brother has visited India,* **and** *he has eaten fast food there.* *My brother has visited India* **and** *eaten fast food there.*
C In some writing, such as in newspapers and magazines, sentences begin with conjunctions like *and* and *but* to emphasize information. Do not do this in academic writing.	*The changes to the menu attracted many new customers.* **And** *the company's profits rose significantly.*

3.1 Connecting Sentences with *And*, *But*, and *Or* (continued)

D Use *and* to connect an independent clause that adds information. You can also use *and* to show a sequence of events.	*He is an excellent cook, **and** I love his recipes.* *This restaurant changed its chef, **and** now it is very popular.*
Use *but* to introduce contrasting or surprising information.	*This is supposed to be a good Mexican restaurant, **but** my Mexican friends don't like it.*
Use *or* to introduce a choice or alternative. It is often used in questions or statements with modals of possibility.	*We could have seafood, **or** we could make pasta.* *Could you prepare the meal, **or** should I ask Sam to prepare it?*

3.2 Connecting Sentences with *So* and *Yet*

A Use *so* to connect a cause and its result.	CAUSE RESULT *Henry doesn't like pizza, **so** we ordered pasta.* *That spice is rare in my country, **so** I substitute a different one.*
Use *yet* to connect contrasting ideas or surprising information. *Yet* sometimes expresses a stronger contrast than *but*.	*Cathy doesn't eat clams, **yet** she eats oysters.* *The restaurant serves wonderful food, **yet** it is known more for its music.*
B Use a comma to combine sentences with *so* and *yet*. Do not use a compound verb.	*Mary is a vegetarian, **so** she eats tofu.* NOT *Mary is a vegetarian so eats tofu.*

Grammar Application

Exercise 3.1 Connecting Sentences with *And*, *But*, *Or*

Complete the sentences about a European supermarket chain that opened stores in the United States. Circle the correct conjunctions. Add commas when necessary.

1 FoodCo opened 100 stores in the United States in 2008, **and** / **but** the managers expected to have great success in certain areas.

2 First, they studied the new market **but** / **and** they even sent anthropologists to study U.S. eating and shopping habits.

3 They opened stores in wealthy neighborhoods **or** / **and** they also opened some in low-income neighborhoods.

4 The trend in the United States is toward "big box" stores[1] **and** / **but** FoodCo decided to open small, convenience-type stores.

[1]**"big box" store:** a very large store that sells almost everything, including food

5 Convenience stores in the United States usually do not sell fresh produce **but/or** FoodCo has changed the definition of *convenience store* with its new stores.

6 FoodCo has positioned itself as a healthy convenience store **and/or** it provides high-quality groceries and produce at reasonable prices.

7 Customers can use FoodCo's shops to pick up last-minute items **but/or** they can do their weekly shopping there.

8 Now shoppers in low-income neighborhoods have a choice. They can buy junk food at a convenience store **but/or** they can buy healthy products at a FoodCo shop.

Exercise 3.2 Connecting Sentences with *So* and *Yet*

Complete the article about Chinese-American dishes. Use *so* or *yet*. Add commas when necessary.

Many Chinese restaurants serve dishes that are not authentic. Chinese restaurant owners wanted to be successful in foreign countries __, so__ they adapted
(1)
dishes to local tastes. Here are some examples: Fortune cookies are popular desserts in many Chinese restaurants _____ they were never popular in China. In
(2)
fact, the cookies were actually invented in Japan and then introduced to the United States by an immigrant in the early 1900s (although some people dispute this and say that a Chinese immigrant invented them first). General Tso's Chicken is another example. No one is absolutely certain of its origin _____ it appears on many
(3)
U.S. Chinese restaurant menus. It's fried chicken with a sweet sauce. Fried chicken is a traditional American dish _____ a clever Chinese restaurant owner probably
(4)
invented it to appeal to American tastes for sweet sauces. Chop suey is another Chinese-American invention. There are many legends about its creation _____
(5)
no one really knows for sure how it came about. In one story, a Chinese-American dishwasher created the dish from leftover bits of meat and vegetables. The man received part of his pay in food _____ he took what he could find at the end
(6)
of the day. Customers asked about the delicious-smelling creation _____ the restaurant manager put it on the
(7)
menu. Some of these dishes may seem inauthentic _____ they have been extremely popular in the
(8)
United States since the 1900s.

Exercise 3.3 Combining Sentences

Combine the sentences about the localization of food. Use the conjunctions in parentheses. Omit the subject and use a compound verb when possible. Add commas when necessary.

1 You can travel to many countries. You can still find dishes from home. (and)

You can travel to many countries and still find dishes from home.

2 I have eaten tacos in China. I have ordered kimchi in France. (and)

I have eaten tacos in China and ordered kimchi in France.

3 You might get an authentic dish abroad. You might find a local version of it. (or)

You might get an authentic dish abroad or find a local version of it.

4 I often find international dishes abroad. They are usually adapted to local tastes. (but)

I often find international dishes abroad, but they are ~

5 Beef isn't eaten in some countries. A fast-food chain might sell lamb burgers. (so)

, so

6 I travel constantly. I never miss food from home. (yet)

, yet

Exercise 3.4 Using *So* and *Yet*

Over to You On a separate piece of paper, complete the answers about local food tastes. Write sentences that are true for you. Discuss your ideas with a partner.

1 How do supermarkets in your neighborhood address local tastes?

Supermarkets in my neighborhood want to address local tastes, so

they have an imported-food section .

2 How might an international food company adapt a product to local tastes?

People in _____ like _____ , so _____ .
　　　　　(name a country)　　　　(food or taste)

3 What inauthentic ethnic dishes are sometimes very popular?

_____ is inauthentic, yet _____ .
(name of dish)

4 Reducing Sentences with Similar Clauses

Grammar Presentation

When you connect sentences that have similar clauses, you can often reduce the words in the second clause.	*Shrimp is one of my favorite foods. Chicken is one of my favorite foods.* *Shrimp is one of my favorite foods, and chicken is, too.*

4.1 Reducing Sentences

A In sentences with *be* as the main verb, use the *be* verb in the reduced clause.	*Their Chinese food isn't very good, but their Thai food is.*
B For other verb forms with auxiliaries, you can reduce the verb form in the reduced clause.	*My brother didn't eat fast food in college, and I didn't, either.*
For the present progressive or past progressive, keep the form of *be* and omit verb + *-ing*.	*The price of beef was rising last month, but the price of chicken wasn't.*
For simple verb forms, use *do/does (not)* or *did (not)*.	*I don't like this restaurant, and Lisa doesn't, either.* *We went out to eat, and so did Victor.*
For the present progressive or past perfect, use *have/has* or *had* and omit the past participle.	*The cost of eating out has risen, and the cost of cooking at home has, too.*
For modals or future forms, use the modal or future form by itself.	*Jason can join us for lunch, and Liz can, too.* *I won't eat fried food, and Greg won't, either.*
C Use *and . . . too* or *and so* to combine two affirmative sentences. Use: • *and* + subject + auxiliary + *too* • *and so* + auxiliary + subject Note that the order of the auxiliary and subject are reversed in *and so* reduced clauses. We usually use a comma before *too*.	AFFIRM. SENT. + AFFIRM. SENT. *I ate there yesterday. She ate there yesterday.* AND + SUBJ. + AUX. + TOO *I ate there yesterday, and she did, too.* AND SO + AUX. + SUBJ. *I ate there yesterday, and so did she.*

4.1 Reducing Sentences (continued)

D Use *and . . . not, either* or *and neither* to combine two negative sentences. Use:

- *and* + subject + auxiliary + *not, either*
- *and neither* + auxiliary + subject.

NEG. SENT. + NEG. SENT.
I don't have any coffee. Kim doesn't have any coffee.

AND + SUBJ. + AUX. + NOT, EITHER
*I don't have any coffee, **and** <u>Kim</u> <u>doesn't</u>, **either**.*

AND NEITHER + AUX. + SUBJ.
*I don't have any coffee, **and neither** <u>does Kim</u>.*

E Use *but* to combine an affirmative and a negative sentence.

AFFIRM. SENT. + NEG. SENT.
The beef is dry. The chicken isn't dry.

AFFIRM. CLAUSE + BUT + NEG. CLAUSE
*The beef is dry, **but** the chicken isn't.*

NEG. CLAUSE + BUT + AFFIRM. CLAUSE
*The chicken isn't dry, **but** the beef is.*

F You can also use *too, so, either,* and *neither* in separate sentences in speaking and less formal writing.

Use *too* and *so* for two affirmative sentences. Use *either* and *neither* for two negative sentences.

*Japanese food is delicious. Korean food is, **too**.*
*Japanese food is delicious. **So** is Korean food.*
*The coffee isn't warm. The tea isn't, **either**.*
*The coffee isn't warm. **Neither** is the tea.*

Exercise 4.1 Reducing Sentences with Similar Clauses

Combine the sentences about food localization in India. Use coordinating conjunctions. If there are two lines, write the sentence in two different ways.

1 Americans like fast food. Indians like fast food.
   Americans like fast food, and Indians do, too.
   Americans like fast food, and so do Indians.

2 Some U.S. food companies are successful in India. Some U.S. food companies aren't successful in India.
   Some ~ , but some (U.S. food companies) aren't.

3 Beef isn't popular in India. Pork isn't popular in India.
   Beef isn't popular in India, and Pork isn't, either.
   Beef isn't popular in India, and neither is Pork.

4 McDonald's adapts its menu to local tastes. Pizza Hut adapts its menu to local tastes.
   McDonald's ~ , and Pizza Hut does, too.
   McDonald's ~ , and so does Pizza Hut.

5 Pizza Hut doesn't serve meat in some regions. McDonald's doesn't serve meat in some regions.
   Pizza Hut ~ , and McDonald's doesn't, either.
   Pizza Hut ~ , and neither does McDonald's,

A Group Work Match the words with pictures of food. Tell the group which foods you have eaten raw.

_b_ **1** eel

_____ **2** jellyfish

_____ **3** sea urchin

_____ **4** seaweed

_____ **5** tuna

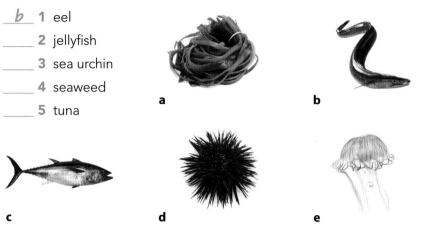

a   b

c   d   e

B Listen to the interview with the chef of a restaurant. Circle *T* if the statement is true. Circle *F* if the statement is false.

1 The chef is talking about Asian dishes that he serves at his restaurant. (T)   F

2 All the dishes he offers are popular with his customers.   T   F

3 The chef has adapted some dishes to local tastes.   T   F

4 The chef does not plan to make any changes to his menu.   T   F

C Listen again. Rewrite the statements to match what the chef says. Use reduced forms.

1 Raw fish is getting more popular. Seaweed salad is getting more popular.

Raw fish is getting more popular _, and so is seaweed salad_ .

2 Tuna has been selling well. Eel hasn't been selling well.

Tuna has been selling well, _____ .

3 Jellyfish didn't sell well last month. Sea urchin didn't sell well last month.

Jellyfish didn't sell well last month, _____ .

4 Spicy noodles have sold well. Cold noodles have sold well.

Spicy noodles have sold well, _____ .

5 This restaurant can't get customers interested in Thai dishes. Our other restaurants can't get customers interested.

This restaurant can't get customers interested in Thai dishes,

_____ .

6 We'll probably stop offering Thai dishes. The other branches will probably stop offering Thai dishes.

We'll probably stop offering Thai dishes, _____ .

7 We won't serve that. Most other Asian restaurants won't serve that.

We won't serve that, _____ .

8 The ice cream has been selling well. The cake has been selling well, too. The ice cream has been selling well, _____ .

5 Avoid Common Mistakes ⚠

1	**Use *or* to connect ideas in a negative sentence.**
	or
	There were no nuts in the vegetarian ~~and~~ the meat dishes.

2	**Use *both*, not *either*, when joining ideas with *and*.**
	both
	They use ~~either~~ butter and oil for cooking.

3	**Use *either*, not *too*, after a negative verb.**
	either
	They do not eat pork, and we don't, ~~too~~.

| 4 | **Do not use a comma when a conjunction joins two phrases.** |
| | *Most local people love durian fruit~~,~~ but dislike the smell.* |

Editing Task

Find and correct eight more mistakes in the paragraphs about food.

Intercultural Dinners

My roommate and I come from different cultures, so ~~either~~ *both* our eating habits and food preferences differ. Fortunately, we have some food preferences in common. I do not eat junk food, and he does not, too. There are no cookies and other desserts in our house. Instead, we have either fresh fruits and nuts for snacks.

5 However, we have some differences. I eat either rice and pasta every day. My roommate, however, thinks meals with rice, and dishes with pasta will make him gain weight, so he does not want to eat them often. Likewise, I do not like to eat a lot of meat and dairy products because I believe they are not healthy. Fortunately, I do not complain about his tastes, and he does not complain about mine, too. When we

10 cook, we try to make food that represents either his culture and mine.

6 Academic Writing

Comparison and Contrast

Brainstorm > Organize > Write > Edit

In this writing cycle (Units 26-28), you are going to write an essay that answers the prompt below. In this unit (26), you will analyze a text and brainstorm and organize ideas about the topic.

> *Not all products and services fit the same business model. Some might have a more successful introduction in a mobile setting. For others, a mobile setting would not be appropriate. Compare and contrast two products or services regarding their potential as mobile businesses.*

Exercise 6.1 Preparing to Write

Work with a partner. Discuss the questions.

1 What influences a person to start a business, their passion to do something or their desire to make money?

2 Describe two modern businesses that reflect the fast-paced nature of the 21st century.

3 How would you define *mobile retail*? Describe an example of a mobile retail business.

4 What other types of businesses might be successful in a mobile setting?

Exercise 6.2 Focusing on Vocabulary

Read the definitions. Complete the sentences with the correct form of the words in bold.

> **aspiring** (adj) wishing to become successful
>
> **component** (n) a part that combines with other parts to form something bigger
>
> **fluctuate** (v) to change frequently from one level to another
>
> **outweigh** (v) to be greater or more important than something else
>
> **proposition** (n) a proposal or suggestion, especially in business
>
> **revenue** (n) the money that a business receives regularly

1 The price of oil has _____ dramatically in recent years, falling from $102 a barrel to just over $26 in 2016, and back up to $75 in 2018!

2 The entrepreneur tried to persuade the bank officers to give him a loan, but they found his business _____ risky and poorly organized.

3 The _____ chef took a lower-level job at a famous New York restaurant to gain experience and connections in the business.

4 The agricultural company convinced the government regulators that the benefits of its new pesticide _____ the risks.

5 The spread of technology and the movement of labor are two _____ of globalization.

6 Amazon's _____ in 2018 was almost $233 billion.

Starting out Mobile

Perhaps you make the world's best peanut butter cookies, or maybe you have always helped your friends and neighbors by fixing their computers. Many businesses are started by people who have hobbies or special talents and want to turn
5 these interests into a business. Yet, scaling up from a hobby to a real business, such as a bakery, restaurant, or store, requires both business know-how and a substantial investment. In reality, many entrepreneurs do not have enough of either the knowledge or the money, but it is often the high financial investment needed
10 to start a brick-and-mortar[1] business that keeps them from taking the first step.

These days, an increasing number of **aspiring** business owners have found a way to make the transition[2] from hobby to business not only more gradual but also less expensive or risky
15 than putting up the money for a building and its equipment right away. They are taking their dreams and talents on the road—in trucks. The first entrepreneurs to do this were in the food business. In recent years, a wave of food trucks have arrived on the scene, serving everything from gourmet muffins to Argentinian
20 empanadas to Korean tacos. Food trucks became a way for aspiring chefs to try out recipes and test the waters before making a big investment in a traditional, brick-and-mortar business.

Beginning on a small scale has its advantages compared with starting a traditional business. The most important of these
25 is the relatively modest size of initial start-up costs. These costs, which consist primarily of the truck, a license, and any required equipment, usually come to $20,000–$30,000, a fraction of what it would cost to start a store or restaurant. Similarly, overhead costs are generally lower. Mobile business owners must pay for gas, of
30 course, but other utility payments are modest. With such tightly controlled costs, mobile businesses often break even[3] in a year or two. In contrast, success comes to brick-and-mortar businesses much more slowly, and they often fail within the first two years. In short, mobile businesses are relatively low-risk **propositions**.

35 The success of food trucks has inspired other entrepreneurs to consider starting out on wheels. Rich Harper once ran a chain of gyms, but his real interest was boxing. In 2005, he bought an old truck, equipped it with some gym equipment, and took to the streets—all for a total start-up cost of $6,000. His business quickly
40 turned a profit and is still going strong. Instead of trying to convince customers to visit his facility in an already crowded market, he brings the boxing ring to customers all over his state.

Today, there are trucks that sell flowers, shoes, clothes, and all kinds of specialty food items. There are also trucks that provide
45 services, such as hair styling, dog grooming, and repair of high-tech devices. While mobile retail has grown steadily in the past decade, it is not without problems. Weather, the fact that gas prices **fluctuate**, and the difficulty of finding a place to park are all challenges that mobile entrepreneurs have to deal with every day.
50 These business owners, however, feel the advantages **outweigh** the disadvantages. In the United States, the mobile food business alone—the largest in the mobile retail sector— generates an average annual **revenue** of over $2 billion.

Once convinced that their business has achieved sufficient
55 success, some successful mobile entrepreneurs move on to open brick-and-mortar locations. Others, like Rich Harper and his boxing gym, are satisfied to stay mobile. In an interesting twist, some brick-and-mortar business owners, like their mobile counterparts, have learned from their competition and have added a mobile
60 **component** to their businesses. The truck sells their products or services and acts as a marketing tool to bring more business into the store. Either as stand-alone businesses, or as extensions of stores, mobile retail appears to be here to stay.

[1]**brick-and-mortar** (adj) existing as a physical building, especially a store
[2]**transition** (n) a change from one state or condition to another
[3]**break even** (idiom) to earn only enough to pay expenses

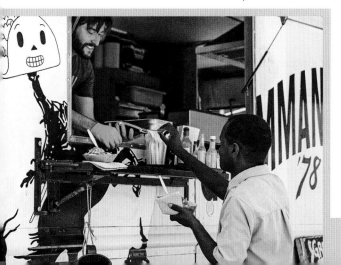

Read the text on page 393. Work with a partner. Discuss the questions.

1 How do many businesses get started?
2 What was the first type of business to take advantage of a mobile setting?
3 What are two advantages of starting on a small scale?

Complete the tasks. Then compare your answers with a partner's.

1 Highlight the conjunctions in paragraphs 1 and 6. Why does the writer include a correlative conjunction in the last sentence of the article?
2 What two things is the writer comparing? Underline the sentences in paragraphs 1 and 2 that help you determine your answer.
3 What is the main idea of paragraph 3?
4 What does the writer conclude after comparing and contrasting these two types of businesses?

Using Signal Words and Phrases to Compare and Contrast

Comparing is showing how two or more things are the **same** or **similar**. **Contrasting** is showing how two or more things are **different**. When writing essays, writers often compare or contrast people, things, or ideas to make their presentations clearer and to focus on advantages and disadvantages. They often use signal words and phrases to alert the reader when they are comparing or contrasting.

In an interesting twist, some brick-and-mortar business owners, **like** their mobile counterparts, have learned from their competition...

These days, an increasing number of aspiring business owners have found a way to make the transition from hobby to business not only **more** gradual but also **less** expensive or risky **than**...

In the first example, the use of **like** signals a similarity between mobile and brick-and-mortar businesses. In the second example, the use of **more** and **less than** signals a difference.

Read each sentence. Indicate if the writer is stating a similarity (S) or a difference (D). Underline the signal words or phrases.

1 In spite of the popularity of eating out, cooking at home is much healthier. _____

2 Hamburgers from the same fast food restaurants in different countries taste the same. _____

3 Unlike the long lines at fast food restaurants in some Asian countries, they are usually shorter in Western Europe. _____

4 Similar to a food truck, a fast food restaurant needs to work quickly and efficiently. _____

My Writing

Using Venn Diagrams

A **Venn diagram** is a graphic organizer that can help you organize your ideas when comparing and contrasting two topics. It consists of two overlapping circles. The special characteristics (differences) of one topic are on the left side, while those of the second topic are on the right side. The shared characteristics (similarities) are in the middle.

Example: "Comparing Fast Food and International Food"

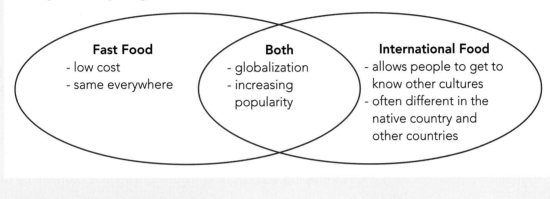

Exercise 6.6 Applying the Skill

Work with a partner. Complete the tasks.

1 Brainstorm at least three products or services that could be set up as mobile businesses.
2 Discuss the advantages and disadvantages of each one.
3 On your own, choose two of the products or services for your essay. Use a Venn diagram to compare and contrast them.
4 Share your Venn diagram with your partner for feedback. Add any new ideas.

Exercise 6.7 Writing a Paragraph

Use your Venn diagram to write a paragraph about the two products or services. Include a topic sentence, at least two similarities or differences with supporting details, and a concluding sentence. Use coordinating or correlative conjunctions to show similarities or differences.

UNIT 27

Adverb Clauses and Phrases

Consumerism

1 Grammar in the Real World

ACADEMIC WRITING

Comparison and contrast

A What are some normal behaviors that can become problems under certain circumstances? Read the web article about shopping addiction. When is shopping an addiction?

B Comprehension Check **Answer the questions.**

1 Why aren't shopping addictions considered a serious problem by most people?

2 What problems can a shopping addiction lead to?

3 What are two ways in which shopaholics can treat their problem?

C Notice **Find the sentences in the article and complete them. Then circle the meaning of the words.**

1 _Even though_ these people do not need more clothes or electronics, they keep buying them.
   (a) The words introduce contrasting ideas.   b The words give a reason.

2 _Because_ shopping may be seen as an amusing addiction, society does not always consider it a serious problem.
   a The word introduces contrasting ideas.   (b) The word gives a reason.

3 _Even though_ shopaholics enjoy the excitement, they often feel depressed or guilty after a shopping trip.
   (a) The words introduce contrasting ideas.   b The words give a reason.

SHOPPING ADDICTION:
When Spending Hurts

Some people have closets filled with new clothes that they do not wear. Others have desks covered with electronics that they 5 never use. **Even though these people do not need more clothes or electronics,** they keep buying them. They cannot help themselves. **Although many** 10 **people like to shop,** some people shop too much. If someone is unable to control spending, he or she may be a shopping addict, or "shopaholic." **Because** 15 **shopping may be seen as an amusing addiction,** society does not always consider it a serious problem. As a result, many people do not recognize they have a 20 problem that needs treatment. However, if this addiction is not treated, it can ruin a person's life.

Shopping can activate[1] chemicals in the brain associated 25 with pleasure, **so some people get a natural "high"[2] while**

shopping. Also, some people shop **because it makes them feel in control.** This often happens 30 **when they face difficulties in their personal or professional lives.** These feelings could be signs of shopping addiction. **While it may appear to some that** 35 **many more women than men are affected by this addiction,** current statistics show that this is not true. The percentage of men addicted to shopping is about the 40 same as the percentage of women (around 5 percent).

Like most addictions, a shopping addiction can cause serious problems. First of all, 45 it is difficult for addicts. **Even though shopaholics enjoy the excitement,** they often feel depressed or guilty after a shopping trip. **Spending** 50 **more money than they have,** many shopaholics have financial problems. **As they spend,** they

may lie to their families about their spending habits. These lies are 55 almost always hurtful and can even destroy the family.

Fortunately, shopping addiction can be treated. **In order to change their behavior,** 60 shopping addicts must admit that they have a problem and then seek help. In addition, shopping addicts should always take a friend along **when they need to** buy 65 something. Most shopping addicts only overspend when they shop alone.

While shopping is usually a harmless activity, an addiction 70 to shopping can cause financial and personal problems. Therefore, people should understand the signs of a shopping addiction **so that they can get help.** Shopping 75 should be a constructive activity, not a destructive one.

---

[1]**activate:** cause something to start

[2]**high:** a feeling of being excited or full of energy

2 Subordinators and Adverb Clauses

Grammar Presentation

Adverb clauses show a relationship between ideas in two clauses. They begin with subordinators, such as *although* and *because*.	*Although she enjoys wearing new clothes, she doesn't enjoy shopping.* *Eric doesn't go shopping often because he doesn't like to spend money.*

2.1 Forming Adverb Clauses

A An adverb clause has a subject and a verb, but it is a dependent clause. It is not a complete sentence.	MAIN CLAUSE DEPENDENT CLAUSE *She shops because it makes her feel good*
B In general, use a comma when an adverb clause begins the sentence.	*Although I sometimes buy things I don't need, I'm not a shopping addict.*

2.2 Using Adverb Clauses

A Use *because* and *since* to give reasons. *Because* is more common.	*Because shopping is necessary, shopping addicts aren't easily recognized.* *Treatment is important for shopping addicts since it is very difficult to overcome this problem on one's own.*
B Use *although*, *even though*, and *though* to show a contrasting idea or something unexpected. *Although* is a little more formal. Use a comma with adverb clauses that include these subordinators, whether they begin or end the sentence.	*Even though shopping addicts enjoy shopping, they feel depressed afterward.* *She spends a lot on clothing, though she doesn't make much money.*
C Use *while* to show contrasting ideas. Use a comma whether the adverb clause begins or ends the sentence.	*Shopping addicts buy things they don't need, while nonaddicts tend to buy mostly things they need.*
D You can use *as*, *since*, *when*, and *while* in adverb clauses to express time relationships.	*It has been six weeks since he went shopping.* *While she was at the mall, she bought many useless things.*

Grammar Application

Exercise 2.1 Adverb Clauses

Combine the sentences about shopping addiction. Use the subordinators in parentheses. Add commas when necessary. Sometimes more than one answer is possible.

1 We are surrounded by advertising messages. It is often difficult to avoid shopping. (since)

   Since we are surrounded by advertising messages, it is often difficult to avoid shopping.

2 Many people feel that it is patriotic to shop. Some politicians say that it is good for the economy. (because)

   Because many people ~,   Some politicians ~.

3 We may not need items. We sometimes want what others have. (even though)

   Even though we may not need items, we ~

4 Shopping addiction seems to be a recent problem. It has almost certainly existed for centuries. (although)

   Although shopping addiction ~,   it has almost -.

5 Addicts may shop to escape negative feelings. Normal people shop to buy things they need. (while)

   Addicts may shop ~, while normal people shop to buy things they need.

6 Normal shoppers use the items they buy. Compulsive shoppers often do not use them. (while)

   While normal shoppers ~,   compulsive ~.

A Complete the interview with a shopping addict. Rewrite each pair of sentences as one sentence. Use one of the subordinators in parentheses.

| Jane | So, Claire, how did you know you were a shopping addict? |

| Claire | I saw a show on TV. I realized I was an addict. (when / since) |

1   *When I saw a show on TV, I realized I was an addict.*

| Jane | I understand that you're getting help. |

| Claire | Yes. My insurance pays for it. I was able to sign up for therapy. (because / although) |

2   _____

| Jane | Is your therapy helping? |

| Claire | Definitely. I've only been in therapy a short time. I'm feeling better already.
(although / when) |

3   _____

| Jane | How are things different now? |

| Claire | I only buy what I really need. I'm spending much less money. (since / although) |

4   _____

| Jane | Describe a recent shopping trip. |

| Claire | I was at the mall yesterday. I only went to one store. (even though / since) |

5   _____

I had a list. I only bought things I truly needed. (since / while)

6   _____

| Jane | Good for you! Thank you for sharing your story with us. |

B Listen to the interview and check your answers.

Group Work   What are some ways to avoid bad shopping habits? Write five sentences using adverb clauses. Use the ideas in the unit and your own ideas.
Decide as a group which two ideas are the most effective and give reasons.

You should take a friend with you when you shop.

3 Reducing Adverb Clauses

Grammar Presentation

Sometimes you can reduce adverb clauses to *-ing* forms. The subject of the main clause must be the same as the subject of the adverb clause.	*While he was shopping*, he bought things he didn't need. *While shopping*, he bought things he didn't need.

3.1 Reducing Adverb Clauses

In many cases, you can reduce adverb clauses. Omit the subject, and use the verb + *-ing*.	*While he was shopping*, he bought a jacket. *While shopping*, he bought a jacket.

3.2 Reducing Clauses That Give Reasons

You can reduce clauses that give reasons when the verb is in the simple past, present perfect, or past perfect. For the simple past, omit the subordinator and the subject, and use the verb + *-ing*. For the present perfect and past perfect, change *have* to *having*. The *-ing* forms usually begin the sentences.	*Because he was cautious*, he didn't spend much money. *Being cautious*, he didn't spend much money. *Since she has gotten help*, she no longer shops so often. *Having gotten help*, she no longer shops so often.

3.3 Reducing Time Clauses

A You can reduce a time clause when the verb is in the present progressive or past progressive. Omit the subject and the form of *be*.	*You can save money while you are going to college.* *You can save money while going to college.* *While he was shopping*, he bought a jacket. *While shopping*, he bought a jacket.
B You can also reduce a time clause with a verb in the simple present or simple past. Omit the subject, and use the verb + *-ing*.	*She started shopping at malls before she realized that shopping was addictive.* *She started shopping at malls before realizing that shopping was addictive.*

Grammar Application

Complete the sentences about Mike and Eric, two hoarders.[1] Rewrite the reason clauses in parentheses as reduced clauses.

1 *Buying new things all the time* , Mike filled his apartment with useless items.
   (because he bought new things all the time)

2 _____ , he took action.
   (because he understood that he had a problem)

3 _____ , he had no savings.
   (because he had spent so much money on clothes)

4 _____ , Eric is now able to keep his
   (since he has received treatment)
apartment much cleaner.

5 _____ , he no longer feels anxious.
   (because he has worked with a therapist)

6 _____ , he no longer hoards useless items.
   (since he has gotten help)

[1]**hoarder:** a person who collects large supplies of things, usually more than he or she needs

Exercise 3.2 Reducing Time Clauses

Complete the sentences about a compulsive spender. Rewrite the time clauses in parentheses as reduced clauses.

1 _While shopping online_ , Amy was ecstatic.
   (while she was shopping online)

2 _While spending money_ , she was in an altered state.
   (while she was spending money)

3 Amy had spent over $30,000 _before getting treatment_ .
   (before she got treatment)

4 _Before spending more money_ , Amy decided to join Debtors
   (before she spent more money)
   Anonymous (DA).[1]

5 _After joining DA_ , Amy learned how to budget.
   (after she joined DA)

6 She also got help with her credit _after starting DA_ .
   (after she started DA)

7 Amy has changed her behavior _since receiving treatment_ .
   (since she received treatment)

[1]**Debtors Anonymous (DA):** an organization that helps compulsive spenders

4 Subordinators to Express Purpose

Grammar Presentation

Some subordinators can express a purpose.	He got help for his shopping addiction **so that** he could feel better. (= He got help for the purpose of feeling better.)

4.1 Using Subordinators to Express Purpose

A Use *so* or *so that* to show a reason or purpose. Clauses with *so that* usually come after the main clause.	People go to psychologists **so that** they can talk about their problems. I keep track of my money **so** I don't spend too much.
B You can also show a reason or purpose with *in order to* or *to* when the subject of the main clause and the adverb clause are the same. Do not repeat the subject.	Shopping addicts buy things they don't need **to** feel good. (= Shopping addicts buy things they don't need so that they feel good.) Shopping addicts may get help **in order to** stop shopping. (= Shopping addicts may get help so that they stop shopping.)

Grammar Application

A Complete the sentences from the book *Consumer World*. Put the subordinators in parentheses in the right place in the sentences.

in order to

1 Psychologists have shown that we actually need very little feel happy. (in order to)

2 Some people buy things feel good about themselves. (to)

3 Some people acquire things they have a sense of who they are. (so that)

4 It's also possible that people acquire things feel secure. (in order to)

5 They buy a lot feel that they are financially secure. (in order to)

6 They buy a lot they are prepared for any emergency. (so that)

7 Find out how little you really need, think about what you would do if you had to move. (to)

8 I think that have true peace of mind, you should have as little as possible. (in order to)

B Group Work **Discuss the questions with your group. Use** *in order to, so, so that,* **and** *to* **in your discussion.**

■ Does owning things make people happy?

■ What are some of the problems that owning things can cause?

■ What do people have to do to be truly happy?

■ What are some ways to live with less?

A *In order to be truly happy, you should focus on people, not things.*
B *I agree, but to have a happy life, you need some possessions.*

C Write sentences about your five best ideas in B. Use subordinators to express purpose.

In order to be truly happy, you should focus on people, not things.
Pretend you are moving so you can decide what to get rid of.

5 Avoid Common Mistakes ⚠

1 **Remember that *even though* is two words, not one.**

even though

I bought a computer bag ~~eventhough~~ I do not own a computer.

2 **Use *even though*, not *even*, to create an adverb clause.**

Even though

~~Even~~ it was late, the store was open.

3 **Do not start a new sentence with *because*, *whereas*, or *although* when the clause refers to the previous sentence.**

store because

I returned the camera to the ~~store. Because~~ I did not really need it.

4 **Remember to use the verb + *-ing* in reduced clauses after words like *after*, *before*, *while*, and *when*.**

watching

When ~~watch~~ ads on TV, some people feel a strong urge to buy the products.

Editing Task

Find and correct eight more mistakes in the paragraphs about addictions.

looking

   After ~~look~~ at research, we see clearly that alcohol and drug addictions are serious physical conditions. Psychologists are now considering adding shopping to the list. Eventhough these experts say that shopping is as addictive as drugs, I disagree that it should be considered a serious addiction.

5   People who argue that shopping is addictive have good reasons. While shop, many people get a good feeling. They like spending money even they may not need to buy anything. However, after go home, they feel regret. They have spent money on something they did not want or need. Because buying something makes them feel a sense of power.

10   However, after examine the situation of over-shopping closely, one can see that many people are victims of advertising. Even they may not plan to buy something, a powerful advertisement can change their mind. If people did not watch so much TV, they would not feel the urge to shop as strongly. In this way, shopping addiction differs from drug and alcohol addictions, which create a chemical change in the body

15   that is very difficult to resist.

   Eventhough shopping too much is a serious problem, it should not be considered an addiction. If advertisements disappeared, society would not have this problem called shopping addiction.

6 Academic Writing

Comparison and Contrast

Brainstorm > Organize > Write > Edit

In Unit 26, you analyzed a text and brainstormed and organized ideas for the writing prompt below. In this unit (27), you will focus on ways to organize comparisons and contrasts and to write concise body paragraphs.

> *Not all products and services fit the same business model. Some might have a more successful introduction in a mobile setting. For others, a mobile setting would not be appropriate. Compare and contrast two products or services regarding their potential as mobile businesses.*

Organizing Comparisons and Contrasts

In formal essays and reports, writers often compare or contrast people, things, or ideas in order to make an argument. There are two common ways to organize a text that compares and/or contrasts topics:

- **Block organization:** The writer discusses all the features (cost, appearance, size) of one topic in a body paragraph and the features of the second topic in a separate body paragraph.
- **Point-by-point organization:** The writer compares and contrasts one feature at a time, usually one feature per paragraph. Point-by-point organization works best when there are clear parallel points for comparison.

Exercise 6.1 Understanding the Skill

Work with a partner. Complete the tasks.

1 Write the correct organizational pattern in each box below.

2 Think about the characteristics of shopping at a brick-and-mortar store and those of shopping online. Choose three characteristics and fill in both outlines.

Organizational pattern: _____	**Organizational pattern:** _____
Shopping in stores _____	Feature 1 _____
Feature 1: _____	Shopping in stores: _____
Feature 2: _____	Shopping online _____
Feature 3: _____	Feature 2 _____
Shopping online _____	Shopping in stores: _____
Feature 1: _____	Shopping online _____
Feature 2: _____	Feature 3 _____
Feature 3: _____	Shopping in stores: _____
	Shopping online _____

Exercise 6.2 Applying the Skill

Read an early draft of a student's essay about the food truck industry. The body paragraphs and conclusion are incomplete. Work with a partner. Discuss the questions.

Roy Choi is considered the pioneer of the modern food truck movement. He was born in South Korea but grew up in Los Angeles, surrounded by incredible diversity--including diverse food. He has worked in fancy restaurants and in food trucks. He was successful in both settings, but it was the dramatic and instant triumph of his first food truck, Kogi BBQ, that really shook up the food world. Choi says that working in each of the two settings taught him important lessons, allowing him to master both cooking and marketing.

Choi went to Culinary school and then started working in hotel restaurants. What he learned in the theoretical world of culinary education did not prepare him for the real world of a busy hotel's kitchen.... [differences between what he was taught and the real world...]

After years of classical cooking, he decided to make the switch to a smaller, less formal setting--a food truck. He wanted... [advantages & disadvantages of the two settings & what he learned]

[Conclusion]

1 Which organizational pattern does the writer use?
2 How could you reorganize the information to follow the other organizational pattern?
3 What would you include in the conclusion?

My Writing

Exercise 6.3 Organizing Ideas

Read the writing prompt on page 406. Use the questions to organize your body paragraphs.

1 Review your work in My Writing in. Unit 26 Do you have three distinct comparisons or contrasts?
2 Create an outline for your body paragraphs.
3 Share your outline with a partner. Use the feedback to edit your outline.

Writing Concisely

Good academic writing is **concise**, which means the writers say what they want to say directly using the fewest number of words possible. One way to write concisely is to reduce clauses to phrases. This not only makes the writing more efficient, but it also demonstrates the ability to use complex sentence structure.

Exercise 6.4 Writing Body Paragraphs

Write your first draft of 2-3 body paragraphs.
- Use signal words and correlative conjunctions to compare and contrast.
- Reduce clauses to make your writing more concise.

28 Connecting Information with Prepositions and Transitions

Technology in Entertainment

1 Grammar in the Real World

ACADEMIC WRITING

Comparison and contrast

A How are video games today different from the games of 5 or 10 years ago? Read the article about a kind of animation technology that is being used in games today. How has it changed the look of video games?

B Comprehension Check Answer the questions.

1 What is "mocap"?

2 In what areas is mocap used?

3 Why isn't mocap used more often in movies and video games?

C Notice Match the words in bold with their meaning.

1 **Because of** the realism that mocap gives its animated figures, a common use for mocap is in video games. _____

2 **Furthermore,** mocap can be used in training for jobs such as firefighting. _____

3 **Despite** the expense, mocap technology is becoming more popular in many different areas. _____

a introduces additional information

b introduces a reason

c introduces contrasting information

MOTION CAPTURE TECHNOLOGY

Computer animation was first introduced in the late 1970s; **however**, today's animation is much more realistic than it was then. While the first animated video game characters moved in only two directions, today's animated
5   game heroes can jump, kick, and spin. The use of sensors[1] to record these movements is called motion capture, or "mocap."

Because of the realism that mocap gives its animated figures, a common use for mocap is in video games.
10 Video game creators use real people to help create their characters. With sports video games, for example, famous athletes are used **instead of** actors. **Consequently,** the games can feature each athlete's unique moves. How does it work? **First**, the athlete puts on a tight suit
15 that has special markers[2] all over it. **Next**, he or she performs a sequence of actions. Video cameras record these movements using the markers. **Finally**, digital information is collected from the markers and the video. This information is used to create the movements of the
20 video character.

Another common use of mocap is in movies. The makers of *Titanic* needed characters that could move realistically in a situation that would have been much too dangerous for a real actor. **As a result**, they used mocap.
25 **Besides being** completely safe, it was a lot cheaper and easier than filming people falling off a sinking ship!

In addition to these uses, motion capture technology is used in medicine. **For instance**, doctors have patients in mocap suits walk on treadmills. The mocap information
30 helps doctors diagnose problems such as weak bones. **Furthermore**, mocap can be used in training for jobs such as firefighting. New firefighters can use mocap games to practice moving through virtual[3] house fires. **Instead of** taking risks in a real setting, they can practice in a virtual
35 reality.

Despite the expense, mocap technology is becoming more popular in many different areas. **Due to** its success so far, who knows what it will be used for next?

---

[1]**sensor:** a device that discovers and reacts to changes in such things as movement, heat, and light

[2]**marker:** a small, reflective dot that is taped to a figure

[3]**virtual:** created by a computer

2 Connecting Information with Prepositions and Prepositional Phrases

Grammar Presentation

Some prepositions and prepositional phrases can connect information to an independent clause. Like subordinators, these prepositions can be used to add information, give reasons, show contrasts, present alternatives, or give exceptions.

Video games look realistic today **because of** improvements in computer animation.

Despite the popularity of animation, most people prefer to watch live-action movies.

2.1 Using Prepositions and Prepositional Phrases to Connect Ideas

A One-word prepositions, such as *besides* and *despite*, and multi-word prepositions, such as *as well as*, *because of*, *in addition to*, and *in spite of*, are followed by nouns, noun phrases, or gerunds.

Besides being very expensive, animated movies can take a long time to produce.

Some animated movies are also popular with adults **in spite of** their appeal to kids.

B Prepositional phrases, like adverb clauses, can come before or after the main clause. Use a comma when the prepositional phrase comes first.

Video games usually use athletes **instead of actors**.

Instead of actors, video games usually use athletes.

2.2 Meanings of Prepositions Used to Connect Ideas

A Use *as well as*, *besides*, and *in addition to* to emphasize another idea.

I enjoy animated movies **as well as** live-action movies.

This TV has 3D technology **in addition to** high definition.

Besides being a talented director, he is an excellent actor.

B Use *as a result of*, *because of*, and *due to* to give reasons.

Because of the high cost of tickets, many people don't go to the movies.

As a result of voters' opinions, the director was nominated for an Academy Award.

The movie's appeal is **due to** its special effects.

2.2 Meanings of Prepositions Used to Connect Ideas *(continued)*

C Use *instead of* to give alternatives.	Let's see a drama *instead of* a comedy. *Instead of* going out, they watched TV at home.
D Use *except* or *except for* to give exceptions. When the main clause is a negative statement, you can also use *besides* to mean "except for."	This composer wrote the music for all the Alien Adventures movies *except* the first one. *Except for* their parents, the audience was mostly children. *Besides* the parents of the children, there weren't any adults in the audience.
E Use *despite* and *in spite of* to show contrasting ideas.	*Despite* being made for children, this movie is enjoyed by adults. *In spite of* its short length, the movie was very powerful.

Grammar Application

Exercise 2.1 Prepositional Phrases to Connect Ideas

Complete the paragraphs about one use of motion capture technology. Use the words in the box. Sometimes more than one answer is possible.

as well as	because of	due to	in addition to	instead of	~~in spite of~~

In spite of the high cost of mocap, its use is expanding. For example, Ford
(1)
Motor Company, a car manufacturer, is using mocap technology to create digital
humans.[1] _Because of_ their human-like behavior, digital humans are used to
(2) *(Due to)*
study people's behavior in cars. _In addition to_ studying driver behavior, engineers
(3) *(As well as)*
are also studying ways to make passengers feel more comfortable. For example,
instead of using a real human, the company uses a short digital female to test
(4)
a short driver's ability to reach the gas pedal.

   Motion capture technology helps the company improve worker safety
as well as driver safety. _Due to_ the technology's ability to
(5) *(In addition to)*   (6) *(Because of)*
replicate workers' movements, the company has reduced the number of assembly
line accidents.

[1]**digital human:** an electronic representation of a person

Complete the sentences about using mocap technology to help athletes recover from injuries and improve their speed. Circle the correct prepositions.

1 (In addition to)/ Because of filmmakers, physical therapists are using motion capture technology to help injured athletes.

2 **As a result of / Instead of** an injury, athletes could lose their careers.

3 An athlete's career could be destroyed **because of / instead of** injuries.

4 Analyzing an injury without motion capture technology is not always accurate, **due to / besides** being time-consuming.

5 With motion capture technology, therapists accurately see the problem **in spite of / instead of** guessing where the problem is.

6 The success of motion capture technology with Olympic athletes is **in spite of / due to** its ability to analyze the athletes' movements at high speeds.

7 **Except for / Despite** the success of motion capture technology with athletes, it cannot replace the hours of practice that athletes need to succeed.

A Combine the ideas about the use of technology in health care. Use the prepositions in parentheses and the underlined words to create prepositional phrases.

1 Many hospitals are no longer using <u>paper medical records</u>. They are using electronic medical records. (instead of)

   Instead of paper medical records, some hospitals are using electronic records.

2 Everyone has <u>quick access to your records</u>. Doctors can share information with each other more easily. (Due to)

   Due to quick access to your records, doctors ~.

3 There are <u>many advantages to electronic records</u>. Some doctors still have serious concerns. (in spite of)

   In spite of many advantages ~, some doctors ~.

4 There should be <u>accurate information in the records</u>. The information could contain data input errors. (instead of)

   Instead of accurate ~, the information ~.

5 There will be <u>a lot of security</u>. Hackers could still steal information from hospitals. (despite)

   Despite a lot of security, hackers ~.

B Group Work Choose an area that is changing because of technology. Use one of the ideas below or your own idea. As a group, write statements that explain the technology, its effects, and the possible advantages and disadvantages of using it. Use prepositional phrases.

- high speed trains
- online learning
- use of cell phones instead of money to purchase products

3 Connecting Information with Transition Words

Grammar Presentation

Transition words are words or phrases that connect ideas between sentences. They are frequently used in academic writing and formal situations.	*It's important not to judge a movie's quality by whether it is animated or not.* **Furthermore,** *you should not assume that a movie with human actors is superior to an animated movie.*

3.1 Using Transition Words

A Transition words join the ideas in two sentences.	*Movie stars often do the voices in animated movies.* **However,** *their fans don't always recognize them.*
Coordinating conjunctions (*but*, etc.), subordinators (*although*, etc.), and prepositions (*in spite of*, etc.) combine two different sentences into one new sentence.	*Music in movies is very important for setting the tone,* **but** *most people don't pay attention to it.* **Although** *animated movies sometimes win the best picture award, they also have their own category.* **In spite of** *having a lot of famous actors, the movie did not get very good reviews.*
B Most transition words occur at the beginning of the second sentence and are followed by a comma. You can also use a semicolon between the two sentences that you combine.	*The studio executives choose a script.* **After that,** *they select a director.* *She is a very talented artist;* **moreover,** *her use of color is exceptional.*
Many – but not all – transition words can go in the middle of the sentence or at the end. When the transition word comes at the end, it is preceded by a comma.	*Most people,* **however,** *associate animation with movies.* *Most people associate animation with movies,* **however.**

3.1 | Using Transition Words (continued)

C The short transition words *so*, *then*, and *also* are often used without a comma. *So* is used at the beginning of a sentence only in informal writing.

Use more formal transition words with the same meanings in academic writing: *afterward*, *in addition*, *therefore*.

My daughter enjoys animated movies a lot. **So** *we take her to them pretty often.* **Then** *she usually wants to stop for a snack on the way home. I am* **also** *usually hungry after a long movie.*

Children often enjoy animated movies. **Therefore***, their parents often take them to the movies.* **Afterward***, it is not unusual to stop for something to eat.* **In addition***, parents often buy a book or souvenir connected to the movie for their children.*

3.2 | Meanings of Transition Words

A To show a sequence or the order of events or ideas, use *first, second, then, next, after that*, and *finally*.

How do animators capture an athlete's movement? **First***, the athlete puts on a special suit.* **Then** *the athlete performs the action.* **Next***, the computer collects digital information.*

B To summarize ideas, use *in conclusion, to conclude*, and *to summarize*.

In conclusion*, technological innovations will change many fields, including animation.*

C To give additional information, use *also, furthermore, in addition*, and *moreover*.

Animation is used in movies, video games, and other entertainment industries. **In addition***, it is used in sports medicine.*

D To give alternatives, use *instead*.

I had expected the movie to be boring. **Instead***, I thought it was quite entertaining.*

E To give contrasting ideas, use *on the other hand* and *in contrast*.

The story was not very original. **On the other hand***, the animation was impressive.*

F To give a result, use *as a result, consequently, therefore*, and *thus*.

The game was designed with animation. **Therefore***, the characters were very lifelike.*

G To give examples, use *for example* or *for instance*.

Many animated movies are very popular. **For example***, Kung Fu Panda and Despicable Me were huge box office hits.*

⊕ DATA FROM THE REAL WORLD

The most common transition words in writing are:	however, so, then, therefore, thus
The most common transition words in conversation are:	anyway, so, then, though

Grammar Application

Exercise 3.1 Transition Words to Show Sequence

A Pair Work Look at the steps involved in computer game design. Can you put them in the correct order? Make guesses with your partner and try to number the steps in order from 1 to 6.

_____ a Make a prototype (a model or "first draft") of the game and test it.

_____ b Work with the marketing team to get the game ready to sell.

__1__ c Decide on the theme and environment of the game.

_____ d Do research on the theme.

_____ e Figure out the goal of the game and the rules.

_____ f Make any necessary changes to the game.

B Now listen to a game designer describing her job. Were your answers correct?

C Listen again and complete the sentences. Use the sequence words in the box. Add commas when necessary.

after that	finally	first	next	second	then

1 _____*First,*_____ I decide on an overall concept for a game.

2 _____ I figure out the goal of the game and the rules.

3 _____ I do research on the theme.

4 _____ I use software to make a prototype of the game.

5 _____ I go back to the computer and make any necessary changes.

6 _____ I work with the marketing people.

Exercise 3.2 Transition Words for Academic Writing

Complete the paragraph about the differences between computer animation and traditional animation. Circle the correct transition words.

Computer-generated animation (CGA) is very popular today. The spectacular effects of CGA in big-budget movies impress many people. Therefore /(However), in my opinion, CGA is not as pleasant to look at as traditional animation (TA). **First / Afterward**, CGA does not require the same skill as TA. Traditional animators draw by hand, and the resulting images look complex and rich in style. **Instead / To summarize**, computer animators use software to produce images. These images often

Computer-Generated Animation

have a cold, hard look to them. **To conclude / Furthermore** ,
(4)
with CGA, objects are often overly bright. This adds to the
unnaturalness of their appearance. **In contrast / Thus** , the
(5)
images from TA are often soft and appear more natural.

In conclusion / Moreover , TA produces better-looking
(6)
images that have more style as well as a lifelike appearance;

on the other hand / therefore , it is better than CGA.
(7)

Traditional
Animation

Exercise 3.3 Using Transition Words

A Look at the brainstorming notes a student made for a paragraph comparing two movies.
Use the words to write sentences to summarize the ideas. Use the notes to help you.

War of the Aliens	The Magical Forest
excellent computer graphics dull plot[1] unappealing characters bad dialog	poor animation interesting story likeable characters good dialog

[1]**plot:** story

had → has

1 excellent computer graphics / in contrast / poor animation

   War of the Aliens had excellent computer graphics. In contrast,
   The Magical Forest had poor animation.

2 excellent computer graphics / however / dull plot

   War of the Aliens had excellent computer graphics. However, it
   had dull plot.

3 furthermore / unappealing characters

   Futhermore, War of the Aliens had unappealing characters.

4 on the other hand / interesting story

   On the other hand, The Magical Forest had an interesting scory.

5 in addition / likeable characters

   In addition, The Magical Forest had likeable characters.

6 moreover / good dialog

   Moreover, The Magical Forest had good dialog.

7 in contrast / bad dialog

   In contrast, War of the Aliens had bad dialog.

8 in conclusion / a better movie than

   In conclusion, The Magical Forest is a better movie
   than War of the Aliens.

B Over to You Think of two movies you have seen that have animation or special effects. Which one was better? Why? Write four to six sentences comparing the two movies. Use transitions to add ideas and show contrasts.

Cowboys in Space *was very popular. On the other hand,* Cowboys in Space II *didn't do very well.*

4 Avoid Common Mistakes ⚠

1 The prepositional expressions *as well as, in spite of, despite,* and *in addition to* are followed by a noun phrase or a gerund, not a subject + verb.

　　　　　the high costs
Despite ~~the costs are high~~, 3D TVs are becoming very popular.

　　　　　　　　　　　　　using
The filmmakers used mocap in addition to ~~they used~~ digital technology.

2 Use *on the other hand,* not *in the other hand,* when contrasting points of view.

　　　　　　　　　　　　　　　　　　　　on
The movie industry has many career opportunities; ~~in~~ the other hand, it is very competitive.

Editing Task

Find and correct four more mistakes in the paragraph about the filmmaking industry.

　　　　　　　　　　　　　　　　　　　　　the slow economy
　　　　Filmmaking is a durable industry. Despite ~~the economy is slow~~, the movie industry is
doing well. People always seem to find money for entertainment. As a result, movie production
companies often hire people because it takes many professionals to create a movie. In addition
to they hire actors and directors, they hire tens of thousands of other professionals that are
5　not well known – for example, grips (people who set up and tear down the sets), production
assistants, and camera operators. The jobs can be exciting and challenging; in the other
hand, some can be low paying. As with most other careers, it is necessary to work hard and
be ambitious to succeed. The work can also be especially tough for production crews – for
example, camera operators, production assistants, and makeup artists – who work up to 18
10　hours a day. Despite they have long hours, these jobs can be difficult to find because there is
a lot of competition for them. In general, moviemaking is seen as a glamorous profession, and
some people want to be a part of that glamor more than anything else. Movies often require
celebrities and artists; in the other hand, they also rely on many people with other skills. It is a
growing industry, too. The Bureau of Labor Statistics states that employment opportunities for
15　people in the filmmaking industry will increase 12 percent between now and 2016. In short, this
industry is competitive, but young people should pursue it if they have an interest in movies.

5 Academic Writing

Comparison and Contrast

Brainstorm > Organize > Write > Edit

In Unit 27, you focused on ways to organize your essay and wrote the first draft of your body paragraphs for the prompt below. In this unit (28), you will write your introduction and conclusion, and then revise and edit your essay.

> Not all products and services fit the same business model. Some might have a more successful introduction in a mobile setting. For others, a mobile setting would not be appropriate. Compare and contrast two products or services regarding their potential as a mobile business.

Connecting the Conclusion to the Introduction

Introductory and concluding paragraphs are connected in several ways, but concluding paragraphs are usually shorter. Conclusions summarize the thesis statement and key ideas in the essay, and they clearly state inferences drawn from the body paragraphs. They also include a final thought or conclusion such as a recommendation, call for action, or request to reconsider ways of thinking. Strong conclusions often return to the hook. For example, if the writer began with a question, the essay should end with a clear answer. If the writer began with an anecdote or story, it should be mentioned in the conclusion.

Exercise 5.1 Applying the Skill

Work with a partner. Read the introductory paragraph of an essay on motion capture movies. Discuss ideas for the concluding paragraph. What will it include?

Have you seen the latest *Avengers* movie? The action and characters are all extremely life-like, and you may feel like you are in the room with them. That is because significant parts were filmed by motion, or performance, capture. Motion capture is a type of film recording that captures the movement of an actor, while the rest of the scene is generated on a computer. It looks and feels very different than traditional filmmaking. While both techniques are popular in today's movies, motion capture has several advantages over traditional filmmaking.

My Writing

Exercise 5.2 Planning and Writing Your Essay

Review your body paragraphs from My Writing in Unit 27. Complete the tasks.

1 Plan your introduction and conclusion.

- What is your thesis? What hook can you use to get your reader's attention?
- What are the main ideas in your body paragraphs?
- What important inferences can you draw from your body paragraphs?
- How can you link your conclusion to your introduction?

2 Write an introduction and conclusion for the ideas and content of your essay.

Exercise 5.3 Revising Your Ideas

1 Work with a partner. Use the questions to give feedback on your partner's essay.

- Which of your partner's ideas seem strongest to you?
- Which of your partner's ideas needs to be explained more clearly?
- What could your partner add or remove to make the essay easier to understand?

2 Use the feedback from your partner to revise the ideas and content of your essay.

Exercise 5.4 Editing Your Writing

Use the checklist to review and edit your essay.

Did you answer the writing prompt completely?	
Did you give some background information on mobile retail in your introduction?	
Did you use an appropriate organizational structure for comparison and contrast?	
Did you use signal words and phrases, and coordinating and correlative conjunctions to compare and contrast?	
Does your concluding paragraph include a final thought for your readers?	

Exercise 5.5 Editing Your Grammar

Use the checklist to review and edit the grammar in your essay.

Did you use coordinating and correlative conjunctions correctly?	
Did you use subordinators and adverb clauses correctly?	
Did you reduce adverb clauses correctly?	
Did you accurately connect information with prepositional phrases and transitions?	
Did you avoid the common mistakes in the charts on page 391, 405, and 417?	

Exercise 5.6 Writing Your Final Draft

Apply the feedback and edits from Exercises 5.3 to 5.5 to write the final draft of your essay.

Appendices

1 Irregular Verbs

Base Form	Simple Past	Past Participle	Base Form	Simple Past	Past Participle
be	was/were	been	hide	hid	hidden
become	became	become	hit	hit	hit
begin	began	begun	hold	held	held
bite	bit	bitten	hurt	hurt	hurt
blow	blew	blown	keep	kept	kept
break	broke	broken	know	knew	known
bring	brought	brought	leave	left	left
build	built	built	lose	lost	lost
buy	bought	bought	make	made	made
catch	caught	caught	meet	met	met
choose	chose	chosen	pay	paid	paid
come	came	come	put	put	put
cost	cost	cost	read	read	read
cut	cut	cut	ride	rode	ridden
do	did	done	run	ran	run
draw	drew	drawn	say	said	said
drink	drank	drunk	see	saw	seen
drive	drove	driven	sell	sold	sold
eat	ate	eaten	send	sent	sent
fall	fell	fallen	set	set	set
feed	fed	fed	shake	shook	shaken
feel	felt	felt	show	showed	shown
fight	fought	fought	shut	shut	shut
find	found	found	sing	sang	sung
fly	flew	flown	sit	sat	sat
forget	forgot	forgotten	sleep	slept	slept
forgive	forgave	forgiven	speak	spoke	spoken
get	got	gotten	spend	spent	spent
give	gave	given	stand	stood	stood
go	went	gone	steal	stole	stolen
grow	grew	grown	swim	swam	swum
have	had	had	take	took	taken
hear	heard	heard	teach	taught	taught

Irregular Verbs (*continued*)

Base Form	Simple Past	Past Participle	Base Form	Simple Past	Past Participle
tell	told	told	wake	woke	woken
think	thought	thought	wear	wore	worn
throw	threw	thrown	win	won	won
understand	understood	understood	write	wrote	written

2 Stative (Non-Action) Verbs

Stative verbs do not describe actions. They describe states or situations. Stative verbs are not usually used in the progressive. Some are occasionally used in the present progressive, but often with a different meaning.

Research shows that the 25 most common stative verbs in spoken and written English are:

agree	dislike	hope	love	see
believe	expect	hurt	need	seem
care (about)	hate	know	notice	think
cost	have	like	own	understand
disagree	hear	look like	prefer	want

Other stative verbs:

appear	deserve	mean	smell
be	feel	owe	sound
belong	forgive	recognize	taste
concern	look	remember	weigh
contain	matter		

Stative verbs that also have action meanings:

be	have	look	taste
expect	hear	see	think
feel	hope	smell	weigh

Using the present progressive form of these verbs changes the meaning to an action.
Can you **see** the red car? (= use your eyes to be aware of something)
I'**m seeing** an old friend tomorrow. (= meeting someone)
I **think** you're right. (= believe)
Dina **is thinking** of taking a vacation soon. (= considering)
I **have** two sisters. (= be related to)
We'**re having** eggs for breakfast. (= eating)
He **is** in his first year of college. (= exist)
She **is being** difficult. (= act)

3 Modals and Modal-like Expressions

Modals are helper verbs. Most modals have multiple meanings.

Function	Modal or Modal-like Expression	Time	Example
Advice less strong	*could* *might (not)*	present, future	He **could** do some puzzles to improve his memory. You **might** try some tips on improving your memory.
stronger	*ought to* *should (not)*	present, future	We **ought to** take a memory class next month. Greg **should** improve his memory.
	had better (not)	present, future	You**'d better** pay attention now.
Past Advice, Regret, or Criticism	*ought to have* *should (not) have*	past	She **ought to have** tried harder to improve her memory. You **should have** made an effort to improve your memory. He **shouldn't have** taken that difficult class.
Permission	*can (not)* *may (not)*	present, future	You **can** register for the class next week. You **may not** register after the first class.
	could (not)	past	You **could** ask questions during the lecture yesterday, but you **could not** leave the room.
formal →	*be (not) allowed to* *be (not) permitted to*	past, present, future	He **was not allowed to** talk during the test, but he **was allowed** to use his books. Students **will not be permitted to** refer to notes during examinations.
Necessity/ Obligation	*have to* *need to* *be required to* *be supposed to*	past, present, future	I **have to** study tonight. She **needs to** quit her stressful job. You **won't be required to** take a test. He **is supposed to** tell you his decision tomorrow.
	must (not)	present, future	You **must** have experience for this job.
Obligation not to/ Prohibition	*must not* *be not supposed to*	present, future	You **must not** talk during the exam. Students **are not supposed to** take their books into the exam room.

Modals and Modal-like Expressions *(continued)*

Function	Modal or Modal-like Expression	Time	Example
Lack of Necessity/ Choices or Options	not have to not need to be not required to	past, present, future	You **didn't have to** bring your notes. You **don't need to** study tonight. You **are not required to** bring your books.
Ability	can (not)	present, future	We **can** meet the professor at noon tomorrow.
	could (not)	past	I **could** understand the lecture, but I **could not** remember it.
	be (not) able to	past, present, future	She **wasn't able to** see very well from her seat.
	could have	past	I **could have** done well on that memory test.
	could not have	past	I **couldn't have** taken the test yesterday. I was in another state!
Probability	can't could (not) (not) have to must (not)	present	Hackers **can't** be interested in my data. He **could** be online now. She **has to** be at work right now. He **must not** be worried about data security.
	may (not) might (not) ought to should (not)	present, future	Your computer **may** be at risk of hacking. That software **might not** be good enough. That password **ought to** be strong enough. It **shouldn't** be difficult to find good software.
	could will (not)	future	The company **could** start using cloud computing next month. My sister **will** probably get a new computer soon.
	can't have could (not) have may (not) have might (not) have must (not) have	past	I **can't have** entered the wrong password! The expert **could not have** given you good advice. The company **may have** been careless with security. I **might have** written the wrong password down. Someone **must have** stolen all the passwords.

4 Noncount Nouns and Measurement Words to Make Noncount Nouns Countable

Category of Noncount Noun	Noun Examples	Measurement Words and Expressions
Abstract concepts	courage, luck, space, time	a bit of, a kind of *You had **a bit of** luck, didn't you?*
Activities and sports	dancing, exercise, swimming, tennis, yoga	a game of, a session of *They played **two games of** tennis.*
Diseases and health conditions	arthritis, cancer, depression, diabetes, obesity	a kind of, a type of *She has **a type of** diabetes called Type 2.*
Elements and gases	gold, hydrogen, oxygen, silver	a bar of, a container of, a piece of, a tank of *We have **tanks of** oxygen in the storage room.*
Foods	beef, broccoli, cheese, rice	a bottle of, a box of, a bunch of, a can of, a grain of, a head of, a loaf of, a package of, a piece of, a pinch of, a serving of, a slice of, a wedge of *I'll take **a serving of** rice and beef.*
Liquids	coffee, gasoline, oil, tea	a bottle of, a cup of, a gallon of, a glass of, a quart of *I would like **a cup of** tea.*
Natural phenomena	electricity, rain, sun, thunder	a bolt of, a drop of, a ray of *There hasn't been **a drop of** rain for three months.*
Particles	pepper, salt, sand, sugar	a grain of, a pinch of *My food needs **a pinch of** salt.*
Subjects and areas of work	construction, economics, genetics, geology, medicine, nursing	an area of, a branch of, a field of, a type of *There are a lot of specialty areas in **the field of** medicine.*
Miscellaneous	clothing, equipment, furniture, news	an article of, a piece of *I need **a piece of** furniture to go in that empty corner.*

5 Order of Adjectives Before Nouns

When you use two (or more) adjectives before a noun, use the order in the chart below.

Opinion	Size	Quality	Age	Shape	Color	Origin	Material	Nouns as Adjectives
beautiful	big	cold	ancient	oval	black	American	cotton	computer
comfortable	fat	free	antique	rectangular	blue	Canadian	glass	evening
delicious	huge	heavy	new	round	gold	Chinese	gold	government
expensive	large	hot	old	square	green	European	leather	rose
interesting	long	safe	young	triangular	orange	Japanese	metal	safety
nice	short				purple	Mexican	paper	software
pretty	small				red	Peruvian	plastic	summer
rare	tall				silver	Thai	silk	training
reasonable	thin				yellow		silver	
shocking	wide				white		stone	
special							wooden	
ugly							woolen	
unique								

Examples:
*That was a **delicious green Canadian** apple!* (opinion before color before origin)
*I saw the **shocking government** report on nutrition.* (opinion before noun as adjective)
*Wei got a **small oval glass** table.* (size before shape before material)

6 Verbs That Can Be Used Reflexively

allow oneself	challenge oneself	hurt oneself	remind oneself
amuse oneself	congratulate oneself	imagine oneself	see oneself
ask oneself	cut oneself	introduce oneself	take care of
be hard on oneself	dry oneself	keep oneself (busy)	talk to oneself
be oneself	enjoy oneself	kill oneself	teach oneself
be pleased with oneself	feel sorry for oneself	look after oneself	tell oneself
be proud of oneself	forgive oneself	look at oneself	treat oneself
behave oneself	get oneself	prepare oneself	
believe in oneself	give oneself	pride oneself on	
blame oneself	help oneself	push oneself	

7 Verbs Followed by Gerunds Only

admit	keep (= continue)
avoid	mind (= object to)
consider	miss
delay	postpone
defend	practice
deny	propose
discuss	quit
enjoy	recall (= remember)
finish	risk
imagine	suggest
involve	understand

8 Verbs Followed by Infinitives Only

afford	help	pretend
agree	hesitate	promise
arrange	hope	refuse
ask	hurry	request
attempt	intend	seem
choose	learn	struggle
consent	manage	tend (= *be likely*)
decide	need	threaten
demand	neglect	volunteer
deserve	offer	wait
expect	pay	want
fail	plan	wish
forget	prepare	would like

9 Verbs Followed by Gerunds or Infinitives

begin	like	regret*
continue	love	start
forget*	prefer	stop*
get	remember*	try*
hate		

*These verbs can be followed by a gerund or an infinitive, with a difference in meaning.

10 Expressions with Gerunds

Use a gerund after certain fixed verb expressions.

Verb expressions	
spend time / spend money waste time / waste money have trouble / have difficulty / have a difficult time	*I **spent time helping** in the library.* *Don't **waste time complaining**.* *She **had trouble finishing** her degree.*

Use a gerund after certain fixed noun + preposition expressions.

Noun + preposition expressions	
an excuse for in favor of an interest in a reason for	*I have **an excuse for not doing** my homework.* *Who is **in favor of not admitting** him?* *He has **an interest in getting** a scholarship.* *He has **a reason for choosing** this school.*

11 Verbs + Objects + Infinitives

advise	force	remind	ask*
allow	get	request	choose*
cause	hire	require	expect*
challenge	invite	teach	help*
convince	order	tell	need*
enable	permit	urge	pay*
encourage	persuade	warn	promise*
forbid			want*
			wish*

* These verbs can be followed by an object + infinitive
or an infinitive only, with a difference in meaning.

Examples:
*My boss **advised me to go** back to school.*
*They **urged the advertisers not to surprise** people.*
*My department **chose* Sally to create** the new ads.*
*My department **chose* to create** the new ads.*

12 *Be* + Adjectives + Infinitives

be afraid	be delighted	be encouraged	be lucky	be sad
be amazed	be depressed	be excited	be necessary	be shocked
be angry	be determined	be fortunate	be pleased	be sorry
be anxious	be difficult	be fun	be proud	be surprised
be ashamed	be easy	be happy	be ready	be upset
be curious	be embarrassed	be likely	be relieved	be willing

13 Verbs + Prepositions

Verb + **about**	Verb + **by**	Verb + **of**	Verb + **to**
ask about	be affected by	be afraid of	admit to
care about	be raised by	approve of	belong to
complain about	Verb + **for**	be aware of	confess to
be excited about	apologize for	consist of	listen to
find out about	apply for	dream of	look forward to
forget about	ask for	be guilty of	refer to
hear about	care for	hear of	talk to
know about	look for	know of	be used to
learn about	pay for	take care of	Verb + **with**
read about	be responsible for	think of	agree with
see about	wait for	be warned of	argue with
talk about	Verb + **from**	Verb + **on**	bother with
think about	graduate from	concentrate on	deal with
worry about	Verb + **in**	count on	start with
be worried about	believe in	decide on	work with
Verb + **against**	find in	depend on	
advise against	include in	insist on	
decide against	be interested in	keep on	
Verb + **at**	involve in	plan on	
look at	result in	rely on	
smile at	show in		
be successful at	succeed in		
	use in		

14 Adjectives + Prepositions

Adjective + **about**	Adjective + **by**	Adjective + **in**	Adjective + **to**
concerned about	amazed by	high in	accustomed to
excited about	bored by	interested in	due to
happy about	surprised by	low in	similar to
nervous about	Adjective + **for**	Adjective + **of**	Adjective + **with**
pleased about	bad for	accused of	bored with
sad about	good for	afraid of	content with
sorry about	ready for	ashamed of	familiar with
surprised about	responsible for	aware of	good with
upset about	Adjective + **from**	capable of	satisfied with
worried about	different from	careful of	wrong with
Adjective + **at**	safe from	full of	
amazed at	separate from	guilty of	
angry at		sick of	
bad at		tired of	
good at		warned of	
successful at			
surprised at			

15 Verbs and Fixed Expressions that Introduce Indirect Questions

Do you have any idea …?	I'd like to know …?	I don't know …?
Can you tell me …?	I wonder / I'm wondering …?	I'm not sure …?
Do you know …?	I want to understand …?	I can't imagine …?
Do you remember …?	Let's find out …?	We don't understand …?
Could you explain …?	Let's ask …?	It doesn't say …?
Would you show me …?	We need to know …?	I can't believe …?

16 Tense Shifting in Indirect Speech

Direct Speech	Indirect (Reported) Speech
simple present She said, "The boss is angry."	**simple past** She **said** (that) the boss **was** angry.
present progressive He said, "She **is enjoying** the work."	**past progressive** He **said** (that) she **was enjoying** the work.
simple past They said, "The store **closed** last year."	**past perfect** They **said** (that) the store **had closed** last year.
present perfect The manager said, "The group **has done** good work."	**past perfect** The manager **said** (that) the group **had done** good work.
will He said, "The department **will add** three new managers."	**would** He **said** (that) the department **would add** three new managers.
be going to She said, "They **are going to hire** more people soon."	**be going to** (past form) She **said** (that) they **were going to hire** more people soon.
can The teacher said, "The students **can work** harder."	**could** The teacher said (that) the students could work harder.
may Their manager said, "Money **may not be** very important to them."	**might** Their manager **said** (that) money **might not be** very important to them.

* Note: *should, might, ought to,* and *could* do not change forms.

17 Reporting Verbs

Questions	Statements				Commands and Requests	
ask	admit	convince	notify	show	advise	request
inquire	announce	exclaim	observe	state	ask	say
question	assert	explain	promise	suggest	command	tell
	assure	find	remark	swear	demand	urge
	claim	indicate	remind	yell	order	warn
	comment	inform	reply			
	complain	mention	report			
	confess	note	shout			

18 Passive Forms

	Active	Passive
present progressive	*People are speaking English at the meeting.*	*English is being spoken at the meeting.*
simple present	*People speak English at the meeting.*	*English is spoken at the meeting.*
simple past	*People spoke English at the meeting.*	*English was spoken at the meeting.*
past progressive	*People were speaking English at the meeting.*	*English was being spoken at the meeting.*
present perfect	*People have spoken English at the meeting.*	*English has been spoken at the meeting.*
past perfect	*People had been speaking English at the meeting.*	*English had been spoken at the meeting.*
simple future	*People will speak English at the meeting.*	*English will be spoken at the meeting.*
future perfect	*People will have spoken English at the meeting.*	*English will have been spoken at the meeting.*
***be going to* (future)**	*People are going to speak English at the meeting.*	*English is going to be spoken at the meeting.*
Questions	*Do people speak English at the meeting?* *Did people speak English at the meeting?* *Have people spoken English at the meeting?*	*Is English spoken at the meeting?* *Was English spoken at the meeting?* *Has English been spoken at the meeting?*

19 Relative Clauses

	Identifying	Nonidentifying
Subject Relative Clauses	Many people **who / that support the environment** recycle.	My sister, **who lives in Maine**, loves being outside.
	Electricity **that / which saves energy** is a good thing.	People power, **which is a way to create energy**, is popular.
	They are the scientists **whose research has won awards**.	Brad Pitt, **whose movies are well known**, gives a lot of money to environmental causes.
Object Relative Clauses	Detectives are people (**who / whom / that**) **I respect tremendously**.	The character Sherlock Holmes, who / **whom Arthur Conan Doyle created**, was a fictional detective.
	Evidence (**which / that**) **criminals leave at the crime scene** is called forensic evidence.	Evidence from criminals, **which we call forensic evidence**, can help police solve cases.
	The person **whose car the thieves stole** was a friend of mine.	Arthur Conan Doyle, **whose medical clinic not many patients attended**, had time to write his stories.
Object Relative Clauses as Objects of Prepositions	There's the police officer (**that / who / whom**) **I spoke to**. (informal) There's the police officer **to whom I spoke**. (formal)	There's Officer Smith, **who / whom I spoke to yesterday**. (informal) There's Officer Smith, **to whom I spoke yesterday**. (formal)
	Police found evidence from the crime scene under the chair (**that / which**) **I was sitting on**. (informal) Police found evidence from the crime scene under the chair **on which I was sitting**. (formal)	The door, **which I entered through**, had been broken during the robbery. (informal) The door, **through which I entered**, had been broken during the robbery. (formal)
Relative Clauses with *Where* and *in Which*	It's a city **where you can find Wi-Fi almost everywhere**. It's a city in **which you can find Wi-Fi almost everywhere**.	The city of Atlanta, **where my sister lives**, is very large. The city of Atlanta, **in which my sister lives**, is very large.
Relative Clauses with *When* and *During Which*	Night is a time **when many students study for exams**. Night is a time **during which many students study for exams**.	Joe prefers to study at night, **when his children are asleep**. Joe prefers to study at night, **during which his children are asleep**.

Relative Clauses (*continued*)

Participle Phrases	Students **concerned with the environment** should get involved in environmental groups on campus.	Millennials, **raised in the era of technology, cell phones, and the Internet**, understand technology very well.
	The expert **giving tomorrow's talk on Millennials** is very well known.	The movie Twilight, **starring Millennials**, is based on a book by Gen Xer Stephenie Meyer.
Prepositional Phrases	The computers **in our classroom** are fast. Young workers **low in self-esteem** are unusual.	
Appositives		Jan Smith, **the president of Myco**, will be speaking at noon today. Jan Smith (**the president of Myco**) will be speaking at noon today. (formal writing)

20 Conditionals

Situation	Tense	*If* clause	Main clause	Example
Real Conditionals	present	simple present	simple present	If a website **is** popular, people **talk** about it.
	future	simple present	future	If you only **listen** to one station, you **will hear** only one opinion.
Unreal Conditionals	present	simple past or past progressive	would, could, might + base form of verb	If I **studied** every day, I **would pass** all my tests. If I **weren't dreaming** all day, I **would pass** all my tests.
	future	simple past	would, could, might + base form of verb	If our school **closed** next year, we **wouldn't have** a place to learn.
	past	past perfect	would have, could have, might have + past participle	If the city **had hired** more teachers, the schools **might have improved**.
Wishes	**Tense**	*that* clause		**Example**
	present	simple past, past progressive, could		I wish (that) schools **were improving**.
	future	were going to, would, could		I wish (that) the teachers **were going to** give us a party.
	past	past perfect		I **wish** (that) I **had studied** more.

Glossary of Grammar Terms

action verb a verb that describes an action.
> I **eat** breakfast every day.
> They **ran** in the 5K race.

active sentence a sentence that focuses on the doer and the action.
> **Jorge played** basketball yesterday.

adjective a word that describes or modifies a noun.
> That's a **beautiful** hat.

adjective clause *see* **relative clause**

adverb a word that describes or modifies a verb, another adverb, or an adjective. Adverbs often end in -ly.
> Please walk **faster** but **carefully**.

adverb clause a clause that shows how ideas are connected. Adverb clauses begin with subordinators such as *because, since, although, and even though.*
> **Although it is not a holiday**, workers have the day off.

adverb of degree an adverb that makes other adverbs or adjectives stronger or weaker.
> The test was **extremely** difficult. They are **really** busy today.

adverb of frequency an adverb such as *always, often, sometimes, never,* and *usually* that describes how often something happens.
> She **always** arrives at work on time.

adverb of manner an adverb that describes how an action happens.
> He has **suddenly** left the room.

adverb of time an adverb that describes when something happens.
> She'll get up **later**.

agent the noun or pronoun performing the action of the verb in a sentence.
> **People** spoke English at the meeting.

appositive a reduced form of a nonidentifying relative clause. Appositives are formed by removing the relative pronoun and the verb *be*, leaving only a noun phrase.
> Jan Smith, **an expert on Millennials**, will be speaking at noon today.

article the words *a/an* and *the*. An article introduces or identifies a noun.
> I bought **a** new cell phone. **The** price was reasonable.

auxiliary verb (also called **helping verb**) a verb that is used before a main verb in a sentence. *Do, have, be,* and *will* can act as auxiliary verbs.
> **Does** he want to go to the library later? **Have** you received the package? **Will** he arrive soon?

base form of the verb the form of a verb without any endings (-s or -ed) or to.

come   go   take

clause a group of words that has a subject and a verb. There are two types of clauses: **main clauses** and **dependent clauses** (*see* **dependent clause**). A sentence can have more than one clause.

MAIN CLAUSE   DEPENDENT CLAUSE   MAIN CLAUSE
I woke up when I heard the noise. It was scary.

common noun a word for a person, place, or thing. A common noun is not capitalized.

mother   building   fruit

comparative the form of an adjective or adverb that shows how two people, places, or things are different.

*My daughter is **older than** my son.* (adjective)
*She does her work **more quickly** than he does.* (adverb)

conditional a sentence that describes a possible situation and the result of that situation. It can be a real or unreal condition / result about the present, past, or future.

If a website is popular, people talk about it. (present real conditional)
If I had studied harder, I would have passed that course. (past unreal conditional)

conjunction a word such as *and*, *but*, *so*, *or*, and *yet* that connects single words, phrases, or clauses.

*We finished all our work, **so** we left early.*
Some more conjunctions are *after, as, because, if, and when.*

consonant a sound represented in writing by these letters of the alphabet: ***b, c, d, f, g, h, j, k, l, m, n, p, q, r, s, t, v, w, x, y,*** and ***z.***

count noun a person, place, or thing you can count. Count nouns have a plural form.

*There are three **banks** on Oak Street.*

definite article *the* is the definite article. Use *the* with a person, place, or thing that is familiar to you and your listener. Use *the* when the noun is unique – there is only one (*the sun, the moon, the Internet*). Also use *the* before a singular noun used to represent a whole class or category.

The *movie we saw last week was very good.*
The *Earth is round.*
The *male robin is more colorful than **the** female.*

dependent clause a clause that cannot stand alone. A dependent clause is not a complete sentence, but it still has a subject and verb. Some kinds of dependent clauses are adverb clauses, relative clauses, and time clauses.

After we return from the trip, *I'm going to need to relax.*

determiner a word that comes before a noun to limit its meaning in some way. Some common determiners are *some, a little, a lot, a few, this, that, these, those, his, a, an, the, much,* and *many.*

These *computers have **a lot** of parts.*
*Please give me **my** book.*

direct object the person or thing that receives the action of the verb.

*The teacher gave the students **a test**.*

direct question a type of direct speech (see **direct speech**) that repeats a person's question.

*The president asked, **"Who were your best employees last month?"***

direct speech (also called **quoted speech**) repeats people's exact words. A direct speech statement consists of a reporting clause and the exact words of a person inside quotation marks.

*The manager said, **"Workers need to use creativity."***

factual conditional *see* **present real conditional**

formal a style of writing or speech used when you don't know the other person very well or where it's not appropriate to show familiarity, such as in business, a job interview, speaking to a stranger, or speaking to an older person who you respect.

Good evening. I'd like to speak with Ms. Smith. Is she available?

future a verb form that describes a time that hasn't come yet. It is expressed in English by *will*, *be going to*, and present tense.

*I'**ll meet** you tomorrow.*

*I'**m going to visit** my uncle and aunt next weekend.*

*My bus **leaves** at 10:00 tomorrow.*

*I'**m meeting** Joe on Friday.*

future real conditional describes a possible situation in the future and the likely result. The *if* clause uses the simple present. The main clause uses a future form of the verb.

*If you only **listen** to one station, you **will hear** only one opinion.*

future unreal conditional describes an imaginary situation in the future. The *if* clause uses the simple past. The main clause uses the modals *would*, *could*, or *might*.

*If teachers **prepared** students better for exams, more students **would pass**.*

gerund the *-ing* form of a verb that is used as a noun. It can be the subject or object of a sentence or the object of a preposition.

*We suggested **waiting** and **going** another day.*

*Salsa **dancing** is a lot of fun.*

*I look forward to **meeting** you.*

habitual past a verb form that describes repeated past actions, habits, and conditions using *used to* or *would*.

*Before we had the Internet, we **used to** go to the library a lot.*

*Before there was refrigeration, people **would** use ice to keep food cool.*

helping verb *see* **auxiliary verb**

***if* clause** the condition clause in a conditional. It describes the possible situation, which can be either real or unreal.

***If it rains tomorrow**, I'll stay home.*

imperative a type of clause that tells people to do something. It gives instructions, directions to a place, and advice. The verb is in the base form.

***Listen** to the conversation.*

***Don't open** your books.*

***Turn** right at the bank and then **go** straight.*

indefinite article *a / an* are the indefinite articles. Use *a / an* with a singular person, place, or thing when you and your listener are not familiar with it, or when the specific name of it is not important. Use *a* with consonant sounds. Use *an* with vowel sounds.

*She's going to see **a** doctor today.*

*I had **an** egg for breakfast.*

indefinite pronoun a pronoun used when the noun is unknown or not important. There is an indefinite pronoun for people, for places, and for things. Some examples are *somebody, anyone, nobody, somewhere, anywhere, nothing, everything*, etc. Use singular verb forms when the indefinite pronoun is the subject of the sentence.

***Everybody** is going to be there. There is **nowhere** I'd rather work.*

indirect object the person or thing that receives the direct object.

*The teacher gave **the students** a test.*

indirect question (also called **reported question**) tells what other people have asked or asks a question using a statement. There are two kinds of indirect questions: *Yes / No* and information questions. Indirect questions follow the *subject-verb* word order of a statement.

*Mia **asked whether** we **would begin** Creative Problem Solving soon.*

*The president asked **who** my best employees **were** last month.*

indirect speech (also called **reported speech**) tells what someone says in another person's words. An indirect speech statement consists of a reporting verb (see **reporting verb**) such as *say* in the main clause, followed by a *that* clause. *That* is optional and is often omitted in speaking.

*He **said** (that) she **was enjoying** the work.*

infinitive *to* + the base form of a verb.

*I need **to get** home early tonight.*

infinitive of purpose *in order* + infinitive expresses a purpose. It answers the question *why*. If the meaning is clear, it is not necessary to use *in order*.

*People are fighting (**in order) to change** unfair laws.*

informal is a style of speaking to friends, family, and children.

Hey, there. Nice to see you again.

information question (also called ***Wh-* question**) begins with a *wh*-word (*who, what, when, where, which, why, how, how much*). To answer this type of question, you need to provide information rather than answer *yes* or *no*.

inseparable phrasal verb a phrasal verb that cannot be separated. The verb and its particle always stay together.

*My car **broke down** yesterday.*

intransitive verb a verb that does not need an object. It is often followed by an expression of time, place, or manner. It cannot be used in the passive.

*The flight **arrived** at 5.30 p.m.*

irregular adjective an adjective that does not change its form in the usual way. For example, you do not make the comparative form by adding *-er*.

good → *better*

irregular adverb an adverb that does not change its form in the usual way. For example, you do not make the comparative form by adding *-ly*.

badly → *worse*

irregular verb a verb that does not change its form in the usual way. For example, it does not form the simple past with *-d* or *-ed*. It has its own special form.

go → *went*   *ride* → *rode*   *hit* → *hit*

main clause (also called **independent clause**) a clause that can be used alone as a complete sentence. In a conditional, the main clause describes the result when the condition exists.

*After I get back from my trip, **I'm going to relax**.*

*If I hear about a good story, **I move quickly to get there and report it**.*

main verb a verb that functions alone in a clause and can have an auxiliary verb.

*They **had** a meeting last week.*

*They have **had** many meetings this month.*

measurement word a word or phrase that shows the amount of something. Measurement words can be singular or plural. They can be used to make noncount nouns countable.

*I bought **a box** of cereal, and Sonia bought **five pounds** of apples.*

modal a verb such as *can, could, have to, may, might, must, should, will*, and *would*. It modifies the main verb to show such things as ability, permission, possibility, advice, obligation, necessity, or lack of necessity.

*It **might** rain later today.*

*You **should** study harder if you want to pass this course.*

non-action verb *see* **stative verb**

noncount noun refers to ideas and things that you cannot count. Noncount nouns use a singular verb and do not have a plural form.

*Do you download **music**?*

noun a word for a person, place, or thing. There are common nouns and proper nouns. (*see* **common nouns, proper nouns**)

COMMON NOUN	PROPER NOUN
*I stayed in a **hotel** on my trip to New York.*	*I stayed in the **Ace Hotel**.*

object a noun or pronoun that usually follows the verb and receives the action.

*I sent **the flowers**. I sent **them** to **you**.*

object pronoun replaces a noun in the object position.

*Sara loves exercise classes. She takes **them** three times a week.*

participle phrase a reduced form of an identifying relative clause. Participle phrases are formed by removing the relative pronoun and the verb *be*. Participle phrases can be used when the verb in the relative clause is in the form verb + *-ing* (present participle) or the past participle form.

*He is the person **using the Internet too much at work**.*

particle a small word like *down*, *in*, *off*, *on*, *out*, or *up*. These words (which can also be prepositions) are used with verbs to form **two-word verbs** or **phrasal verbs**. The meaning of a phrasal verb often has a different meaning from the meaning of the individual words in it.

passive sentence a sentence that focuses on the action or on the person or thing receiving the action. The object is in the subject position.

English was spoken at the meeting.

past participle a verb form that can be regular (base form + *-ed*) or irregular. It is used to form perfect tenses and the passive. It can also be an adjective.

I've studied English for five years.

The frightened child cried.

past progressive a verb form that describes events or situations in progress at a time in the past. The emphasis is on the action.

They were watching TV when I arrived.

past unreal conditional describes a situation that was not true in the past. Past unreal conditionals describe something that was possible but did not happen. The *if* clause uses the past perfect. The main clause uses the modals *would have*, *could have*, or *might have* and the past participle form of the verb.

If we hadn't had a hurricane, the schools wouldn't have closed.

phrasal verb (also called **two-word verb**) consists of a verb + a particle. There are two kinds of phrasal verbs: separable and inseparable. (*see* **particle, inseparable phrasal verbs, separable phrasal verbs**)

    VERB + PARTICLE

They came back from vacation today. (inseparable)

Please put your cell phone away. (separable)

phrase a group of words about an idea that is not a complete sentence. It does not have a main verb.

across the street   in the morning

plural noun a noun that refers to more than one person, place, or thing.

students   women   roads

possessive adjective *see* **possessive determiner.**

possessive determiner (also called **possessive adjective**) a determiner that shows possession (*my*, *your*, *his*, *her*, *its*, *our*, and *their*).

possessive pronoun replaces a possessive determiner + singular or plural noun. The possessive pronoun agrees with the noun that it replaces.

My exercise class is at night. Hers is on the weekend. (hers = her exercise class)

preposition a word such as *to*, *at*, *for*, *with*, *below*, *in*, *on*, *next to*, or *above* that goes before a noun or pronoun to show location, time, direction, or a close relationship between two people or things. A preposition may go before a gerund as well.

I'm in the supermarket next to our favorite restaurant.

The idea of love has inspired many poets.

I'm interested in taking a psychology course.

prepositional phrase a reduced form of an identifying relative clause. Prepositional phrases are formed by removing the relative pronoun and the verb *be,* leaving only a prepositional phrase.

*The computers **in our classroom** are fast.*

present perfect a verb form that describes past events or situations that are still important in the present and actions that happened once or repeatedly at an indefinite time before now.

*Lately scientists **have discovered** medicines in the Amazon.*

*I**'ve been** to the Amazon twice.*

present perfect progressive a verb form that describes something that started in the past, usually continues in the present, and may continue in the future.

*He **hasn't been working** since last May.*

present progressive a verb form that describes an action or situation that is in progress now or around the present time. It is also used to indicate a fixed arrangement in the future.

*What **are** you **doing** right now?*

*I**'m leaving** for Spain next week.*

present real conditional (also called **factual conditional**) describes a situation that is possible now and its result. Present real conditionals describe general truths, facts, and habits. The *if* clause and the main clause use the simple present.

*If you **control** the media, you **control** public opinion.*

present unreal conditional describes an imaginary situation in the present. The *if* clause uses the simple past or past progressive. The main clause uses the modals *would*, *could*, or *might*.

*If I **studied** every day, I **could pass** all my tests.*

pronoun a word that replaces a noun or noun phrase. Some examples are *I*, *we*, *him*, *hers*, *it*. (*see* **object pronoun, subject pronoun, relative pronoun, possessive pronoun, reciprocal pronoun, reflexive pronoun.**)

proper noun a noun that is the name of a particular person, place, or thing. It is capitalized.

Central Park** in **New York City

punctuation mark a symbol used in writing such as a period (.), a comma (,), a question mark (?), or an exclamation point (!).

quantifier a word or phrase that shows an amount of something. In addition to measurements words, some other quantifiers are *much, many, some, any, a lot, plenty, enough,* etc.

*We have **three bottles** of juice and **plenty of** snacks.*

quoted speech *see* **direct speech**

reciprocal pronoun a pronoun (*each other, one another*) that shows that two or more people give *and* receive the same action or have the same relationship.

*Mari and I have the same challenges. We help **each other**. (I help Mari, and Mari helps me.)*

reflexive pronoun a pronoun (*myself, yourself, himself, herself, ourselves, yourselves, themselves*) that shows that the object of the sentence is the same as the subject.

*I taught **myself** to speak Japanese.*

regular verb a verb that changes its form in the usual way.

live → live**s**

wash → wash**ed**

relative clause (also called **adjective clause**) defines, describes, identifies, or gives more information about a noun. It begins with a relative pronoun such as *who, that, which, whose*, or *whom*. Like all clauses, a relative clause has both a subject and a verb. It can describe the subject or the object of a sentence.

People **who have sleep problems** *can join the study*. (subject relative clause)

There are many diseases **that viruses cause**. (object relative clause)

relative pronoun a pronoun (*who, which, that, whose, whom*) that connects a noun phrase to a relative clause

People **who** *have sleep problems can join the study*.

There are many diseases **that** *viruses cause*.

reported question *see* **indirect question**

reported speech *see* **indirect speech**

reporting verb a verb used to introduce direct speech or indirect speech. *Say* is the most common reporting verb. Other such verbs include *admit, announce, complain, confess, exclaim, explain, mention, remark, reply, report, state*, and *swear*, and *tell*.

The president **said**, *"We will change our system of rewarding employees."*

The president **stated** *that they would change their system of rewarding employees.*

result clause *see* **main clause**

sentence a complete thought or idea that has a subject and a main verb. In writing, it begins with a capital letter and has a punctuation mark at the end (. ? !). In an imperative sentence, the subject (*you*) is not usually stated.

This sentence is a complete thought.

Open your books.

separable phrasal verb a phrasal verb that can be separated. This means that an object can go before or after the particle.

Write down *your expenses.*

Write *your expenses* **down**.

simple past a verb form that describes completed actions or events that happened at a definite time in the past.

They **grew up** *in Washington, D.C.*

They **attended** *Howard University and* **graduated** *in 2018.*

simple present a verb form that describes things that regularly happen such as habits and routines (usual and regular activities). It also describes facts and general truths.

I **play** *games online every night.* (routine)

The average person **spends** *13 hours a week online.* (fact)

singular noun a noun that refers to only one person, place, or thing.

He is my best **friend**.

statement a sentence that gives information.

Today is Thursday.

stative verb (also called **non-action verb**) describes a state or situation, not an action. It is usually in the simple form.

I **remember** *your friend.*

subject the person, place, or thing that performs the action of a verb.

People use new words and expressions every day.

subject pronoun replaces a noun in the subject position.

Sara and I are friends. We work at the same company.

subordinator a conjunction that connects a dependent clause and an independent clause. Some common subordinators include *although*, *because*, *even though*, *in order to*, *since*, and *so that*.

Although many people like to shop, some people shop too much.

superlative the form of an adjective or adverb that compares one person, place, or thing to others in a group.

*This storm was **the most dangerous** one of the season.* (adjective)

*That group worked **most effectively** after the disaster.* (adverb)

syllable a group of letters that has one vowel sound and that you say as a single unit.

There is one syllable in the word lunch *and two syllables in the word* breakfast. (*Break* is one syllable and *fast* is another syllable.)

tag question consists of a verb and pronoun added to the end of a statement. Tag questions confirm information or ask for agreement. The tag changes the statement into a question.

*They don't live in Chicago, **do they?*** *Geography is interesting, **isn't it?***

tense the form of a verb that shows past or present time.

*They **worked** yesterday.* (simple past)

*They **work** every day.* (simple present)

third-person singular refers to *he*, *she*, and *it* or a singular noun. In the simple present, the third-person singular form ends in *-s* or *-es*.

*It **looks** warm and sunny today. **He washes** the laundry on Saturdays.*

time clause a phrase that shows the order of events and begins with a time word such as *before*, *after*, *when*, *while*, or *as soon as*.

Before there were freezers, people needed ice to make frozen desserts.

time expression a phrase that functions as an adverb of time. It tells when something happens, happened, or will happen.

*I graduated **in 2020**. She's going to visit her aunt and uncle **next summer**.*

transitive verb a verb that has an object. The object completes the meaning of the verb.

*She **wears** perfume.*

two-word verb *see* **phrasal verb**

verb a word that describes an action or a state.

*Alex **wears** jeans and a T-shirt to school. Alex **is** a student.*

vowel a sound represented in writing by these letters of the alphabet: ***a, e, i, o,*** and ***u.***

Wh- question *see* **information question**

Yes/No question begins with a form of *be* or an auxiliary verb. You can answer such a question with *yes* or *no.*

*"**Are** they going to the movies?" "**No**, they're not."*

*"**Can** you give me some help?" "**Yes**, I can."*

Index

a/an, 130, 148–49

action meanings of verbs, 8

active sentences vs. passive sentences, 278–79, 292

adjectives
   and, 138
   be, A9
   commas, 138
   infinitives, 200
   modifying nouns, 138
   order before nouns, A6
   prepositions, A10

adverbs/adverb clauses and phrases (*see also* time clauses), 396–98
   past perfect, 59–60
   present perfect, 36, 42
   present progressive, 5–6
   reducing, 401
   showing degrees of certainty, 73
   simple past, 20, 23, 41, 60
   simple present, 4, 12
   subordinators, 398, 401, 403

a few (of), 130, 151, 152

after
   future events, 86
   -ing forms of the verb, 404
   past perfect, 60
   simple past, 22–23

agent in passive sentences, 278, 284

a great deal of, 151

a little (of), 151

all (of), 151, 152

a lot (of), 151, 152, 157

already, 36, 41, 91

also, 413, 414

although, 398, 404, 414

and, 138, 380, 384–85, 391
   and . . . either, 389
   and neither, 389
   and . . . not, 389
   and so . . ., 388
   and . . . too, 388

another, 167–68

anybody/anyone, 170, 173, 307

anything, 170

anywhere, 170

appositives, 339, 343, A14
   commas, 339

articles
   definite, 148, 149
   indefinite, 148–49
   omission of, 149

as, 398

as a result (of), 411, 415

as soon as, 22, 86

as well as, 411, 418

auxiliary verbs (*see also* modals and modal-like expressions)
   conjunctions, 384, 388, 389
   negative questions, 210, 217
   reducing sentences, 388, 389
   tag questions, 212, 217

be
   followed by adjectives and infinitives, A9
   future, 103
   irregular forms, A1

passive sentences, 278–79, 286, 293, 298, 301
   reducing sentences, 388
   relative clauses, 338, 339, 343
   simple present, 71
   stative verb, 8, 44, A2
   tag questions, 212
   time clauses, 401

be able to, 108–09, A4

be allowed to, 103, 111, A3

because (of), 398, 404, 411

before
   future action, 91
   past perfect, 55, 60
   reduced clauses, 404
   simple past, 22–23
   time clauses, 86

be going to, 68, 70, 73–74, A14
   future events, 86
   future progressive, 76
   indirect speech, A11
   ongoing events, 87
   passive forms, A12
   vs. *will*, 73–74

be permitted to, A3

be required to, 103, 104, A3, A4

besides, 411

be supposed to, 103, 104, 111, A3

both, 391
   both . . . and, 380, 381

but, 380, 384–85, 389, 414

by
   after adjective, A10
   after verb, A9
   future action, 91

introducing an agent in passive sentences, 278
past perfect, 55
reflexive pronouns, 165

by the time, 60

can / cannot / can't (see also could)
indirect speech, A11
modals, 103, 108–09, 116, 117, 122, 123, A3, A4

can't have, 123, A4

certainly, 73, 76

clauses (*see* object relative clauses; relative clauses; subject relative clauses)

commas
adjectives, 138
adverb clauses, 398
appositives, 339
conjunctions, 384, 385, 391
direct speech, 250
identifying object relative clauses, 307
identifying subject relative clauses, 307
if clauses, 349, 351, 357
nonidentifying object relative clauses, 326
nonidentifying subject relative clauses, 310
prepositional phrases, 411
that clauses, 232
time clauses, 22–23, 87
too, 388
transition words, 414

conditionals, real / unreal (*see* real conditionals; unreal conditionals)

conjunctions, 378–80
auxiliary verbs, 384, 388, 389
commas, 384, 385, 391
coordinating, 380, 414
correlative, 380–81
modals, 384
parallel structure, 388–89
reducing sentences, 388–89

consequently, 415

coordinating conjunctions, 380, 414

correlative conjunctions, 380–81

could / could not / couldn't (see also can) conditionals, 365, A15
direct speech, 254
indirect speech, 254, A11
modals, 100, 103, 116, 117, 118, 119, 122, 123, A3, A4
wishes, 371

could have / could not have / couldn't have
conditionals, 369, A14
modals, 109, 123

count nouns (*see also* nouns), 130
definite articles, 148–49
indefinite articles, 148–49
quantifiers, 151–52

definite articles, 148, 149

definitely, 73, 76

despite, 411, 418

determiners
show possession, 152
usage, 130, 131

did not have to, 111

didn't use to, 26

direct questions, 243

direct speech, 248–50, 261

due to, 411

each other, 168

either
reducing sentences, 389
vs. *whether*, 245

even, 404
even though, 398, 404

even if, 352

ever, 36

everybody / everyone, 170, 173

everything, 170

everywhere, 170

few (of), 151

for
after adjective, A10
after verb, A9
present perfect, 36, 37

for example, 415

for instance, 415

furthermore, 415

future, 68
modals, A3–A4
passive forms, A12
time clauses, 84–85, 86–87

future perfect, 84–85, 91–92
passive forms, A12
vs. future perfect progressive, 91

future perfect progressive, 84, 91–92
prepositions, 91
time clauses, 91
vs. future perfect, 91

future progressive, 68, 76

gerunds (*see also -ing* form of the verb), 176–78, 181–82, 185, 187
after verbs, A7
common fixed expressions, 182
expressions with, A8
nouns + *of*, 185
object of preposition, 181, 187
object of sentence, 179
passive sentences, 298
prepositions, 187, 411, 418
subject of sentence, 179, 187
subject-verb agreement, 179, 187
vs. infinitives, 197–98
vs. present progressive, 179

get, passive sentences, 295–96, A1

had better (not), 100, A3

had to, 104

has / have (see also future perfect; past perfect; present perfect)
forms, A1
stative verb, 8, 44, A2

has / have to, 103, 104, 116, 117, A3, A4

however, 415

how long

habitual action, 43
   present perfect progressive, 44
how much/how many, 44, 238
identifying object relative clauses
   (*see also* object relative clauses;
   relative clauses)
   object of preposition, 327
   vs. nonidentifying object
      relative clauses, 325
identifying subject relative
   clauses (*see also* relative
   clauses; subject relative
   clauses), 306–07, 322–23
   commas, 307, 329
   subject-verb agreement, 307
   vs. nonidentifying subject
      relative clauses, 309–10
if clauses
   commas, 349, 351, 357
   conditionals, A14
   future real conditionals,
      351–52, 357
   future unreal conditionals,
      364–65
   indirect questions, 268–69
   noun clauses, 240–41, 243
   past perfect, 373
   past progressive, 365
   past unreal conditionals,
      368–69, 373
   present real conditionals,
      348–49, 357
   present unreal conditionals,
      364–65, 373
   questions, 349, 357
   real conditions with modals
      and modal-like expressions,
      354
if . . . not, in real conditions, 352
imperatives
   future real conditions, 354
   indirect, 270–71
   present real conditions, 354
in
   after adjective, A10
   after verb, A9
   present perfect, 37

in addition (to), 411, 414, 415, 418
in contrast, 415
indefinite articles, 148–49
indefinite pronouns, 170
indirect imperatives
   infinitives, 270
   requests and advice, 270–71
indirect questions, 243, 266,
   268–69, A10
indirect speech, 248–49, 253–54
   tense shifting, 253–54, A11
   without tense shifting, 253
infinitives, 192–93
   after adjectives, 200, A9
   after nouns, 200
   after verbs, 194–95, A7
   after verbs + objects, 195, A8
   indirect imperatives, 270
   negative, 203
   not with *if*, 241
   passive sentences, 298–99
   reduced noun clauses, 239
   vs. gerunds, 197–98
   with *whether*, 241
information questions, 268
-ing form of the verb (*see also*
   gerunds), 2
   adverb clauses, 401
   future progressive, 76, 84, 85,
      91, 95
   modals and modal-like
      expressions, 125
   past perfect progressive, 52,
      62, 65
   present perfect progressive,
      34–35, 43–44, 46
   present progressive, 4, 5–6, 9,
      13, 18, 21, 24, 29, 70
   reduced clauses, 404
   relative clauses, 338
   used as a noun, 178
in order to, 403
in spite of, 411, 414, 419
instead (of), 411, 415
intransitive verbs, 282–83

irregular verbs, A1–A2
just, 36
likely, 73, 76, 118
little (of), 151
many (of), 130, 151
may (not)
   indirect speech, A11
   modals, 103, 116, 117, 118, 119,
      122, 123, A3, A4
may (not) have, 123, A4
maybe, 73
measurement words, 134, A5
might (not)
   indirect speech, 254, A11
   modals, 100, 116, 117, 118, 119,
      122, 123, A3, A4
   real conditionals, A14
   unreal conditionals, 365, A14
might (not) have, 123, 369, A4, A14
   might (not) want to, 100
modals and modal-like
   expressions (*see also* auxiliary
   verbs), 98–99, 100–01, 114,
   A3–A4
   conjunctions, 384
   expressing ability, 124–25
   expressing advice and regret,
      100–01, 111
   expressing future probability,
      118–19
   expressing past probability,
      122–23
   expressing permission,
      necessity, and obligations,
      103–04
   expressing present probability,
      116–17
   expressing probability, 114,
      116–17, 118–19
   future time, A3
   indirect imperatives, 270
   negative questions, 210
   past participles, 122
   past time, A3
   present time, A3
   progressive verbs, 119

real conditions, 354
    tag questions, 212
    unreal conditionals, 365
    wishes, 371
modifying nouns, 128, 138
most (of), 152
most likely, 70
must (not)
    future probability, 125
    modals, 103, 104, 116, 117, 122, 123, A3, A4
must (not) have, 123, A4
need (to)
    modals, 103, 104, A3
    stative verb, 8, A2
negative infinitives, 203
negative questions, 208–10
    answering, 210, 217
neither, 389
    neither . . . nor, 380, 381
never, 35
nobody, 169
non-action verbs (*see also* stative verbs), 8, A2
noncount nouns (*see also* nouns), 128–32, A5
    definite articles, 148–49
    quantifiers, 151–52
    singular vs. plural, 141
    used as count nouns, 134
none of / no, 151, 152
nonidentifying object relative clauses (*see also* object relative clauses; relative clauses), 325–26
    commas, 326
    vs. identifying object relative clauses, 325
nonidentifying subject relative clauses (*see also* relative clauses; subject relative clauses), 309–10
    commas, 310
    vs. identifying subject relative clauses, 309–10

no one, 170, 173
not a lot of, 151, 152
not any (of), 151, 152
nothing, 170
not many (of), 151
not much (of), 151
not only . . . but also, 380, 381
not . . . until, 86
not yet, 36
noun clauses, 236, 238
    if / whether, 240–41, 243, 245
    wh- words, 238–39, 245
nouns (*see also* count nouns; noncount nouns), 128
    count, 130, 148–49
    infinitives, 200
    irregular plurals, 131
    modifying, 128, 138
    noncount, 130, 131–32, 134, 148–49, A5
    plural forms only, 131
    same singular and plural forms, 131
    singular vs. plural, 130
nowhere, 170
object pronouns vs. reflexive pronouns, 165
object relative clauses (*see also* identifying object relative clauses; nonidentifying object relative clauses; relative clauses), 320–21
    objects of prepositions, 326–27
objects
    in passive sentences, 282–83
    of prepositions in object relative clauses, 326–27
    used with infinitives, 195, A8
once
    simple past, 22–23
    time clauses, 86
one another, 168
on the other hand, 415, 418
or, 380, 384–85

or not, 240
other(s), 167–68, 173
ought (not) to, 100, 116, 117, 118, 119, 254, A3, A4
ought to have, 92, A3
participles, past (*see* past participles)
passive, 276–78, 284, 290–91
    agent, 278, 284
    be, 293, 298, 301
    be going to, 292–93, A12
    by + agent, 278
    common verbs, 279, 235
    future perfect, A12
    gerunds, 298
    get, 295–96
    infinitives, 298–99
    intransitive verbs, 282–83
    modals, 292–93
    objects, 282–83
    past forms, 278–79
    past participles, 278–79, 283, 286, 293, 295, 298, 301
    past perfect, 279, A12
    past progressive, 279, A12
    present forms, 278–79
    present perfect, 278–79, A12
    present progressive, 278–79, A12
    questions, A12
    relative clauses, 338
    simple future, A12
    simple past, 279, A12
    simple present, 278–79, A12
    transitive verbs, 282–83
    vs. active sentences, 279–80, 292, A12
past
    modals, A3
    that clauses, 227–28
    unreal conditionals, 368–69
past participles
    conditionals, A14
    irregulars, A1–A2
    modals and modal-like expressions, 100–01, 109, 111, 122

passive sentences, 278–79, 283, 286, 293, 295, 298, 301
reducing sentences, 388
relative clauses, 338
past perfect, 52, 54–55
background information, 55, 65
common verbs, 56
completed actions, 65
conditionals, A15
passive sentences, 279, A12
reducing adverb clauses, 401
reducing sentences, 388
time clauses, 59–60
vs. simple past, 55
past perfect progressive, 52, 62
background information, 62, 65
past progressive, 18, 20
background activities, 20
conditionals, A14
describing an ongoing action, 23
if clauses, 365
indirect speech, A11
passive sentences, 279, A12
reducing sentences, 388
reducing time clauses, 401
stative verbs, 20
time clauses, 23
two actions in the same clause, 22–23
vs. simple past, 20
perhaps, 73
permitted to, 103
personal pronouns vs. reciprocal pronouns, 168
possession with determiners, 152
prepositions and prepositional expressions, 408, 411, 414
after adjectives, A10
after verbs, A9
commas, 411
future perfect progressive, 91
past perfect, 55
relative clauses, 339, A13–A14

present (*see also* simple present), 346, 348
if clauses, 348–49, 357
imperatives, 354
modals, A3
that clauses, 227
present perfect, 34, 36–37
adverbs, 36, 40
completed actions, 44, 46
habitual actions, 43
indirect speech, A11
passive sentences, 278, 279, A12
reducing adverb clauses, 401
reducing sentences, 388
stative verbs, 44
time clauses / expressions, 36, 86
vs. present perfect progressive, 43, 46
vs. simple past, 40–41
present perfect progressive, 34–35, 43
habitual actions, 43
ongoing actions, 44, 46
vs. present perfect, 43–44, 46
present progressive, 2, 4–5, 68, 70
adverbs, 4–5
expressing ongoing events, 87
indirect speech, A11
passive sentences, 278–79, A12
reducing sentences, 388
reducing time clauses, 401
relative clauses, 338
stative verbs, 8, A2
vs. gerunds, 179
vs. simple present, 3–4
probability with modals and modal-like expressions, 114, 116–17, 118–19
probably, 70, 73, 76, 118
pronouns, 162
indefinite, 170, 173
other / another, 167–68
reciprocal, 168
reflexive, 164–65, 173

relative, 306–07, 322–23, 326, 327, 338–39
punctuation (*see* commas; quotation marks; semicolons)
quantifiers, 151
count nouns, 151–52
noncount nouns, 151–52
use / non-use of *of*, 152
questions direct, 243
indirect, 243, 244, 268–69, A10
information, 268
negative, 208, 210
passive forms, A12
tag, 208–09
yes / no, 268
quite a few (of), 151
quotation marks
in direct speech, 250, 261
real conditionals
future, 351–52, 354, 357
modals, 354
present, 348–49, 354
recently, 36
reciprocal pronouns, 168
vs. personal pronouns, 168
reduced relative clauses (*see also* relative clauses)
appositives, 339
participle phrases, 338
prepositional phrases, 339
reducing adverb clauses, 401
reducing sentences, 388–89
reducing time clauses, 401
reflexive pronouns, 164–65
by, 165
common verbs, 165
imperative, 165
position, 165
vs. object pronouns, 165
relative clauses (*see also* identifying object relative clauses; identifying subject relative clauses; nonidentifying object relative clauses; nonidentifying subject relative

clauses; object relative clauses; reduced relative clauses; subject relative clauses), 332–33
  identifying vs. nonidentifying, A13–A14
  present participles in, 338
  reduced, 338–39
  when, 334–35
  where, 334, 335

relative pronouns, 306–07, 322–23, 326–27, 338–39
  object relative clauses, 322–23, 326–27
  omission of, 338–39
  reduced relative clauses, 338–39
  subject relative clauses, 306–07
  verb agreement, 307

reporting verbs, 256, 258, A11

say, 253, 258, 270, A1

semicolons, 414

should (not), *shouldn't*
  indirect imperatives, 270
  modals, 100, 101, 116–17, 118, 119, 270, A3, A4
  probability, 114, 116, 118–19, A3, A4

should (not) have, *shouldn't have*, 100, 101, A3

simple past, 18, 20
  adverbs, 20, 23, 41
  completed past actions, 26, 27, 40
  conditionals, A14
  indirect speech, A11
  irregular verbs, A1–A2
  passive sentences, 279
  reducing adverb clauses, 401
  reducing time clauses, 401
  stative verbs, 20
  time clauses, 22–23, 60
  vs. past perfect, 55
  vs. past progressive, 20
  vs. present perfect, 40–41

simple present (*see also* present), 2, 4, 12, 71
  adverbs, 4, 12
  conditionals, A14
  expressing an action that interrupts another action, 87
  if clauses, 248, 351
  indirect speech, A11
  passive sentences, 278–79, A12
  reducing time clauses, 401
  special meanings, 12
  stative verbs, 8
  time clauses, 86, 91
  vs. present progressive, 4–5

since, 36, 37, 398

so, 384, 385, 389, 403, 414, 415

so that, 403

so far, 36

some (of), 130, 151, 152

somebody / someone, 170, 307

something, 170, 307

somewhere, 170

speech, direct (*see* direct speech)
  speech, indirect (*see* indirect speech)

stative verbs, 8, A2
  future perfect, 92
  future perfect progressive, 92
  present perfect, 44
  simple past vs. past progressive, 21

still, 36

subject relative clauses (*see also* identifying subject relative clauses; nonidentifying subject relative clauses; relative clauses), 304, 306, 315
  avoiding repetition, 315
  whose, 312–13

subject-verb agreement
  gerunds, 179
  identifying subject relative clauses, 307
  present perfect, 46

subordinators, 410

adverb clauses, 398
  combining sentences, 414
  expressing purpose, 415
  reducing adverb clauses, 401

tag questions, 208–09, 212–13
  affirmative vs. negative, 213
  answering, 213

tell, A1
  indirect imperatives, 270–71
  infinitives, 270
  passive, 283
  reporting verb, 258

that, 307, 309, 315, 323, 326, 327, 329, A13–A14
  identifying object relative clauses, 323, 327, A13
  identifying subject relative clauses, 307, A13
  nonidentifying object relative clauses, 326, 327, A13
  nonidentifying subject relative clauses, 309, A13
  reduced relative clauses, 338
  that clauses, 222–24, 227–28
    after adjectives, 229
    after nouns, 229–30
    commas, 232
    indirect speech, 253
    past verbs, 227–28
    present verbs, 227
    wishes, A15
  wishes, 329

the, 130, 131, 148–49

then, 349, 414, 415

therefore, 414, 415

these, 130

this, 130

those, 130

though, 398

thus, 415

time clauses / expressions / phrases / words (*see also* adverbs)
  commas, 22, 87
  future, 86–87
  future perfect progressive, 91

past perfect, 59–60
past progressive, 24
present perfect, 36, 86
reducing, 401
simple past, 20, 23–24, 60
simple present, 86, 91
unreal conditionals, 365

to
    after adjective, A10
    after verb, A9
    expressing purpose, 403
    preposition vs. infinitive, 203

too, 388, 389, 391

transition words, 408, 410, 413–14
    commas, 414
    common phrases, 413–14
    semicolons, 414

transitive verbs, 282–83

unless, in real conditions, 352

unreal conditionals, 363–64, A14
    future, 364–65
    modals, 365
    present, 364–65

until
    past perfect, 55, 60
    simple past, 22
    time clauses, 86

use/used to, 26, 29

verbs
    followed by gerunds, A7
    followed by infinitives,
        194–95, A7, A8
    followed by objects, A8
    followed by prepositions, A9
    intransitive, 282–83
    irregular, A1–A2
    non-action, 8, A2
    reflexive, A6
    reporting, 256, 258, A11
    stative, 8, A2
    transitive, 282–83

want
    followed by infinitives, 195,
        203, 299, A7
    followed by objects, 195, 203,
        A7

stative verb, 8, A2

was/were able to (*see also can;
    could*), 109

wh- words
    indirect questions, 268
    noun clauses, 238–39

what, 238–39, 329
    noun clauses, 238–39

when, 239
    adverb clauses, 398
    expressing ongoing events, 87
    future real conditionals, 357
    if clauses, 349
    noun clauses, 239
    past perfect, 60
    past progressive, 23
    reduced adverb clauses, 404
    relative clauses, 334, 335, 342,
        A14
    simple past, 22–23
    simple present, 87
    time clauses, 86
    vs. *while* in the past, 24

whenever, if clauses, 349

where
    noun clauses, 239
    relative clauses, 334, 335, 343,
        A14

whereas, 404

whether
    noun clauses, 240–41
    vs. *either*, 245

which
    noun clauses, 239
    object relative clauses, 323,
        326, 327, A13
    reduced relative clauses, 338
    relative clauses, 334, 335
    subject relative clauses, 307,
        309, A13

while
    adverb clauses, 398
    expressing ongoing events, 87
    past progressive, 24
    reduced adverb clauses, 404
    simple present, 87

vs. *when* in the past, 24

who/whom
    noun clauses, 239
    object relative clauses, 323,
        326–27, A13
    reduced relative clauses, 338
    subject relative clauses, 307,
        309, A13

who's, vs. *whose*, 315

whose
    object relative clauses, 323,
        326, A13
    subject relative clauses,
        312–13, A13
    vs. *who's*, 315

will (not)/won't
    expressing ongoing events, 87
    future, 86, 87
    future perfect, 95
    future progressive, 76
    indirect speech, A11
    modals, 103, A4
    predictions and expectations,
        73
    probability, 118
    quick decisions, 74
    requests, offers, and promises,
        73
    vs. *be going to*, 73–74

wishes, 371, A14

would
    conditionals, 365, A14
    describing past events, 26, 27,
        29
    expressing wishes, 371, A14
    tense shifting in indirect
        speech, A11

would have, 369, A14

yes/no questions, 268

yet
    coordinating conjunctions,
        284, 285
    present perfect, 36, 40
    simple past, 40

Credits

Acknowledgements

The authors and publishers acknowledge the following sources of copyright material and are grateful for the permissions granted. While every effort has been made, it has not always been possible to identify the sources of all the material used, or to trace all copyright holders. If any omissions are brought to our notice, we will be happy to include the appropriate acknowledgements on reprinting and in the next update to the digital edition, as applicable.

Key: U = Unit

Text

U17: Figure 1 adapted from Organization for Economic Cooperation and Development (OECD), Online Education Database, retrieved September 13, 2019, from https://stats.oecd.org/Index.aspx. See Digest of Education Statistics 2018, table 603.20. Reproduced with kind permission; Figure 2 adapted from OECD (2019), 'Education and earnings: Level of earnings relative to median earnings' by Educational Attainment, OEC. Stat, https://stats.oecd.org/Index.aspx?DataSetCode=EAG_EARNINGS, accessed on August 1, 2019. Reproduced with kind permission.

Photography

The following photos are sourced from Getty Images.

U14: Viaframe/Corbis; George Rose News; Monkeybusinessimages/iStock/Getty Images Plus; PhotoAlto/Eric Audras/Brand X Pictures; **U15:** IP Galanternik D.U./E+; MPI/Archive Photos; Darren pearson (dariustwin)/Moment; Seb_ra/iStock/Getty Images Plus; **U16:** okeyphotos/iStock/Getty Images Plus; H. Armstrong Roberts/ClassicStock/Archive Photos; Hulton Archive; **U17:** Comstock Images/Stockbyte; Jon Feingersh/DigitalVision; Monkeybusinessimages/iStock/Getty Images Plus; Jacoblund/iStock/Getty Images Plus; **U18:** Bloom Productions/DigitalVision; Hero Images; Vm/E+; Caiaimage/Agnieszka Olek; **U19:** SDI Productions/E+; Caiaimage/Caiaimage/Robert Daly/OJO+; **U20:** julief514/iStock/Getty Images Plus; Jose A. Bernat Bacete/Moment; Istanbulimage/E+; Kosamtu/E+; NoDerog/iStock/Getty Images Plus; **U21:** GIPhotoStock/Cultura; Echo/Juice Images; Photobalance/iStock/Getty Images Plus; Maciej Lulko/Moment; **U22:** gorodenkoff/iStock/Getty Images Plus; Steve Allen/Stockbyte; Monty Rakusen/Cultura; Stephen Chernin; Andersen Ross Photography Inc/DigitalVision; **U23:** NurPhoto; PeopleImages/E+; JGI/Tom Grill; Johnny Greig/E+; Juanmonino/E+; Simon Marcus Taplin/Corbis; **U24:** bruev/iStock/Getty Images Plus; Bloomberg Creative Photos; Skynesher/iStock/Getty Images Plus; Franckreporter/E+; **U25:** onfilm/E+; 1001nights/E+; Huntstock/Brand X Pictures; Kickstand/iStock/Getty Images Plus; Joshuaraineyphotography/iStock/Getty Images Plus; Stocktrek Images/Richard Roscoe; **U26:** martinedoucet/E+; Lew Robertson/Photolibrary; Will Heap/Dorling Kindersley; ilietus/iStock/Getty Images Plus; SolStock/E+; Cgissemann/iStock/Getty Images Plus; chengyuzheng/iStock/Getty Images Plus; MIXA Co. Ltd.; LUNAMARINA/iStock/Getty Images Plus; Troscha/iStock/Getty Images Plus; GlobalP/iStock/Getty Images Plus; **U27:** Csondy/E+; Michaelpuche/iStock/Getty Images Plus; Carlos Ciudad Photography/Moment; Gavin Jackson/ArcaidImages; **U28:** Handout; BSIP/Universal Images Group.

The following photos are sourced from other libraries.

U15: ClassicStock/Alamy Stock Photo; **U19:** Keith Crowley/Alamy Stock Photo; **U21:** WENN Ltd/ Alamy Stock Photo; **U24:** Artur Marciniec/Alamy Stock Photo; **U25:** FEMA/Alamy Stock Photo; **U26:** Catinsyrup/Shutterstock; **U28:** Everett Collection Inc/Alamy Stock Photo.

Illustrations

Maria Rabinky; Monika Roe; Rob Schuster; Shelton Leong.

Audio

Audio production by John Marshall Media.

Typeset

Q2A Media Services Pvt. Ltd.